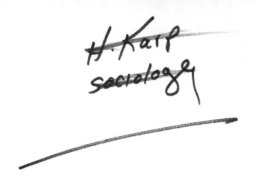

US EXPANSIONISM

US Expansionism

The Imperialist Urge in the 1890s

DAVID HEALY

THE UNIVERSITY OF WISCONSIN PRESS

Madison, Milwaukee, and London 1970

Published 1970
The University of Wisconsin Press
Box 1379, Madison, Wisconsin 53701

The University of Wisconsin Press, Ltd.
27–29 Whitfield Street, London, W.1

First printing

Printed in the United States of America
Impressions, Inc., Madison, Wisconsin

ISBN 0-299-05851-4; LC 71-121769

TO ANN ERICKSON HEALY
this book is fondly
and gratefully dedicated.

Table of Contents

Acknowledgments

LIKE MOST scholars, the author of this work owes a great deal to his colleagues. When the project was merely an idea, I found my thinking stimulated by fortunate contact with Professors Raymond Betts, of Grinnell College, and Pierre Boulle, now of McGill University. Here at the University of Wisconsin–Milwaukee I have benefited by the counsel and criticism of an embarrassing number of my fellows. Of those who gave so ungrudgingly of their time and knowledge, I must mention by name Professors A. Theodore Brown, Keith Bryant, Bruce Fetter, Lillian Miller, Roland Stromberg, and Walter Trattner. To these should be added Professor Eugene Trani of Southern Illinois University, and Miss Martha Beier, who made the index. The faults of the book are mine alone.

As usual, the greatest contribution of all came from my wife, to whom this book is dedicated.

US EXPANSIONISM

Introduction

THE 1890s, as every textbook declares, saw the United States emerge as a world power. The decade witnessed war scares with Chile and Great Britain, as well as a successful war with Spain. It saw the creation of a modern and fast-growing navy, the annexation of several important pieces of overseas territory, and the establishment of a major protectorate; it ended on a note of declining martial enthusiasm and mounting concern about the risks and responsibilities which had accompanied victory.

In an age when even "limited" wars are tragically long and bloody, it is difficult to take the Spanish-American War and its surrounding events entirely seriously. Yet that conflict, though brief in duration and mercifully unsanguinary, undoubtedly accompanied and hastened great changes in the national role of the United States. Both the relatively small scale of the war and the importance of its results were as obvious to contemporary observers as to subsequent historians. While John Hay described it in a famous phrase as "a splendid little war," President David Starr Jordan of the Leland Stanford University concluded that the real crisis would come when the war was over. Speaking to his students in the month of Dewey's victory at Manila Bay, he voiced the questions that troubled him: "What will be the reflex effect of great victories, suddenly realized strength, the patronizing applause, the ill-concealed envy of great nations, the conquest of strange territories, the raising of our flag beyond the seas?" As Jordan said, it was all very new and bewildering: "It is un-American; it is contrary to our traditions; it is delicious; it is intoxicating." Such was the confusion of emotions with which Americans viewed their future in 1898, and went on to complete an episode ever since controversial in the nation's history.

Several decades ago, the noted historian Samuel F. Bemis branded the expansionist activities of the United States in the 1890s a "great aberration," and this assertion provides a convenient point of departure for evaluating them. If they represented an aberration, it must be asked, an aberration from what? Not, certainly, from the behavioral norms of the period itself, which marked the high point of modern imperialism in the rest of the world. A better case might be made that they were an aberration from the nation's own past, yet only after granting that a sustained and triumphant expansion had heretofore been a central theme of its development. Was this older expansionism utterly dead in the post-Civil War years, and was the new expansionism so fundamentally different in nature as to be unrelated to the old?

We may ask, finally, whether imperialism was an aberration of logic, an emotional binge having little relation to reality and foreign to the nation's needs. Unquestionably the imperialist movement had a large emotional content. Furthermore, the more rational motives for a program of territorial expansion were apparently lacking. The United States possessed ample territory, large amounts of which were still only lightly populated and partially developed. Americans were not seeking overseas areas to which they could emigrate, and no significant number of them ever went to the lands annexed in 1898. Isolated between two oceans, the nation was menaced by no strong neighbors. Of all the world's powers, the United States faced the smallest visible threat to its security, and had the slightest reasons for strategically motivated advances. Finally, the United States had already built up an enormous foreign trade without the trouble and expense of colonies or large armaments, and made American economic competition respected and feared in Europe. Thus at first glance, it would seem difficult to have made a reasoned appeal for territorial acquisitions. Yet the fact remains that many expansionists saw overseas expansion, whatever else it was, as also a problem-solving device, aimed at ameliorating social, economic, and security problems of the first importance. If their actions seem illogical today, it may be in part because we have forgotten the reasoning which produced them.

One way to explore these questions is to listen to the voices of the expansionists themselves, in all their vigor and diversity. While men's explanations of their own actions are not necessarily dependable, they constitute at least a first step toward understanding. There are, of course, pitfalls into which the earnest inquirer may fall. For example, while it is useful to classify imperialist appeals into categories grouped about economic factors, social factors, and the like, to separate them is in one sense arbitrary, for they were but differing aspects of an integrated body of assumptions. Although individuals might stress one or another facet of the movement, all were mutually reenforcing, and can be completely understood only in terms of their mutual relationships. Nor is it profitable to argue overly much about whether the "real" motives of the imperialists were selfish or altruistic. Had the American public seen no national advantage in imperialism, they would never have embarked upon it merely to do good; yet, had they seen no good in it, it is extremely doubtful that enough of them could have been persuaded to support it only for the sake of expediency. Both appeals acting together were no more than adequate to summon the minimum support needed for the success of the "large policy." Neither was necessarily a mere rationalization of the other, and neither can be dismissed as "secondary." To be politically viable, democratic foreign policy must be able to make a plausible case that it combines expediency and morality. The grounds upon which the desired actions are made moral are of prime importance to the historian, whatever their abstract merit may appear to him, since their nature and effectiveness tell much about the society for which they were formulated.

Let us, then, examine the expansionist urge as it appeared in the

United States during the closing years of the nineteenth century. But in order to do that, we must first notice some corresponding phenomena in the world at large, which had no small influence upon the American mind.

PART I
The Setting

1 A World of Empires

IT WAS in 1897 that the long reign of Victoria, Queen of England, reached the round sum of sixty years. It was a remarkable reign, everyone agreed, and the world was prepared to take notice of the unique anniversary. So was the British government, which saw in the occasion an opportunity to promote closer ties among the many and dispersed components of the British Empire. The resulting Diamond Jubilee, a more brilliant version of the Golden Jubilee of ten years before, was planned along lines sufficiently spectacular and imperial to satisfy Benjamin Disraeli himself, had he been alive to witness it. Imperial unity was the theme, and the magnitude and splendor of the British Empire was the chosen backdrop against which the pageant was to unfold; every portion of the Queen's far-flung possessions must be represented. As Jubilee Week approached, London became the focus of gathering thousands, some from the ends of the earth, while the newspapers of the world reported in detail the city's awesome preparations.

The American newspaper reader received his full share of Jubilee news, for nowhere outside of England was the press coverage fuller than in the United States. To fashionable Americans, the great June celebration in London promised to be the major social event of the year, and hundreds of the wealthy crossed the Atlantic to take part. Eastern society in particular took up the Jubilee as its own, which was only to be expected in a group whose daughters were beginning

9

to marry into the leading English families, and among whom a presentation at the English court was the ultimate seal of social acceptability. Only a few years earlier, a young English diplomat had noted the eagerness of the American smart set to identify with London society, about which they spoke "much as Scotch ministers talk about heaven, [with] half familiarity and half awe."[1]

Ordinary Americans, too, were interested in the Jubilee, if only because it was held to be the outstanding spectacle of its kind in recent times. The statistics alone were staggering. Fifty thousand troops participated in the great procession of June 22nd, including contingents from over thirty different colonial possessions. Eleven colonial prime ministers rode in state coaches, each with a guard of soldiers from his own colony. The Queen herself was followed by forty-two mounted princes from all over Europe. Crowds lined the entire seven-mile-long parade route, although the total turnout was less than had been expected, and some of the speculators in grandstand seats and other vantage points found it necessary to lower their prices in order to do business. That night, the city's principal buildings and bridges were electrically lighted, while across the length and breadth of England 2,500 beacon fires burned for local celebrants.

On the following Sunday, the Navy matched the Army's parade with an enormous naval review at Spithead. The Royal Navy alone sent 170 warships without, the Admiralty proudly announced, depleting any of its powerful forces on foreign stations; twenty foreign navies were represented as well. With every ship festooned and outlined in strings of electric lights, the scene after dark was not soon forgotten.[2] But then, everything about the Jubilee was overpowering. As a New York *Tribune* writer commented, "It was a dreamlike picture which fired the imagination of the dullest sightseer and convinced reflecting men that it symbolized the greatness of a world-wide empire."[3]

The *Tribune,* of course, led all the New York papers in the quantity and enthusiasm of its Jubilee coverage. It began running daily front-page reports from London well before Jubilee Week began, and on the day after the great procession its editors gave

most of page one and all of page two to columns of ecstatic description. This was no mere coincidence, for the *Tribune*'s influential
editor, Whitelaw Reid, headed the official United States Jubilee
delegation as Special Envoy to the Queen. Reid was presumably
in sympathy with such colonial displays, for he currently advocated
the extension of United States control over Cuba and Hawaii,
though one of the *Tribune*'s reporters in London rather wistfully
pointed out that even these prizes would be "but small and insignificant compared with the imperial domain which now fills and
fascinates the English imagination." Or, as the Chicago *Record*
put it, the Jubilee festivities presented "the most imposing outward
display of the political, social, and military factors of modern
civilization which the world has yet witnessed."[4]

The point underlying all this pageantry was clear enough to the
thoughtful observer: the world was still a world of empires, and
the British Empire was still incomparably the largest and most
imposing. All of the great powers, however, had colonial possessions
and were ambitious for more; in all the world the United States
now seemed the most important exception to the prevalence of
national land-hunger. A glance about the globe showed imperial
activity almost everywhere. Africa was undergoing continental partition: the British and French were the principal rivals, soon to
practice brinkmanship in the Nile Valley, but Germany too had
vigorously entered the lists. Of the lesser powers, Portugal still held
large African colonies and Spain smaller ones, while the Italians,
smarting from their recent and humiliating failure to conquer
Abyssinia, remained penned in their foothold on the Red Sea. In
southern Asia, England's sprawling Indian Empire swept across
Burma to the borders of China and Siam, with the Malay States as
an outlyer, while the French hung on China's southern flank in their
Indo-Chinese colonies. The rich islands of the Dutch East Indies
were still a vigorous relic of the past, in contrast to the declining
power of Spain in the Philippine Archipelago. In the broad reaches
of the Pacific, the British, and their Australian and New Zealand
subjects, competed for islands with Germany, France, and even,
at times, the United States.

Even in relatively stable North America, it was difficult to ignore the huge neighboring areas of Canada, Labrador, and Newfoundland, or the polyglot state of the West Indies, divided among five European flags and two local ones.

In the general advance of European dominion, China seemed marked as the country next to be overrun. By 1897, Russian influence had penetrated deeply into that decaying kingdom, and before the year was out the German seizure of Kiao-Chow would appear to be the signal for a general struggle. Great Britain and Japan were already alert to the possibilities, while France hoped to expand her influence in the far south.

Americans, then, saw about them in 1897 not only a world of empires, but of dynamic and fast-growing empires. In the thirty years from 1870 to 1900, Great Britain alone added four and three quarter million square miles of territory to her holdings, an area considerably larger than the total United States. In the same period, the French acquired three and a half million square miles, and the Germans one million. European subjugation of virtually the entire Eastern Hemisphere appeared probable, if not inevitable, in the near future; after all, the process was already far advanced.[5]

The men and nations responsible for this seemingly endless extension of European power had long since formulated the most conclusive justifications for their activities. The English, who led in the work, also seemed the most confident about its necessity and righteousness. By the 1890s, they had evolved a philosophy and a literature of empire to which imperialists in the other countries turned to bolster their own cases. But beneath all the arguments, Victorians knew that imperialism was necessary if for no other reason than that it represented progress. And progress meant, simply, the improvement of the human condition, and ultimately of man himself.

Belief in human progress had been dented a bit by the upheavals accompanying the French Revolution and the Napoleonic Wars, but the advance of the nineteenth century saw a revival in England of a renewed and strengthened confidence. On the simplest level, it seemed obvious that the exploding productivity and new technological skills that characterized the era must make possible the betterment of man's lot on earth. For the first time in history, it seemed possible that want might eventually retreat before plenty, although present poverty was still an ugly and widespread reality. Improved travel and communications must gradually erase ignorance and isolation, erode away the misunderstandings between peoples, and facilitate the gathering and distribution of the new plenty. As Thomas Babington Macaulay wrote, "every improvement of the means of locomotion benefits mankind morally and intellectually as well as materially,"[6] and the nineteenth century achieved, in the railroad and the steamship, the greatest advances in transportation that history had witnessed. Advancing and increasingly applied science was learning to control disease, and making way against the ultimate enemy, Death himself. Cheap, mechanized printing loosed floods of knowledge to the public at large, and would surely result in the development of a more enlightened and virtuous population than any before seen. In every civilized community, the possibilities of the future appeared limitless.

Unfortunately, it also appeared that most of the world's communities were not really civilized. To the Victorian, the world was sharply divided between civilized men—those of European culture, commanding the new science and technology, politically organized in centralized and relatively homogeneous nation-states, disposing armed forces of a wholly new order of efficiency and destructiveness—and barbarians, who shared few or none of these attributes. As the gap between western society and all the others grew wider, a dilemma presented itself. Was one to believe in the perfectibility of man, or only of some men? Was one to work for the betterment of humanity, or merely that portion of it born in the advanced countries? It seemed that western civilization, already the custodian of Christianity and the opportunity for eternal life, had become the dispenser of earthly salvation as well. It seemed so, at least, if one assumed that all men shared a common humanity, and were equally susceptible to civilization as well as to salvation. This assumption, however, could no longer be taken for granted. The nineteenth century saw a marked decline in belief in the equality of man. A growing emphasis upon the importance of race accompanied a new conviction that the regions which had produced such superior achievements must be inhabited by superior men. The result, by the end of the century, was a general European belief in white superiority. But if men were in fact unequal, to what extent *did* they share a common humanity? Perhaps the backward peoples were unequal to the task of acquiring civilization.[7]

Such perplexities, though challenging, could be largely overcome through the use of evolutionary social theories. These, in turn, grew out of the Victorian fondness for universal laws, valid for all times and places. The rapid pace of change had become upsetting; it tended to undermine old generalizations with a distressing regularity. The Victorians, therefore, developed scientific laws of change itself, and the result, for a time, seemed magic. The irresistible torrent of change was now seen to flow through visibly defined channels, and to obey laws of its own which a careful observer might deduce. Chief among these laws was that of evolution: in response to the demands of their environment, individuals, species, and, by a bold extension, races and societies, evolved through time into ever higher forms—abler, better adjusted to their needs, more intelligent, perhaps even nobler. This process of evolution now became the principal mechanism of progress, and of history. Thus Walter Bagehot could say, in 1872, "Everyone now admits that human history is guided by certain laws." The working of these laws, generation after generation, meant a continuous improvement "which makes each civilization not a set of detached dots, but a line of colour, surely enhancing shade by shade."[8]

A generation earlier, Herbert Spencer had proclaimed in his magisterial way that the final advent of human perfection was "removed out of the region of probability into that of certainty" by those same laws, which Spencer was confident he had laid bare.[9] In the meantime, the professional acceptance of Charles Darwin's conclusions about the biological evolution of species seemed to lend the prestige of science to parallel theories of social evolution, or to what came to be called Social Darwinism.

The evolutionary approach had multiple advantages: it not only established and explained the workings of progress, but it allowed for both the perfectibility and the inequality of man. The various human sub-groups, it developed, were at different stages in the universal process of evolution; some peoples were far ahead of the others. It went without saying that white Europeans headed the list, with those from Northern and Western Europe at the very top of the evolutionary ladder. Yet all groped toward the common goal, and all could hope — in the very long run — to achieve the same perfection. The images of childhood and maturity came to symbolize the relation of the advanced to the backward peoples, and immediately suggested the operative function of the relationship: parental tutelage. As the parent raised and trained the child, so the superior peoples — the white Europeans — should lead their inferiors toward civilization. Like children, these backward peoples needed constraint and authority, lest they do damage to themselves and to others; like children, they could be bright, charming, and precocious, but seldom "steady," responsible, or of really sound judgment. Yet they bore within themselves the seeds of future manhood, for good or for evil, depending on the rearing. The conclusion was inescapable: it was not only possible for the civilized to lead the backward toward the light, it was actually their moral duty to do so. If the task was hard, and its duration long—as long as the foreseeable future—then this opportunity and duty could fittingly be called, at last, "the White Man's Burden."[10]

In 1893 John W. Burgess, a prominent professor at Columbia College in New York, attempted to familiarize his countrymen with some of these considerations. He found many of them sadly lacking in a true understanding of "the mission of the Teutonic nations," since they tended to view colonial conquests as unwarrantable interference in the affairs of others. Burgess was particularly exercised at the notion that the subject peoples concerned should be allowed to determine their own fate. Those who so argued were, he felt, naive. "They do not appear to give due consideration to the fact that by far the larger part of the surface of the globe is inhabited by populations which have not succeeded in establishing civilized states," and which lacked the capacity to do so. Such populations must submit to outside tutelage, Burgess insisted. "There is no human right to the status of barbarism. The civilized states have a claim upon the uncivilized populations, as well as a duty towards them, and that claim is that they shall become civilized." If the barbarians resisted, they must be coerced; if they proved hopelessly obdurate, then as a last resort they must be expelled or exterminated, but they must not stop the march of civilization. "There is a great deal of weak sentimentalism abroad in the world concerning this subject," the eminent professor complained.[11]

Put in these terms, the advance of progress must have seemed uncomfortably like that of a juggernaut to its dismayed beneficiaries, but Burgess, who owed his inspiration to German thought and training, dwelt rather more on the harsh realities of coercion than many Victorians would have preferred. He had nevertheless defined, however unpleasantly, a duty which his English contemporaries certainly believed to exist. Yet duties without rewards are notoriously apt to go untended. It is important that the later Victorians thought it right, and perhaps necessary, to carry their culture to alien areas; it is equally important that they thought they saw advantage in it.

Almost everywhere, the colonial relation was regarded by imperialists as mutually beneficial. As we have seen, the colonial power was to bring its new subjects order, stability and enlightenment, modern medicine and eternal salvation. The popular Scottish lecturer, J. A. Cramb, asserted in 1900 that "imperialism . . . is patriotism transfigured by a light from the aspirations of universal humanity." The colonial peoples and their lands, on the other hand, could bring their masters material gain. They produced raw materials used by modern industry, as well as food to sustain the industrial masses. Civilization needed the rubber and tin, tea and coffee, gold and diamonds, bananas and petroleum, of the non-western world, and especially of the tropics. Late in his career one of England's colonial overlords of Africa, Sir Frederick Lugard, explained the European viewpoint: "the tropics are the heritage of mankind, and neither, on the one hand, has the suzerain Power a right to their exclusive exploitation, nor, on the other hand, have the races which inhabit them a right to deny their bounties to those who need them." This Dual Mandate, as it came to be called, resembled a contractual obligation: the backward peoples owed to civilized society whatever natural bounties civilization required for its use, while the civilized world had an obligation to spread the blessings of progress among the barbarians.[12]

Actually, the economic role of the colonial peoples was defined far more broadly than the terms of the Dual Mandate would suggest. Colonial areas were expected not only to produce needed raw materials, but to consume the manufactures of the mother country, and to provide additional opportunities for its business enterprises. In the last third of the nineteenth century Europe suffered from periodical industrial depressions, chronic unemployment, and financial instability. Many business and political leaders came to accept a "glut theory" to explain these economic ills. Put simply, the theory held that owing to technological advances, productivity in the industrial countries was increasing far faster than their populations could ever be expected to increase. Thus production had permanently outrun the demands of the home market, and economic health could be restored only by selling the surplus goods in the non-industrial areas of the world. The creation of a colonial empire would provide new markets for the mother country, as the native populations were introduced to industrial products and taught to desire them. As they acquired civilization, so would they become consumers.

No one put the matter more clearly than Jules Ferry, Premier of France and principal prophet of French imperialism. "The colonial policy," he wrote, "is the daughter of the industrial policy. For the rich states where capital abounds and rapidly accumulates, and the manufacturing regime is constantly on the increase ... exportation is an essential factor of public prosperity and the field for the use of capital, as the demand for work is measured by the extent of the foreign market . . . . European consumption is saturated; one must move out into other parts of the globe for new classes of consumers, under pain of throwing modern society into bankruptcy."[13] Joseph Chamberlain voiced similar views in England. He said in 1888: "If tomorrow it were possible . . . to reduce by a stroke of the pen the British Empire to the dimensions of the United Kingdom, half at least of our population would be starved." Later, Chamberlain told a workers' audience in Birmingham that the expansion of the Empire was the government's principal weapon against unemployment. If England should lose any important part of her colonies, he warned, "the first to suffer would be the workingmen of this country." Thus capitalists and workers alike were assured that overseas possessions served their own material interests, and if some were skeptical, many believed, or hoped, that it was true.[14]

Nor were the benefits of empire merely economic. If colonies brought wealth, they also brought strength. The national consolidation of Germany and its startling victory over France in 1870, the steady growth of Russia and the United States, the modernization of Japan, the emergence of two rival European alliance systems—all led to a preoccupation with national security as well as prosperity. Colonial rivalries themselves added to the tension, and the world seemed to be coalescing into ever larger political units and combinations, the largest of which must come to dominate the rest. An early statement of the resulting fears came in 1883 from the distinguished English historian, John R. Seeley. Seeley thought that "the same inventions which make vast political unions possible, tend to make states which are on the old scale of magnitude unsafe, insignificant, second-rate. If the United States and Russia hold together for another half century, they will at the end of that time completely dwarf such old European states as France and Ger-

many, and depress them into a second class. They will do the same
to England, if at the end of that time England still thinks of herself
as simply a European state . . . ."

Seeley advocated the federation of England and her overseas
settlement colonies into a single English-speaking union. He expressly rejected the idea that "an artificial union of settlements and
islands scattered over the whole globe," which were "connected by
no tie except the accident that they happen all alike to acknowledge
the Queen's authority," could constitute the super-state he had in
mind, and he emphasized the distinction between colonies inhabited by those of English language and descent and those inhabited
by subject aliens. Others, however, were less interested in such
distinctions, and Englishmen tended to regard their empire as
enhancing their security, not only through the control of specific
strategic points, but by virtue of sheer overpowering mass. There
was comfort in seeing the globe so splashed and spotted with red;
the Jubilee was an attempt to bring alive the meaning of those
colored areas on the map. Nations either grew or declined; was
there a clearer proof of growth and vitality than that steady extension of dominion which still swelled the British Empire?[15]

Such were the assumptions which justified imperialism and made
it rational to its practitioners. European rule over the backward
peoples represented a necessary stage in the inevitable march of
progress, as well as adding to the present well-being of the world.
A few far-sighted thinkers were already envisioning the state of
affairs which would follow the fulfillment of the imperialist mission.
Among these was Charles H. Pearson, an Englishman who viewed
the future from the vantage of the 1890s, and reacted to it with
mixed emotions. The imperialist duty, he felt, could not be shirked:
"We are bound, wherever we go, to establish peace and order; to
make roads, and open up rivers to commerce; to familiarize other
nations with a self-government which will one day make them
independent of ourselves." If the duty were properly performed,
the day must come at last when the more numerous non-white
races had been developed to a point of virtual equality with white

civilization. They would then conduct their own government and commerce, possess armies and navies, achieve education and social grace; they would be "represented by fleets in European seas, invited to international conferences, and welcomed as allies in the quarrels of the civilized world." When this should happen, "the citizens of these countries will then be taken up into the social relations of the white races, will throng the English turf, or the salons of Paris, and will be admitted to intermarriage. It is idle to say," conceded Pearson, shaken by his vision, "that if all this should come to pass, our pride of place will not be humiliated. We were struggling among ourselves for supremacy in a world which we thought of as destined to belong to the Aryan races and to the Christian faith . . . . We shall wake to find ourselves elbowed and hustled, and perhaps even thrust aside by peoples whom we looked down upon as servile, and thought of as bound always to minister to our needs." Even so, Pearson neither shrank from his conclusions nor questioned the process by which they would be brought about. Europe must continue, he insisted, "to carry peace and law and order over the world, that others may enter in and enjoy it." Yet it was bitter to think of the end of European primacy: "In some of us the feeling of caste is so strong that we are not sorry to think we shall have passed away before that day arrives."[16]

Few, however, followed the logic of imperialism so ruthlessly to its end, and at any rate that end, as everyone knew, was very far off. The pace of the civilizing process was not to be measured in years, but in generations or even centuries. Had it not taken thousands of years to bring western civilization to where it now so proudly stood? It was hardly likely, then, that the hordes of barbarism could be hustled into a similar state of grace within a few decades. For the foreseeable future, European dominion was safe; beyond that lay only matter for remote speculation.

All of this was not to say that everyone in Europe, or even in England, was a thoroughgoing imperialist. There existed in England an old and sturdy anti-imperialist tradition, of which Herbert Spencer himself was a vigorous exponent. Nor had every statesman

who presided over the growth of the British Empire a philosophical
commitment to the process. One prime minister, Lord Salisbury,
declared irritably that Africa had been invented to plague the
Foreign Office, and viewed oriental adventures with a lackluster
eye. " . . . I agree with you," he wrote Joseph Chamberlain in 1897,
"that 'the public' will require some territorial or cartographic con-
solation in China. It will not be useful, and will be expensive; but
as a matter of pure sentiment, we shall have to do it."[17] Not only
public opinion, but existing colonial responsibilities, drove the
government and its distant satraps to new frontier advances; a
large empire provided a powerful motivation for a larger one. Yet,
after making all allowances, the mystique of empire stood very
high in the 1890s, and public men were rare whose thinking was
not in some way influenced by it.

   Much of the world view of late-Victorian Englishmen was shared
by their American contemporaries. Americans, too, believed in
progress, and saw a gulf between western civilization and non-
western barbarism; they too sought to find universal laws of history,
and enthusiastically embraced evolutionary social theories. White
men were as confident of their superiority in the United States as
ever they were in England, and desired new markets as keenly as
their cousins across the sea. Most Americans, it is true, thought less
about the international implications of their assumptions than did
the Europeans. Still accustomed to feeling isolated in the western
hemisphere, and lacking colonial territories or subjects, they preferred to leave world affairs to those more immediately concerned
with them, and to notice them, if at all, casually and with relative
detachment. But when the United States itself became embroiled
in colonial problems, it tended at first to look to the English experience as well as to its own. When Elihu Root became Secretary of
War in 1899, with the responsibility of pacifying and governing
the new island territories, his response was characteristic. "The
first thing I did after my appointment," he wrote, "was to make out
a list of a great number of books which cover in detail both the
practice and the principles of . . . colonial government under the

English law," and for the next few months he spent his spare time
in reading them.[18]

It was not, however, as a model to copy, but as a threat to repel,
that European empire-building first came to play an important part
in the American foreign policy of the 1890s. With the powers of
Europe well along in their self-appointed task of partitioning the
Eastern Hemisphere among themselves, the possibility that they
might also turn their attention to the Western Hemisphere could
not be ignored. Many of the Latin American nations were weak
and vulnerable; it was even questioned whether some of them
should really be called "civilized." Europeans had large financial
interests in Latin America, and the British, at least, had great
diplomatic influence there as well. Such factors raised the specter
of a colonial "scramble" in the New World to parallel that in the
Old.

At first such a possibility seemed unthinkable, for it clashed with
United States traditions and with the hallowed Monroe Doctrine.
There had, of course, been a good deal of anxiety about European
incursions during the American Civil War, when the Union was too
distracted to prevent them. The Spanish had then provoked a small
naval war with the West Coast countries of South America, and
had temporarily reannexed the troubled Republic of Santo Domingo. A more serious threat to hemispheric security appeared
simultaneously in Mexico, where a joint British-Spanish-French
debt-collecting expedition evolved into a full-fledged French invasion. When the French erected a new government headed by
Archduke Maximilian of Austria, now styled Emperor of Mexico
and maintained in power by 40,000 soldiers of France, people in
the United States began to take alarm. The French venture, however, ended disastrously, owing to a combination of stout Mexican
resistance and United States diplomatic pressure. Indeed, the whole
affair came to symbolize for Americans the triumphant vindication
of the Monroe Doctrine, which had been made good against a
great European power.[19]

Yet periodic straws in the wind suggested that Europe still

harbored dangerous aspirations in the New World. One such occurrence was the announcement in 1879 of a French project to build a ship canal across the Isthmus of Panama. Since the leading figure in the scheme was Ferdinand de Lesseps, the famed builder of the Suez Canal, the possibility of its success could not be lightly dismissed. Men had long envisioned an isthmian canal across Central America, and Americans had assumed that when it was built, they would build it. Such a waterway would have enormous strategic importance and hardly less commercial significance; both Congress and the President were shocked at the prospect of its control by a European power.

The French government was quick to dissociate itself from the canal project, explaining that de Lesseps represented only a group of private citizens of several nationalities. To President Rutherford B. Hayes, this assurance was inadequate. The leadership and capital of the canal company were largely French; the company would inevitably look to the French government for protection in time of need. In a special message to Congress, Hayes declared: "The policy of this country is a canal under American control. The United States can not consent to the surrender of this control to any European power or to any combination of European powers." The issue was of "paramount concern to the people of the United States," he warned.[20]

Fortunately for Hayes and his successors, the Panama Canal Company was beset with practical difficulties and crippled by inadequate management, and within a few years it virtually ceased operations. The dangers from the French receded, and as the end of the century approached it was the English who were singled out as the nemesis of hemispheric security. Looking to England for social and cultural leadership, seeking her capital, yet fearing her economic rivalry, both jealous of and admiring her imperial power and prestige, Americans had cast the English in an ambivalent role by the 1890s, and seriously suspected them of plotting the systematic encirclement of the United States.

For one thing, Great Britain had a far stronger position in the

Western Hemisphere than any other outside nation. Her territories covered as much of North America as did those of the United States itself; her possessions dotted the Caribbean, and touched both Central and South America. The British economic and diplomatic influence were paramount in South America; the British merchant marine led in the hemisphere's carrying trade, and her naval power was potentially dangerous even when far removed from American waters. All this was serious enough, but in the 1890s the conviction grew in the United States that the British intended to expand their already formidable power in the New World. The crisis came in 1895, when, to the fearful, many threads seemed suddenly to draw together. In South America, a decades-old boundary dispute between Venezuela and British Guiana came to a head, with the bone of contention an enormous tract of lightly populated jungle country claimed by both nations. As the British hardened their position toward Venezuela, declaring that their claim to much of the disputed area was no longer subject to negotiation, they appeared to many to be pushing forward the boundaries of their empire in a way long familiar in India, Burma, and Africa.

At the same time, in the spring of 1895, English warships seized the port of Corinto in Nicaragua to collect a disputed indemnity from the Nicaraguan government. The English left after collecting their money, but this sudden exercise of force in Central America added to the unease caused by their Venezuelan policy. Another source of nervousness was Hawaii, where the old native monarchy had been overthrown in 1893 by a revolutionary government which sought annexation to the United States. President Grover Cleveland had rejected the Hawaiian advances, charging the preceding Harrison administration with complicity in the Hawaiian Revolution, and leaving the ultimate fate of the islands in doubt. In numerous though unsupported rumors, the British were charged with having designs on Hawaii, possession of which would give them a naval control of the Pacific comparable to that which they already held in the Atlantic. As a direct result of all these factors, the British were astonished in 1895 to find themselves involved in a diplomatic crisis with an aroused and defiant United States, the roots of which lay in American fears that European imperialism was seeking entry into the New World.[21]

Senator Cushman Davis of Minnesota, who in two years would become Chairman of the Senate Committee on Foreign Relations, voiced these fears in May, 1895, in a speech which traced British aggression and aggrandizement through British Honduras, Nicaragua, Venezuela, and Hawaii. The United States government should have intervened to prevent the British seizure of Corinto, Davis said, and must certainly intervene in the Venezuelan boundary dispute, while the immediate annexation of Hawaii was imperative to prevent its use by "a hostile power."[22]

What Davis stated briefly, his younger colleague, Senator Henry Cabot Lodge of Massachusetts, developed at length. During a Senate speech in March, 1895, Lodge produced a huge map of the world on which was marked, with large red crosses, every British naval base. Dramatically he pointed out the evidence of British encirclement. "That red line which goes down the Atlantic coast shows the foresight of England. Does anyone suppose that that naval station at the Bermudas was placed there because England did not have enough naval stations? She put it there because it is only a little over 600 miles from New York." Similarly, British naval stations in the Falkland Islands, the Fiji Islands, and at Vancouver marked the outlines of a system of Pacific control. Only the central point, the Hawaiian Islands, was lacking to complete it. "They are the key of the Pacific," Lodge announced, concluding passionately if a bit incoherently that "there in the one place where the hand of England has not yet been reached out, to throw away those islands is madness."[23]

Senator John T. Morgan of Alabama followed Lodge's speech with another along the same lines, in spite of the declaration of Senator Richard F. Pettigrew of South Dakota that he was "tired of hearing Senators upon this floor, whenever they wish to put through a measure which they advocate, talk to the American people about the fear of England." To Lodge, however, the danger was a deadly reality. If the British were allowed to make territorial gains in the Americas, he wrote shortly after this exchange, France and Germany would do the same. "These powers have already seized the islands of the Pacific and parcelled out Africa. Great Britain cannot extend her possessions in the East. She has pretty nearly reached the limit of what can be secured in Africa. She is now turning her attention to South America. If the United States are prepared to see South America pass gradually into the hands of Great Britain and other European powers and to be hemmed in by British naval posts and European dependencies, there is, of course, nothing more to be said." But the Republican senator was clearly not so prepared, and neither, it developed, was the Democratic administration of Grover Cleveland.[24]

On July 20, 1895, Secretary of State Richard Olney sent a long despatch to the United States Ambassador in London, with instructions to give a copy of it informally to the British Prime Minister, Lord Salisbury. Salisbury, who was his own Foreign Minister, must have found this missive startling reading; President Cleveland referred to it approvingly as "Olney's twenty-inch gun," and it voiced United States opposition to European expansion in the Americas in words which could have come from Senator Lodge himself.

Olney too saw the British course in the Venezuelan dispute as thinly veiled expansionism, and he declared that "the safety and welfare of the United States are . . . concerned with the maintenance of the independence of every American state as against any European power . . . ." European threats to the integrity of American states would "justify and require the interposition of the United States," Olney said, coupling the point with a large claim: "Today the United States is practically sovereign on this continent, and its fiat is law upon the subjects to which it confines its interposition." This was because "its infinite resources combined with its isolated position render it master of the situation and practically invulnerable as against any and all other powers." But this situation would be drastically altered by any successful European incursion, for the other European powers would rush to exploit any weakening of the

Monroe Doctrine. Each would seize American territory: "What one power was permitted to do could not be denied to another, and it is not inconceivable that the struggle now going on for the acquisition of Africa might be transferred to South America." The weaker countries would soon be conquered, "while the ultimate result might be the partition of all South America between the various European powers."

> The disastrous consequences to the United States of such a condition of things are obvious. The loss of prestige, of authority, and of weight in the councils of the family of nations, would be among the least of them. Our only real rivals in peace as well as enemies in war would be found located at our very doors. Thus far in our history we have been spared the burdens and evils of immense standing armies and all the other accessories of huge warlike establishments, and the exemption has largely contributed to our national greatness and wealth as well as to the happiness of every citizen. But, with the powers of Europe permanently encamped on American soil, the ideal conditions we have thus far enjoyed can not be expected to continue. We too must be armed to the teeth, we too must convert the flower of our male population into soldiers and sailors, and by withdrawing them from the various pursuits of peaceful industry we too must practically annihilate a large share of the productive energy of the nation.

"How a greater calamity than this could overtake us," Olney concluded, "it is difficult to see." It was, therefore, up to the British to explain themselves. "Being entitled to resent and resist any sequestration of Venezuelan soil by Great Britain, [the United States] is necessarily entitled to know whether such sequestration has occurred or is now going on." The test of whether or not such was the case was to be, specifically, whether or not the British would submit their claims to arbitration. Only thus could they prove that they were engaged, not in aggression, but in a legitimate boundary dispute.[25]

Even Olney's amazing note failed to bring a quick response from London, and it was followed in December by a special message to

Congress from the President himself. Cleveland again insisted that England arbitrate the boundary issue, asked Congress to send a United States commission to determine what territory rightfully belonged to Venezuela, and promised that the government would "resist by every means in its power" any British attempt to take such territory. The result was an international sensation, and, ultimately, British agreement to submit to arbitration. Though Cleveland's opponents regarded his course as unnecessarily belligerent, there was a general and justified feeling that the affair had brought about a significant change in the international position of the United States. The world was given notice that no outside imperialism could enter the Western Hemisphere unchallenged, whatever the fate of the rest of the world.

At the same time, however, the threat of such a prospect had forced the phenomenon of imperialism upon the attention of Americans, and led them to think more seriously about their foreign relations. The immediate effects were at least twofold. One was the growing advocacy of a sort of prescriptive imperialism, a conviction that the United States should seize desirable areas before a rival power got them. Most notably applied to Hawaii, this consideration would henceforth find a place in the discussions of almost any foreign territory in which the United States took an interest. In addition, some Americans came increasingly to incorporate imperialist assumptions into their thinking about their own nation's problems. Even the idea of an American empire began to seem less alien; if overseas colonies were of such benefit to Europe, perhaps they could help to cure the ills of the society and economy of the United States.

After new island territories had actually been secured in 1898, the European example served still another purpose. This was a different kind of expansion for the United States, exciting yet somewhat disquieting, and expansionists sought to fit it into the frames of reference available to them. In their efforts to do so, they coupled appropriate aspects of their own past with borrowings from current European thought. Among the intellectual devices employed, one of the most successful was the amalgamation of American expan-

JOHN BULL: "It's really most extraordinary what
training will do. Why, only the other day I thought
that man unable to support himself."

— *The Inquirer*, Philadelphia.
Reprinted in the *Literary Digest*, Aug. 20, 1898.

sion and British imperialism into an all-embracing Anglo-Saxon
mission. The concept of a common trans-Atlantic Anglo-Saxondom
was hardly a novelty, but seldom before had it been applied so
directly to foreign policy. In a magical transformation, the nemesis
of 1895 became the blood brother of 1898. The Venezuelan crisis
ended in English concessions which cleared the air and calmed old
suspicions. On the heels of this came England's wartime role as
the only European nation friendly to the United States, and a burst
of English journalistic writing which welcomed the advent of the

Americans into the ranks of the civilizing powers. The Americans, it developed, were fellow Anglo-Saxons, and thus qualified by race and heredity to take up the White Man's Burden. So said the *Fortnightly Review* of London, whose editors believed that there was "no question that Americans are as capable as any other persons of their race of becoming successful managers of colonies which are mainly populated by inferior stocks."[26]

The British, who were beginning to feel concerned about their international isolation, toyed with the possibilities of a partnership of the English-speaking world. Even before the war Sir Walter Besant, a leading Anglo-Saxonist, had drawn glittering pictures of a union of the two peoples, dwelling upon the immense amount of territory which they jointly controlled. "We have the whole of North America, an immense possession, glorious in the present, destined to become far more glorious in the future. We have the whole of Australia, the whole of India, the whole of New Zealand; we have rich and beautiful islands; we have Burma, Singapore and the settlements of the Far East; we have a vast extent of territories in Africa, we have strongholds in the Mediterranean, we occupy Egypt: the whole round world is dotted here and covered there with the possessions of the Anglo-Saxon race . . . if it were one united federation of states it would be the greatest, the richest, the most powerful empire, republic or state that history has ever recorded."[27]

A flamboyant and crusading English editor, William T. Stead, had long been the prophet of such a fruition. He struck this note in 1890 in the first issue of his new *Review of Reviews*, where he declared his "deep and almost awestruck regard for the destinies of the English-speaking man" and called for "fraternal union with the American Republic." Years later, in 1902, Stead entitled a special supplement to his review *The Americanization of the World*. Seeing the United States emerging as the greatest of world powers, he argued that only by union with her could Great Britain retain a share, at least, of preeminence. Like Besant he revelled in the sheer size of the resulting empire, but he insisted further on its "providential mission" to "secure peace to the world," presumably by enforcing it on everyone else. The Anglo-Saxons had, after all, "despoiled the Portuguese, the French, and the Dutch, and have left to the German and the Italian nothing but the scraps and knucklebones of a colonial dominion." Indeed, "the rest of the world cuts but a poor figure compared with the possessions of the English-speaking allies," Stead remarked complacently. In view of all that was to be gained, and of the realities of power, Stead urged his countrymen to subordinate narrow nationalism to a broader racial patriotism. "We live in the day of combinations. Is there no Morgan who will undertake to bring about the greatest combination of all—a combination of the whole English-speaking race?" And like a Morgan merger, the result would harmonize economic rivalries between the two industrial giants.[28]

This was heady stuff, but it was not entirely new to Americans. John Fiske, who also looked to the "English race" to bring the world peace, order, and liberty, had said much the same things back in the 1880s. Believing that "the conquest of the North American continent by men of English race was unquestionably the most prodigious event in the political annals of mankind," Fiske looked to the time, already in sight, when the two great branches of that "race" should dominate the world. "Obviously the permanent peace of the world can be secured only through the gradual concentration of the preponderant military strength into the hands of the most pacific communities." The overwhelming power of the Anglo-Saxons would thus end major wars; their economic competition would force all other peoples to modernize and rationalize their own societies. Europe must eventually federate to survive, and as nationalism declined, free trade and international cooperation would take over. In time, the influence of a united Anglo-Saxondom would make over the world in its own image.[29]

It should be noted, in all fairness, that both Stead and Fiske hated war and opposed conquest. They spoke essentially of peaceful and evolutionary developments, not of militant coercion of the rest of the globe. Both were upset at what they regarded as perversions of their visions to more strictly imperialist ends, but their readers had a distressing tendency to be intrigued by their goals rather than their methods. On the other hand, few in England or America thought seriously of the political union of their two countries. The English often spoke of an alliance, while American expansionists saw merely a rather mystical, but distinctly reassuring, community of roles in world affairs. The English had been doing this sort of thing successfully for years, and as an integral part of an over-arching Saxondom, American society could be viewed simply as coming of age and taking up its proper and predestined share of the task. The rather condescending English assurances that this was true served, in the moment of transition, to provide corroboration from high authority.

Many in England, conversely, saw in the entry of the United States into the colonial game, not only the creation of a potent international partner, but assurance that colonial acquisition did in fact make sense. Imitation was the sincerest form of flattery; it was taken also as an independent verification of the validity of empire. Thus British and American expansionist movements strengthened each other in the late 1890s. This mutual intensification was strongest in 1898; in the following year the Boer War on the one hand, and the Philippine War on the other, quickly damped the fervor of the colonialists in both countries. Furthermore, as Americans buckled down to the task of administering their new dependencies, they found their own methods and principles rather than blindly following the British example. After the initial shock of change, they were less in need of external reenforcement and guidance.[30]

While the Anglo-Saxonist wave crested, however, it was pervasive and influential, carrying along men of affairs as well as writers and intellectuals. Joseph Chamberlain, who had emerged as a principal figure in Salisbury's cabinet, publicly asserted that "even war itself would be cheaply purchased if in a great and noble cause the Stars and Stripes and the Union Jack should wave together over an Anglo-Saxon alliance." On another occasion he declared that the Americans "are our kinsfolk and we shall never forget it." In already familiar words he pictured a partnership of the two people which "would be a guarantee of the peace and the civilization of the world."[31]

On the American side, that same Richard Olney who had so recently bearded the British lion during the Venezuelan dispute, now found that there was "a patriotism of race as well as of country—and the Anglo-American is as little likely to be indifferent to the one as to the other." He implied that his own late thunderings at Perfidious Albion had been merely the "liberties of speech which only the fondest and dearest relatives indulge in." Similarly, Ambassador John Hay told the English that there was "a sanction like that of religion which binds us to a sort of partnership in the beneficent work of the world." The two peoples, he said, were "joint ministers of the same sacred mission of liberty and progress, charged with duties which we cannot evade by the imposition of irresistible hands." Even Theodore Roosevelt, long suspicious of British ambitions, concluded that "it is for the good of the world that the English-speaking race in all its branches should hold as much of the world's surface as possible."[32]

There was, of course, a good deal of resistance to all this on the part of the many Americans who could not think of themselves as Anglo-Saxon. Even German-Americans tended to see the whole idea as an English trick, despite efforts to include them under the broader rubric of Teutonism. Nor could everyone so quickly abandon the ancient distrust of England, or the traditional aversion to foreign entanglements. It was further true that Englishmen and Americans often envisaged divergent goals while employing a common rhetoric. Yet at its short-lived peak, the glittering wave of Anglo-Saxon generalities swept much of the public before it, and marked a genuine, if limited, mingling of the two streams of British imperialism and American expansionism.

2 Destiny and Dollars

"WE HAVE done something out of line with American history," Benjamin Harrison asserted in 1900. The troubled ex-president spoke of the recent acquisition of a colonial empire. A small, reserved man with a chilly manner, Harrison appeared to his contemporaries an "iceberg in politics," and they must have wondered at the vehemence of his belated reaction against the annexations of 1898. As president, he had himself advocated a more active foreign policy, and even attempted to secure added territory. Yet he found outright imperialism alien to the American tradition, and so did many of his countrymen.[1]

There were, nevertheless, assumptions deeply rooted in the American past which harmonized with imperialist assumptions, as well as serious problems in the present to which imperialists claimed to possess the solution. Thus at least some elements of current European thinking fell on fertile ground in the United States, and were assimilated into the national outlook. In the main, these elements were those which Americans could equate with traditions and concepts they already considered their own, and which they could apply to issues which then seemed important to them.

A central tradition, as Theodore Roosevelt never tired of pointing out, was expansionism. "Throughout a large part of our national career our history has been one of expansion," Roosevelt wrote, "the expansion being of different kinds at different times. This expansion is not a matter of regret, but of pride."[2] In its first century of national life the United States had advanced, stage by inexorable stage, across an entire continent. The story of this triumphal march was one which Americans never tired of hearing, and which still thrilled them in retrospect. Running for the Senate in 1898, the young orator Albert J. Beveridge moved an Indiana audience to wild excitement simply by recounting the nation's successive acquisitions of territory. He began by sketching the ample boundaries of 1789. "The timid souls of that day said that no new territory was needed, and, for an hour, they were right. But Jefferson, through whose intellect the centuries marched, . . . Jefferson, the first imperialist of the Republic—Jefferson acquired that imperial territory which swept from the Mississippi to the mountains, from Texas to the British Possessions, and the march of the flag began. The infidels to the gospel of liberty raved, but the flag swept on." Next came the Floridas, seized by General Andrew Jackson and President James Monroe. "Then Texas responded to the bugle call of liberty, and the march of the flag went on. And at last we waged war with Mexico, and the flag swept over the Southwest, over peerless California, past the Golden Gate to Oregon, and from ocean to ocean its folds of glory blazed." It was enough to start Beveridge's audience cheering, and it was indubitably a part of the American heritage.[3]

Not only had the nation expanded across vast territories, but it had done so in the firm belief that Providence had decreed the outcome. With a boundless faith in their own institutions and enterprise, Americans saw themselves as expanding the frontiers of freedom, bringing forth riches from the waste places of the continent, and carrying forward civilization. They called the process Manifest Destiny, never doubting that it fulfilled God's own plan.[4]

No important addition of territory had been made, it was true, since the purchase of Alaska in 1867. Many thought that the march of destiny ended with the crossing of the continent. Others hoped for the eventual annexation of the rest of North America, but felt that the time was unpropitious for that action. Yet there were always some who urged projects of expansion in and out of season, and who kept the idea alive and relevant. Commodore Matthew C. Perry, the famed "Opener of Japan," hoped in the 1850s to lay the foundations of American power in the Far East. He suggested the establishment of naval bases in the Ryukyu and Bonin Islands, and called for a United States colony in Formosa, but found the government preoccupied with affairs closer to home. Other pre-Civil War expansionists, usually Southerners eager to augment the political power of the slave states, advocated the acquisition of Cuba, Nicaragua, or northern Mexico. These projects were blocked by anti-slavery forces, and forgotten during the Civil War, only to be revived in new forms after Appomattox.[5]

The outstanding post-Civil War expansionist was William Henry Seward, secretary of state under Presidents Abraham Lincoln and Andrew Johnson. In the late 1860s, Seward attempted to buy the Virgin Islands from Denmark, and explored the possibility of purchasing Cuba, Puerto Rico, Greenland, and Iceland. He gave strong diplomatic backing to schemes for the American construction of an isthmian canal. After bargaining for naval bases in Haiti and Santo Domingo, he advocated outright annexation of one or both of those countries. He counted upon the future annexation of Hawaii, and eventually of Canada and Mexico, by voluntary agreement of the inhabitants, and envisioned their incorporation into the union as a number of full-fledged states.[6]

None of these hopes was realized; the purchase of Alaska was Seward's only successful act of expansion. Yet the tradition of expansion was real enough, and men like Perry and Seward pointed the way toward its later revival. Their schemes, and those of other men like them, were clearly the fruit of American ideas, not foreign thinking, and in retrospect they helped to bridge the apparent gap between manifest destiny and imperialism. Carl Schurz, the German-American editor and politician, complained during the debate over Hawaiian annexation in 1893 that "whenever there is a project on foot to annex foreign territory to this Republic, the cry of 'manifest destiny' is raised to produce the impression that all opposition to such a project is a struggle against fate."[7]

Thus the idea of expansion never really died in the United States; neither was it ever found entirely separated from the concepts of progress and mission. From colonial times, Americans had seen themselves as building a new and better society which they thought the very embodiment of progress. To the general nineteenth-century optimism about the future, Americans added their faith in democracy and their enthusiasm for the amazing success story which was, to them, American history. As Andrew Carnegie wrote in 1893, "The old nations of the earth creep on at a snail's pace; the Republic thunders past with the rush of an express."[8]

Progress, after all, was tangibly present for everyone to see. The sweep of the frontier across the west, the peopling of an empty wilderness with tens of millions of souls, the planting of farms, and the growth of cities where savagery had reigned, the rush of invention, the amazing productivity of American industry—was this not progress on a grand scale? There were of course critics like Henry George, whose book, *Progress and Poverty*, dwelt upon the mass of human misery that had somehow managed to survive all this tangible achievement untouched; the conundrum posed by George was undoubtedly a puzzler, and growing labor and agrarian unrest made it hard to ignore. Yet most Americans still felt pride in what the nation had so far accomplished. By the end of the 1890s, the United States had become the world's first industrial nation, as well as the greatest exporter of agricultural products, and her people were, collectively, the richest society ever known.[9] Surely it was still a nation marked for special ends; the question was what new achievements the future would bring.

If Americans persisted in high hopes for their future, they also thought it their mission to promote liberty. Most felt that the nation had served this mission by creating a viable democratic society, by opening that society as a haven to the Old World's oppressed, and by setting an example of freedom as a model for the rest of mankind. While European civilization could bring enlightenment to barbarians, Americans hoped to enlighten Europe itself, not to

mention lesser places; for generations they had thought of themselves as a New World improving upon the Old.[10] The Victorian
insistence, however, upon the division of the globe between civilized and uncivilized societies in time affected American perspec-
tives too. Interest in the further democratization of Europe began
to give way to speculation about the American role in the march
of civilization.

The historian and lecturer John Fiske wrote in 1885 that "the
two great branches of the English race have the common mission
of establishing throughout the larger part of the earth a higher
civilization and more permanent political order than any that has
gone before," thereby claiming for the United States an equal
partnership with England in spreading progress.[11] In the following
year a reform-minded protestant clergyman named Josiah Strong
published *Our Country,* a best-selling book which also affirmed an
American world mission. Strong thought the Americans a people
unique in history. Occupying a huge, rich, contiguous territory,
located midway between Europe and the Orient, they combined a
special love of civil liberty with American Protestantism, which he
described as a "pure, spiritual form of Christianity." They were
energetic and practical, with a knack for money-making and a
tradition of social mobility. Furthermore, they had demonstrated
a genius for colonizing. Already well along toward creating the
good society at home, they must export their special gifts to the
less fortunate. "God has two hands," Strong wrote. "Not only is He
preparing in our civilization the die with which to stamp nations,"
but "He is preparing mankind to receive our impress." While certain
that the Almighty intended that American influence should mold
the world, the author confessed that "the exact nature of that influence is, as yet, undetermined." The method and timing of its
application was likewise for the future to determine; what was
beyond question was the special destiny of the United States.[12]

Vague as this was, it again raised the question whether the
American mission could continue to be fulfilled only at home, or
whether it required going out into the world in a missionary role.

In the 1890s, this question received increasing scrutiny, with the case for overseas action gathering adherents. One was Richard Olney, who had been secretary of state during the Venezuelan crisis. In a vigorous speech delivered shortly before the outbreak of the Spanish-American War, he attacked those content to set the world an example: "Posing before less favored peoples as an exemplar of the superiority of American institutions may be justified and may have its uses. But posing alone is like answering the appeal of a mendicant by bidding him to admire your own sleekness, your own fine clothes and handsome house and your generally comfortable and prosperous condition. He possibly should do that and be grateful for the spectacle, but what he really asks and needs is a helping hand. The mission of this country, if it has one, as I verily believe it has, is not merely to pose but to act . . . ." Great Britain and other powers went forth to do the world's work, Olney said, while the United States remained in isolation, playing the part of a sluggard.[13] At almost the same time, Ambassador John Hay wrote his President from London: "It is a pity we have so many men among us who do not and who cannot believe in the American people and in their glorious destiny . . . . The greatest destiny the world ever knew is ours."[14]

Besides a heritage of expansionism and a conviction of mission, Americans could find in their tradition another element in common with imperialist thought: a widespread belief in the inequality of races. Beyond and beneath an acceptance of Social Darwinism and other theories of inequality lay a whole national lifetime of practice. In the beginning, it was the Indian who was dehumanized. Frontier life soon convinced white men that their savage foes were in fact sub-human "red devils," and it became a truism that the only good Indian was a dead Indian. Unassimilated into white society, the Indian was pushed along ahead of the frontier, and at last herded onto segregated "reservations," selected chiefly for their worthlessness to white settlers. A second category of inferiors came with the institution of Negro slavery, which not only insisted upon the innate inferiority of the Negro, but subjected him to a harsh bondage and to sweeping controls over every aspect of his life. Three centuries of usage so firmly fixed the conviction of black inferiority that it survived the end of slavery almost unimpaired. A third non-white group classed as inferior was the Oriental, and particularly the Chinese, immigrant, who came to the West in considerable numbers in the second half of the nineteenth century. Brought in as cheap labor to build the railroads and work in the mines, the coolie enraged local whites by his competition on the job market as well as by his alien race and customs, and soon suffered, like the Negro and the Indian, from legal restrictions and extra-legal assaults.

By the end of the century, even certain groups of European whites felt the stigma of inferiority. As European immigration to the United States swelled in volume, it also changed in origin from the countries of northern and western Europe to those of the south and east. These Slavic, Jewish, and Mediterranean peoples brought social norms which diverged widely from those of the United States, or of northwest Europe; they seemed backward and alien to many Americans. These so-called "new immigrants," while not actually barred from full membership in their adopted society, were received with oft-voiced suspicions that they would prove to be inherently inadequate to the task of assimilating.

All of these prejudices were in play near the century's end. The feeling against the Indian, it is true, appeared less intense than before. Having gone down to final defeat, the Red Man ceased to be a threat; he even began to receive the sympathy of a few idealists. Chinese immigration ended with a federal ban in 1882, although those Chinese already in the United States continued to suffer from nativist hostility. It was thus the much larger groups of Negroes and recent immigrants from Europe who bore the brunt of prejudice in the 1890s. It was widely held that the current crop of immigrants was incapable of becoming good citizens, and they were often charged with entire responsibility for the slums and municipal corruption that marked the rapid growth of big cities in that era. Critics claimed, too, that they imported alien, radical ideologies to undermine democracy. The American Protective Association, organized in the 1880s to combat the influence of immigrants and Roman Catholics, added a religious bias to the nativist one, and gained a half million members in the next decade. In 1891, newspaper reports characterized a group of striking Slavic coal-miners in Pennsylvania as "Huns," while in 1895 a leading American poet described the newcomers collectively as "a wild motley throng . . . bringing with them unknown gods and rites," and "tiger passions," whose "strange tongues" were loud with "accents of menace alien to our air."[15]

Even this reaction was mild, however, compared to the nation's consignment of the Negro to new forms of legal inequality. The great anti-slavery crusade of the Civil War had faded into failure and disillusionment during Reconstruction, to be followed in the 1880s and 1890s by growing Northern apathy toward the Southern race problem. Wearied of struggling against the apparently unshakeable racism that survived Confederate defeat, and having salved their consciences with the destruction of institutional slavery, white liberals began to lose their enthusiasm for the cause. Protests against the resubmergence of the Southern Negro became cursory, and ended as mere party rhetoric used by Republicans to berate Democrats. Beginning in the 1890s, state legislation in the South virtually withdrew the freedmen's political rights, while the system of legalized segregation known as "Jim Crow" developed in luxuriant detail and found Federal sanction in a series of Supreme Court decisions. Sardonically, Professor William Graham Sumner of Yale pointed out that "we have made friends with the Southerners. They and we are hugging each other . . . . The Negro's day is over. He is out of fashion."[16]

It was clear that the words of the Declaration of Independence which declared that "all men are created equal" had long since acquired a special meaning: they applied to white men with origins in a limited area of northwest Europe, and they co-existed with a general conviction that everyone else shared in a varying degree of inferiority. Thus Americans went far to conquer in advance one of the most formidable contradictions to arise from their coming adventure in imperialism, that of practicing an institutionalized inequality while professing an egalitarian ideology. They had done it at home for years.

Not only did imperialist assumptions find support in important aspects of the American outlook, but they did so at a time when the makers of American foreign policy were increasingly preoccupied with foreign markets and political hegemony in the western hemisphere. In the 1880s, both Congress and the Executive became concerned about the tendency of the Latin American countries to sell their mineral and agricultural staples in the United States, only to spend the proceeds for goods produced in Europe. They viewed this both as another facet of the rising tide of European influence, and as a loss of needed sales to an American economy which seemed dangerously vulnerable to the fluctuations of the business cycle. In 1884, President Chester Arthur appointed a commission to investigate Latin American market prospects, and to recommend measures for increasing exports to that area. In the words of Senator John F. Miller of California, "the time has come now . . . when new markets are necessary . . . in order to keep our factories running. Here lies to the South of us our India . . . . " And S. O. Thacher, one of Arthur's three commissioners, reported at the end of his labors: "Peace, progress, and the manifold blessings of contented producing classes wait on the footsteps of any measure that shall insure to our laborers, our farmers, and our manufacturers a fair chance in the markets of Central and South America."[17]

Many of the commission's recommendations resembled the suggestions of the dynamic and imaginative James G. Blaine, Senator from Maine and secretary of state under President James A. Garfield. Blaine thought it urgently necessary to diminish European influence in the hemisphere, increase that of the United States, and move to secure greatly increased sales for the nation's products in the countries to the south. To achieve these goals he advocated a program that eventually included such items as the building of an isthmian canal under American control, federal merchant marine subsidies to improve sea communications, the negotiation of reciprocal trade agreements to lower tariff barriers, and the establishment of an international silver coinage acceptable in every American republic, thus eliminating difficult problems of currency exchange. Blaine particularly desired a pan-American conference to draw the Americas together politically and to enhance the opportunities for United States leadership.[18]

Garfield's assassination, which led to Blaine's resignation from the cabinet, wrecked his first move toward his cherished pan-American conference; his unsuccessful try for the presidency as the Republican candidate in 1884 was a further blow. But in 1889, with his reappointment as secretary of state by the newly elected President Benjamin Harrison, began a period of more active foreign policy and rising interest in the hemisphere. Blaine's long sought Conference of American Republics, cancelled in 1882 by the Arthur administration, convened at last in 1889. It proved something less than a complete success, as the Sister Republics were wary of *Yanqui* ambitions and uneager for new trade agreements. While its concrete achievements were debatable, however, it symbolized the advent of a new tempo of events.[19]

Harrison, Blaine, and Secretary of the Navy Benjamin Tracy agreed on the need for a larger navy and for the acquisition of overseas bases from which it could operate. They took a stiff tone toward other nations in hemispheric affairs: Blaine intensified a controversy with Great Britain over the degree to which the United States could control the taking of seals in the Bering Sea, and Harrison went to the brink of war with Chile as a result of a series of minor irritations and of a Valparaiso brawl in which some sailors were killed. As the end of his presidency approached, Harrison unsuccessfully attempted to secure the annexation of the Hawaiian Islands. He wrote Blaine in 1891 that while "not much of an annexationist," he felt that "in some directions, as to naval stations and points of influence, we must look forward to a departure from the too conservative opinions which have been held heretofore."[20]

The drive for a modern navy also began in the 1880s, at a time when the existing naval forces were so few and obsolete as to equal, in the face of any major opponent, no navy at all. Beginning in 1883, Congress authorized the construction of a succession of modern steel warships. In 1890, under Tracy's leadership, battleships were added to the smaller warships already in progress, and by the eve of the war with Spain thirteen heavy vessels were built or building, together with some two dozen lighter craft.[21]

In part this spurt of activity reflected fear of European aggression. Secretary Tracy included a reference to a hypothetical attack on New York in his annual report for 1890, and the burning of Washington by the British during the War of 1812 stood as an oft-cited example of the dangers of an unguarded coast. National pride played a role, too; it was humiliating to find that little Chile had two battleships when the United States had none. The American drive for export markets came also to be linked with naval needs. Not only did our growing foreign commerce require protection, but heightened trade rivalries would increase the probability of war.[22]

So reasoned the navy's Policy Board in an 1890 report. At the moment, the report said, the nation was fairly safe. "We fear no encroachments upon our territory, nor are we tempted at present to encroach upon that of others . . . . We have no colonies, nor any apparent desire to acquire them . . . . " Most of the nation's foreign commerce was carried on in foreign ships. "All of these reasons combine to make the United States self-contained to a greater degree than any other important nation," and accordingly lessened the chances of conflict with other countries. "But there are not wanting indications that this comparative isolation will soon cease to exist, and that it will gradually be replaced by a condition of affairs which will bring this nation into sharp commercial competition with others in every part of the world . . . . In the adjustment of our trade with a neighbor we are certain to reach out and obstruct the interests of foreign nations." This greatly increased the danger of war. In fact, the board was so certain of future crises that it asked for funds to build over two hundred additional warships, a request which was indignantly rejected by an astonished Congress.[23] Nevertheless, the naval expansion program went forward at a steady, if less ambitious, pace, reflecting in one more way the new sensitivity to overseas affairs.

Beginning in 1893, a prolonged business depression greatly accentuated interest in the economic side of foreign relations. There had been numerous depressions, "panics," and financial crises in nineteenth-century America, but this latest attack struck with unprecedented severity. A year after it began, the historian Henry Adams wrote: "Everyone is discussing, disputing, doubting, economizing, going into bankruptcy, waiting for the storm to pass, but no sign of agreement is visible as to what has upset us, or whether we can cure the disease. That the trouble is quite different from any previous experience, pretty much everyone seems to admit . . . . " To Adams, the collapse seemed inconceivable. "Here, in this young, rich continent, capable of supporting three times its population with ease, we have had a million men out of employment for nearly a year, and the situation growing worse rather than better. Society here, as well as in Europe, is shaking, yet we have no bombs, no violence, and no wars to fear."[24]

The economic crisis added tension to other social issues. Labor unrest had become endemic, and in the presidential election campaign of 1896, years of agrarian protest came to a head as William Jennings Bryan, the Democratic candidate, boldly proclaimed the western farmer's defiance of eastern financial interests. The depression became the occasion for reviewing society's weak spots and articulating its stresses. Discussions of the immigration question, urban problems, and class conflicts led to a more fundamental questioning of the very quality of American society, and whether or not it was "degenerating." Some observers raised the disquieting possibility that the depression might prove permanent. In a much discussed article entitled "What Are Normal Times?" one writer suggested that the boom times of the 1880s had resulted from special and non-recurring factors, and could not be expected to return. Chief among these special factors was the great frontier phase of western development, which was now losing its dynamism. The conclusion was gloomy: "We have been steadily, but inevitably, forced out of our old conditions of exceptional well-being, which came from our possession of a virgin continent, and have been brought into the competitive struggle in which all other civilized nations are engaged . . . . In a word, we are in the great world-struggle for existence."[25]

"Normal times," in short, meant among other things a continuing quest for export markets abroad. They also meant, to many, that an era was ending, and that it was time to re-examine old policies and ideas to determine if they had become obsolete, and to seek new approaches better suited to changing conditions. Thus the eve of the Spanish-American War found a nation in some ways puzzled and frustrated, undergoing what one historian has called a "psychic crisis," and ready to entertain novel notions in foreign policy as well as in domestic affairs.[26]

Some of this ferment found expression in the public press. "Marse" Henry Watterson, famed editor of the Louisville *Courier-Journal*, sounded the new note in 1896: "We are no longer a squalid Democracy, secure chiefly by reason of our isolation, a Pariah among the governments of men. We are a Nation—with the biggest kind of an N—a great imperial Republic destined to exercise a controlling influence upon the actions of mankind and to affect the future of the world as the world was never affected, even by the Roman Empire . . . . The struggle of the future will be the survival of the fittest. Why should we not begin to look about how things are going and to cast about for our particular interest and glory?" Watterson's clarion call was echoed the following year in a curious effusion written by Murat Halstead, a well-known Ohio editor and political figure. In a frothy and loosely reasoned magazine article, Halstead reproached the nation's leaders, both past and present, for their failure to secure northwestern Canada and Vancouver for the United States, and announced that destiny also decreed the annexation of Cuba "in good time." He raised the threat of foreign incursion: the Germans were infiltrating into South America and the West Indies, while the numberless hordes of Asia would soon attempt to cross the Pacific and challenge America. War was in the offing; the nation must arm as befitted a great power. It must embrace glamorous, though unspecified, projects of action. "Shall we not go on where the honors and the glories await us as the Power that is competent, if we will, to speak for half the globe?" And in the same year, the editor of *The Illustrated American* spoke of "the growing 'empire doctrine,' or the doctrine that it is the obvious duty of our country to increase its domain . . . . "[27]

The outbreak of war in 1898 brought scenes that, for a time, satisfied even the most heated imaginations. The armed forces of the United States fought successfully in exotic and widely separated areas, and the government suddenly found itself exercising responsibility in such farflung tropical territories as Cuba, Puerto Rico, Hawaii, and the Philippines. To the American people, already curiously torn between complacency and alarm, between faith in their destiny and uncertainty about their future, was presented a new paradox. Their fledgling empire seemed in many ways a proper product of their past history and traditions; in many other ways, it seemed to violate them.

3 Evolution of the New Imperialism: The Philippines

THE YEAR 1898, during which the United States gained an empire, came near the zenith of the empire-building activities and aspirations of Europe. Those Americans familiar with ideas and events in the Old World found it natural, therefore, to associate the actions of their own country with the global march of imperialism. To Captain Alfred Thayer Mahan, the United States Navy's prestigious historian and theorist, the current American expansionism appeared to be "but one phase of a sentiment that has swept over the whole civilized European world within the last few decades.... Every great state has borne its part in this common movement," he pointed out.[1] Furthermore, the American expansionist tradition seemed to provide precedent for imperialist ventures. Leading expansionists thus pictured the United States, to which territorial growth was second nature, and which shared the world mission of the favored Anglo-Saxon race, as having reached maturity and taken up its proper position in the onward march of western civilization.

Yet there was no lack of critics to point out the difference between the old expansion and the new. Running for president a second time in 1900, William Jennings Bryan charged that his opponents sought to confuse imperialism with traditional expansion, and attacked their effrontery in daring to claim Jefferson as a supporter of their policy: "The forcible annexation of territory to be governed by arbitrary power differs as much from the acquisition of territory to be built up into states as a monarchy differs from a democracy." The Democratic party, its standard-bearer insisted, did not oppose expansion "when expansion enlarges the area of the Republic and incorporates land which can be settled by American citizens, or adds to our population people who are willing to become citizens and are capable of discharging their duties as such."[2]

The fact is that "expansion," in the 1890s, meant several distinct things. The traditional process of adding contiguous territory destined for statehood, or even the acquisition of a network of small overseas base areas to protect or expand foreign trade, differed importantly from the annexation of distant areas with large, alien populations. This last form of expansion was what most people meant by "imperialism," and, while there were many anti-imperialists in America, there were few anti-expansionists. Thus traditional ideas of expansion survived to exert a powerful influence in the new era of the 'nineties, even upon imperialists themselves.

One traditional goal still widely discussed in the 'nineties was the annexation of Canada. Alternately waxing and waning for more than a century, interest in Canadian annexation took an upswing in the late 1880s. Canadians, for their part, were concerned about both their economic and their political future. Union with the United States would insure their goods free entry into their principal market, and tie them to the world's most dynamic economy. It would also end the anomalous position of a country which was no longer a colony and not yet a nation. Also, the revival of Anglo-French tensions within the dual Canadian society made the prospect of merging with another "Anglo-Saxon" nation more tempting to the dominant British sector in Canada; the French would be hopelessly outnumbered as a part of the United States. Traditional loyalties to the British Empire joined with a growing sense of Canadian identity and nationalism to outweigh the appeals of annexation among most Canadians, but there was sufficient interest north of the border to permit the founding in 1892 of a Continental Union League, representing annexationists in both Canada and the United States.[3]

In the latter country, the hope of acquiring Canada was as old as nationhood. There had been no attempt at conquest since the unsuccessful ventures of 1775 and 1812, but the purchase of Alaska in 1867 stirred a renewed interest in peaceable union. This interest was enhanced in 1869 by the remarkable proposal of Senator Charles Sumner that the United States should accept Canada in satisfaction of claims arising from Great Britain's violations of neutrality during the Civil War. President Ulysses Grant and his Secretary of State, Hamilton Fish, were also Canadian annexationists, but nothing came of their approaches to the British government. While interest slackened again in the 1870s and 1880s, it never died, and the remaining unionists included such Republican party leaders as James G. Blaine and Senator John Sherman of Ohio.[4]

The increased interest in the subject which brought forth the Continental Union League lasted longer in the United States than in Canada, and caught up men with a variety of political viewpoints. Early members of the League included John Hay, Theodore Roosevelt, Andrew Carnegie, and Charles A. Dana, editor of the New York *Sun.* Carnegie and Dana co-signed an appeal for money donations to the League in 1893, declaring that continental union would "deliver the Continent from any possible complications and add enormously to the power, influence, and prestige of North America." The reasoning was sufficiently persuasive to move a wealthy New York lawyer named Elihu Root to send $25. More importantly, continental union became official Republican doctrine. The Republican platform of 1896 called for "the eventual withdrawal of the European powers from this hemisphere," and "the ultimate union of all English-speaking parts of the continent by the free consent of its inhabitants."[5]

Almost as traditional an object of American expansionism as Canada was Cuba, and more recently Hawaii had also consistently interested Americans. In an 1897 editorial, the New York *Tribune* sketched the nation's continuity of purpose regarding these two areas: "for three-quarters of a century the 'historic policy' of the

United States has favored the annexation of Cuba and held it to be, eventually, inevitable. For half a century it has regarded the annexation of Hawaii as a probable and perhaps desirable contingency. To that policy nearly every American statesman of commanding rank has been committed." In support of his argument, the *Tribune* writer marshalled Thomas Jefferson, John Quincy Adams, Henry Clay, Daniel Webster, William L. Marcy, William H. Seward, Edward Everett, and James G. Blaine.[6]

The *Tribune* was on sound historical ground. In 1823, Secretary of State John Quincy Adams described Cuba and other West Indian islands as "natural appendages" to North America, while, to President James Monroe, Cuba formed a part of the mouth of the Mississippi. Not only was the United States destined to include all of North America, according to these expansionists, but, by a sort of geographical affinity, the nearby islands ought naturally to come with the rest. Ultimately the principle was extended all the way to Hawaii, now regarded as the natural outpost of the continent. To Senator Henry Cabot Lodge, the continental United States was the "citadel" and Hawaii a "necessary outwork," one of the "outlying islands which ought to belong to us." Senator George Frisbie Hoar of Massachusetts, a leading Senate anti-imperialist, supported the annexation of Hawaii from 1893 on, though only after repeated soul-searchings. But when the islands were finally annexed in 1898, he complained that expansionists had recently shifted their ground; instead of seeing Hawaii as the ultimate natural frontier, they now spoke of it as a stepping-stone to the farther shores of the Pacific. Hoar could support the first view as traditionally American; the second he rejected.[7]

This expanded continentalism, stretched to the limit in all directions, was reflected in other ways. In 1886, the United States opened a long dispute with Great Britain over the control of seal hunting in the Bering Sea with the claim that the entire sea was a *mare clausum*—a closed sea. Its waters were equivalent to the territorial waters of the United States, the government declared, in a claim which it was ultimately forced to abandon. In 1889, an American

ex-diplomat went even further. George H. Bates, who had been a
United States special commissioner in the long and troublesome
negotiations over Samoa, wrote an article arguing that those small
and distant islands lay within the jurisdiction of the Monroe Doctrine, which Bates thought ought to apply to the entire western
hemisphere. Admittedly, Samoa was not very near to the Americas
—not even Bates could claim it as a "natural appendage"—but it,
with Hawaii, constituted "special applications" of the hallowed
doctrine, Bates said.[8]

However broadly interpreted, the central focus of traditional
expansionism was the North American continent and its environs.
This essential continentalism set limits upon its aspirations, albeit
extraordinarily generous ones: even the most grandiose of expansionists hesitated to project their visions beyond the bounds of the
western hemisphere.

Another limitation to traditional expansion concerned the political status of territorial acquisitions. Up to now, Americans had
normally assumed that major territorial additions would progress
through the stages of development first formulated in the Northwest Ordinance of 1787, beginning with a standardized territorial
form of government and ending in full and equal statehood. The
process was still in operation in the continental United States, with
Oklahoma, Arizona, and New Mexico yet in territorial status, as
well as thinly populated Alaska. It was by no means obvious to
everyone that the new acquisitions should not be brought under
the familiar system that had served so well for all the others.

It was particularly common to view Cuba as one or more future
states. Senator Lodge took this view during the Spanish-American
War; he regarded a Cuban protectorate as "too complicated and
too unnatural for our form of government." Across the Senate aisle
a long-time Democratic "jingo" and expansionist, Senator John T.
Morgan of Alabama, took it for granted that "when these people
should grow up into a sufficient capacity they would be welcomed
and received even as States in the American Union. . . . " Morgan
was confident that a mass immigration from the United States to

Cuba would "Americanize" the island and soon fit it for statehood. Appointed to a commission to recommend to Congress the proper form of government for Hawaii, the Alabama senator again urged statehood, this time immediate, but was overruled by his more cautious colleagues. On the other hand, he thought Puerto Rico fit for no more than local autonomy under a United States protectorate.[9]

Such views provoked rage and alarm in men like Whitelaw Reid. The influential editor of the New York *Tribune* had been the unsuccessful Republican candidate for vice-president in 1892, and was one of the United States delegates to the peace conference which ended the war with Spain. Favoring creation of a genuine colonial empire, Reid was horrified at the idea of "admitting anybody and everybody to full partnership in the American union." He complained: "It has been only a little while since one could get anybody in Congress to admit the possibility of dealing with the Sandwich Islands [Hawaii] in any other way than by making them a state in the union." Worse yet, "Everybody seemed to consider it natural, as well as certain, that Cuba would come in some day as a state." To Reid, such a course "would . . . be humanitarianism run mad, a degeneration and degradation of the homogeneous, continental Republic of our pride . . . . " United States Ambassador to Germany Andrew Dickson White agreed entirely with Reid in his opposition to admitting alien areas to the union; he found Cuban statehood "a fearful prospect." But if Cuba were to be annexed at all, he thought, it must be as a state; she was too large, too near, and too well developed to accept less, even if the American political tradition should permit it. His conclusion reflected that of anti-imperialists in general: since the former Spanish islands were not appropriate areas for statehood, and since statehood was the only legitimate and practicable goal for such territories, they should not be annexed at all.[10]

There remained, of course, the possibility of evading the issue. Senator Lodge suggested that Puerto Rico and Hawaii could be organized as territories in the usual way, and then simply left in that status indefinitely, theoretically preparing for statehood, but never actually admitted. "When you reflect that we have kept New Mexico as a territory for more than fifty years although it is entitled to be a state," Lodge pointed out, "you can see how easy it is going to be to keep an outlying possession in a territorial condition." Not every mind was so flexible as that of Senator Lodge, however, and to many the statehood question lay near the heart of the controversy over expansion. In December of 1898, Senator George G. Vest of Missouri introduced a joint resolution that hit the issue squarely. It resolved "that under the Constitution of the United States no power is given to the Federal Government to acquire territory to be held and governed permanently as colonies . . . . [A]ll territory acquired . . . , except such small amount as may be necessary for coaling stations . . . and similar governmental purposes, must be acquired and governed with the purpose of ultimately organizing such territory into States suitable for admission into the Union." Vest's resolution touched off a major debate on the expansion question, highlighted by the arguments of leading figures on each side. Senator William E. Chandler of New Hampshire found the discussion helpful. "The right of the U.S. if we see fit, to hold a colony not as an integral and equal part of the nation seemed to me to grow clearer last winter as the debate went on," he wrote afterward. As usual, other listeners reached the opposite conclusion. What was clear was that the real question was not that of expansion, but of what kinds of expansion were permissible.[11]

It was the acquisition of the Philippine Islands which raised this question in its most acute form. Sprawling, populous, and located halfway around the world, the Philippines seemed to fit no previous category of American expansion. They had no conceivable geographic link with the Americas. Their population, remarkable for its diversity, was utterly alien, and the idea of Philippine statehood struck most people as simply grotesque. Annexation of the islands meant, therefore, the colonial rule of a distant, non-white people. To observers at the time, as to those since, it was the Philippine case which represented most clearly a break with past policies,

and which occupied the center of interest and debate. It was there
that the anti-imperialists concentrated their main efforts, and found
their greatest support and unity. It was, in fact, only on the Philippine issue that the anti-imperialists could reach a consensus, for
their leaders found it possible to accept a wide variety of expansionist projects elsewhere. In spite of grave reservations about
imperialism, and without regard to party affiliation, they betrayed
expansionist leanings almost to a man. Democratic leader William
Jennings Bryan wished to retain coaling stations in the Philippines
and Cuba, and advocated the annexation of Puerto Rico if her
people approved, though he was opposed to annexing unwilling
populations. Another Democratic view was expressed by Senator
Horace Chilton of Texas in a letter to Bryan: "It seems such a
conflict with the traditions of the Democratic party to argue against
expansion on this hemisphere . . . . If you lay down a principle
which . . . is equivalent to opposition to *all expansion,* I feel that
you will fatally weaken the chances of the Democratic party to win
popular approval." Chilton had a suggestion which would eliminate
the awkward problem of the Philippines: "Why not draw the line
on the same general circle with the Monroe Doctrine?" In short,
expansion was acceptable as long as it stayed within the hemisphere. Former Secretary of State Richard Olney, of the Cleveland
wing of the party, strongly opposed taking the Philippines, but
held the acquisition of Cuba to be necessary and inevitable. Nor
did he object to keeping a naval base in the Philippines; one forti-
fied base, he thought, would be far easier to defend than the whole
archipelago, and would accomplish the nation's entire strategic
purpose there.[12]

Republican anti-imperialists were equally ambivalent. Andrew
Carnegie, already a Canadian annexationist, also favored acquiring
Puerto Rico and Cuba if the inhabitants of those islands approved,
and he was confident that this approval would soon be forthcoming.
"I am no little American," Carnegie declared. "The day is coming
when we shall own all these West Indian islands. They will gravi-
tate to us of their own accord." Carnegie was even willing to take

Hawaii, as long as it come willingly. Senator Hoar not only voted for Hawaiian annexation, but approved of the Platt Amendment which made a United States protectorate of Cuba in 1901. Such a relationship seemed to Hoar merely a proper application of the Monroe Doctrine, and he said as much; a protectorate, after all, was a very different thing from a colony. The powerful Republican Speaker of the House, Thomas B. Reed, was an uncompromising anti-expansionist who almost single-handedly staved off the annexation of Hawaii for a year. Yet Reed argued in 1897, not that further territorial growth should cease forever, but that it must wait until the present national domain was more fully developed, and its sectional differences eased. His was a gradualist view of expansion: "Too much food may mean indigestion . . . . There is no need to hurry . . . . those empires which hope for eternity can wait."[13]

Among the political independents, or Mugwumps, Carl Schurz was one of those who regarded Canadian annexation as highly desirable and in harmony with the national traditions. Canada was contiguous, its people could easily be assimilated, and the several provinces as easily converted into states of the union, Schurz declared. Neither did he reject overseas bases. In 1898, he warned President William McKinley against acquiring any large colonies, insisting that "we shall . . . be able to get coaling stations and naval depots wherever we may want them," without taking on the burdens of colonial empire.[14]

It was clearly not expansion in general to which all of these people were opposed; it was merely the wrong kind of expansion, and they agreed that Philippine annexation exemplified that wrong kind. It is therefore useful to determine when and how the Philippines became a part of the expansionists' program. The first important point to be noted is that, prior to the war with Spain, no one in the United States even thought of acquiring the Philippines. Late in 1896, in one of the rare pre-war references to those islands, an article in the Atlanta *Constitution* discussed their future. The author believed that Spain's position in the Philippines was becoming hopeless because of native revolts, and predicted rivalry between Russia and Japan to take them over from Spain. There was no hint that the United States might have any interest in the matter at all, yet between 1895 and 1898 the expansionist program was clearly articulated and well publicized.[15]

Senator Lodge proclaimed that program in its most ambitious form: the annexation of Hawaii, the maintenance of United States influence in Samoa, the construction of an isthmian canal under United States control, the establishment of some form of control over Cuba, the expansion of the navy, and the acquisition of "at least one strong naval station" in the West Indies. In addition, Lodge was an ardent continental unionist; he eagerly awaited Canadian annexation, though admitting that "I should not think that we should go to war for it."[16] Few important expansionists had wider aspirations than Lodge, and none of them mentioned the Philippines. Whitelaw Reid advocated taking Hawaii in the present and Cuba in the future. Senator Morgan of Alabama called for a Nicaraguan canal under United States control, the annexation of Hawaii, and an enlarged navy. Theodore Roosevelt shared Morgan's aims, but also wished to see every European power driven out of the Americas. He thought that "every foot of American soil, including the nearest islands . . . , should be in the hands of independent American states, and so far as possible in the possession of the United States or under its protection." Henry Adams was another who hoped to see Europe evicted from the hemisphere, but Adams declared in 1898 that "the Philippines are not, and were not, in my scheme."[17] Alfred Thayer Mahan himself testified after the war that the expansionist group had failed to foresee the Philippine adventure. "Their vision reached not past Hawaii," he confessed, declaring that "the expansionists themselves, up to the war with Spain, were dominated by . . . purely defensive ideas," which centered on "the Antilles, Cuba, the Isthmus, and Hawaii."[18]

It was the prospect of war with Spain that first brought the Philippines within the circle of American policy, and it was an obscure group of naval planners who connected the islands with the coming war. In 1895, the navy began to study the strategic implications of a Spanish war. Reporting in June, 1896, the planning group envisioned such a war as an essentially naval one. The main American fleet would blockade Cuba, cutting off the supplies of the Spanish forces there and collaborating with the Cuban insurgents. Other naval units would blockade the Philippines and attack Manila, in order to put further pressure on the government of Spain. Lacking military power on land, the natural strategy of the United States was to use its superior naval strength to strike at Spain's vulnerable overseas empire.[19]

This 1896 plan became the object of debate within the navy, and when the McKinley administration took office in 1897, the projected Manila attack had been shelved for a substitute assault on the Canary Islands. To settle the controversy, the new civilian heads of the navy, Secretary John D. Long and Assistant Secretary Theodore Roosevelt, initiated another study of war plans. The result, submitted in June, 1897, restored the Philippine operation. "For the purpose of further engaging the attention of the Spanish navy, and more particularly in order to improve our position, when the time came for negotiations with a view to peace," the new planning board recommended an attack on Manila by the Asiatic Squadron. If successful, the squadron could aid the Philippine insurgents in overthrowing Spanish control, "in which case, we could probably have a controlling voice, as to what should become of the islands, when the final settlement was made."[20]

Once war was imminent, civilians as well as naval planners saw logic in attacking the archipelago. During the Congressional debate on the war resolutions, Senator Elkins insisted that the United States must take the entire Spanish empire as a war indemnity, to be disposed of as seemed best, and specifically named the Philippines, along with Cuba and Puerto Rico, as territory to be seized. Speaking in more purely strategic terms, Albert J. Beveridge told a Boston audience that Spain must be attacked "at her weakest point before we strike her at her strongest points . . . . The Philippines are logically our first target." It was, however, the news of Commodore George Dewey's victory at Manila Bay on May 1,

1898, that first made the general public aware of the existence of those hitherto obscure islands. Simultaneously with Dewey's victory came the government's decision to send an army to occupy Manila. To the public, the two events together signified that the archipelago was as good as conquered. Suddenly everyone was discussing what should be done with "the captured islands," though the discussion suffered from an almost total lack of accurate information on the subject. "Many of our readers may learn with surprise," said one editorial attempt to fill the void, "that in population and commerce the Philippines are much superior to Cuba; the population of the former is about 7,000,000 as compared with Cuba's 1,500,000" while the foreign trade of the Philippines was described as double that of Cuba.[21]

During the month of May, press reaction to the Philippine question developed rapidly. The Springfield, Massachusetts, *Republican* held that it was out of the question to return the islands to Spanish oppression, but equally unthinkable to keep them; an editorial suggested that they be sold to the highest bidder. The New York *Mail and Express* also spoke of a possible "auction" of the islands, but proposed alternatively that they might be traded to Great Britain in exchange for the British West Indies. The Chicago *Inter-Ocean*, which within a few months would be urging annexation, declared that there was "no part of the globe less suited to form a part of the United States than these Philippine Islands," and suggested their partition among several other powers. Whitelaw Reid's expansionist New York *Tribune*, however, cautioned the country against attempting to settle in advance questions about which it lacked full knowledge, while the Philadelphia *Record* thought that "the retention of some part of the Philippine group . . . may become inevitable."[22]

Public figures also began to express themselves. William Jennings Bryan and ex-President Grover Cleveland agreed that the war must not be prostituted to purposes of conquest, and both opposed taking the Philippines. "Shall we contemplate a scheme for the colonization of the Orient merely because our fleet won a remarkable victory in the harbor of Manila?" Byran asked. But another Democrat, Louisville editor Henry Watterson, predicted that the Pacific basin would become the center of the world's activities, and declared that the Philippines, along with the other war conquests, must remain American. "To surrender territory acquired by the outlay of so much blood and treasure would be a wanton and cowardly abandonment of obligations and opportunities literally heaven-sent, for they were not originally contemplated by anybody . . . ."[23]

Taken by surprise, many expansionists wavered at first on the Philippine issue. Just before leaving Washington to join his "Rough Riders," Theodore Roosevelt told Assistant Secretary of State John Bassett Moore that those islands lay far beyond the United States' sphere of influence, and warned against their acquisition.[24] In a month he had changed his mind, perhaps infected by the enthusiasm of his close friend Senator Lodge. Lodge thought the Philippines offered "vaster possibilities than anything that has happened to this country since the annexation of Louisiana," but even Lodge's confidence was somewhat shaken by the reservations of his mentor, Captain Mahan. "I myself, though rather an expansionist, have not fully adjusted myself to the idea of taking them, from our own standpoint of advantage," Mahan wrote Lodge. Nevertheless, it would be hard to withdraw entirely, and Mahan hoped for a compromise settlement by which the United States would take only the island of Luzon, and leave the rest of the archipelago to Spain. In August, Lodge advised the Secretary of State that the United States should take all of the Philippines, keep only Luzon, and trade the remainder to England "in exchange for the Bahamas and Jamaica and the Danish West Indies, which I think we should be entitled to ask her to buy and turn over to us." By autumn, however, the Massachusetts senator was determined to keep the entire group if possible.[25]

Alabama's Senator Morgan found the Philippine problem a knotty one. In June, 1898, he thought that the United States should take only a few naval bases. The Filipinos ought to receive their independence, while the Americans must assist them in creating a new nation. "A policy of colonization by conquest, or coercion, is repugnant to our national creed," Morgan pointed out. A month later he was still opposed to annexing territory "in countries that are outside the American sphere," but favored keeping a military base on Luzon to guard the Filipinos against foreign intervention and domestic upheaval. This amounted to an informal American protectorate, but would constitute neither colonization nor conquest, the senator thought. In any case, Morgan feared too much contact between the races. Negro slavery in America, he believed, had had a civilizing influence on the Negroes, but a "degenerating effect" upon the whites. He feared that, in a similar way, "to hold Asiatics in political subjection would be paralyzing to the energies and the noble aspirations that should always characterize the race called Anglo-Saxon."[26]

In spite of these doubts, the Senator ultimately approved of the annexation of the Philippines. Upon reflection, he afterwards said, he decided that the islands could only be ruled and defended as a unit, and that their continuing need for American tutelage would require that the United States possess sovereignty over them all. By 1900, Morgan was eager to "solve" the Negro problem in the South by resettling the Negroes in the Philippines. He always insisted, however, that once annexed, the Filipinos must be given United States citizenship and legal equality, and he fought hard but unsuccessfully to have this principle embodied in the Philippine Organic Act of 1902.[27]

The evolution of popular thought on the Philippines question was reflected in the editorial statements of national magazines like *The Outlook*. Following Dewey's victory, the *Outlook's* editors were opposed either to annexing the islands or to giving them back to Spain; they were unfit for statehood, while to make them a mere colony would violate the spirit of American institutions, and continued Spanish tyranny was out of the question. As an alternative, the *Outlook* favored selling them to Great Britain, keeping only a naval station. The British were experienced at colonial rule and would safeguard the welfare of the Filipinos, while the United States would be recompensed by the sale price for its trouble in the matter. By July the *Outlook* still opposed annexation, but saw an American duty to provide freedom, equal rights, and schools to the islanders. "What America wants is not territorial expansion, but expansion of civilization," one editorial declared, but it did not explain how this could be done in the absence of United States control. Later in the summer the editors seemed to favor a temporary protectorate, and argued that Americans were as capable of governing colonies as anyone else. October's issues displayed a growing self-confidence: "the radical difference between the expansionist and the continentalist — that is, between the one who believes that American ideas and institutions are good for the whole world, and the one who thinks they are adapted only to the continent of North America—is not that the former is an imperialist and the latter a democrat, but that the former is a more radical, a more enthusiastic, and a more optimistic democrat than the latter." The last step came in January, 1899, when the editors found it "pretty clear" that the nation's duty to the Philippines "cannot be performed by simply leaving the government to the people of the islands."[28]

A comparable evolution was reflected in the mind of the President himself, for McKinley's position changed rapidly during the period of fighting. In the early months of 1898 he had worked hard to avoid war with Spain, but once the conflict began he personally ordered the implementation of Dewey's planned naval attack on Manila. More important, he soon ordered an army force sent to Manila to operate with the navy. The decision to send ground forces to the Philippines emerged from a meeting between the President and his service chiefs on May 2, 1898, even before the arrival of reliable news about the previous day's battle of Manila Bay. The new plan was formally announced in an army general order of May 16.[29]

This, rather than Dewey's naval attack, was the crucial step toward permanent United States involvement in the Philippines. The dispatch of ground troops to the distant archipelago encouraged Senator Lodge to write Theodore Roosevelt, late in May, that "the Administration is now fully committed to the large policy that we both desire." Just how large a policy, however, was still uncertain. At the beginning of June, McKinley confided to his Secretary of State his willingness that the Philippines should remain Spanish, except for "a port and necessary appurtenances, to be selected by the United States," if the war could be ended at once. This, of course, was a month before the land and naval victories in Cuba which led the Spanish to request an armistice, and may have reflected the President's desire to evade the test of battle. But on June 14, still before the coming battles, and before the first American troops appeared in the islands, McKinley changed his position on the Philippines. It now appeared that the insurgents had become a factor in the situation, and that the disposal of the islands must for the present be left an open question.[30]

By mid-July, McKinley was reportedly in favor of keeping not only Manila, but the entire island of Luzon, the largest and most populous of the archipelago. So matters still stood when the President met with his new peace commission for the first time in mid-September. It was out of the question to give up Manila, he told the group, and probably unwise to hold the city and bay without also retaining the whole of Luzon, the island in which they were situated. Beyond this he was not then inclined to go. Nevertheless, he raised the possibility that it might be necessary for defense purposes to acquire some of the smaller nearby islands as well, and expressed a desire to hear expert military and naval advice on the matter.[31]

The initiation of actual peace negotiations forced the President to crystallize his thinking, and by late October he had come to favor taking all of the Philippines. "The interdependency of the several islands, their close relations with Luzon, the very grave problmem [*sic*] of what will become of the part we do not take," he wrote, had led him to conclude "that duty requires we should take the archipelago."[32] The peace commission was soon advised of the President's thinking, and the treaty of peace embodied the transfer of the Philippines to the United States. From an early desire to keep a base at Manila, McKinley's aspirations had grown steadily, ending in a determination to annex the former Spanish colony as a unit. He had tested public opinion by a summer speaking tour through the eastern United States, found it sufficiently favorable, and taken the plunge when the time came.

Other samplings of public opinion confirmed that of the astute President. The *Literary Digest* took a nationwide poll of the views of newspaper editors on the Philippines during the summer of 1898, and published the results in September. Of the newspapers which responded, eighty-four favored United States ownership of the entire group, while sixty-six preferred to keep only a naval station. Of those who wished only the naval station, most apparently foresaw Philippine independence, although the poll did not make this clear. Seventeen papers, on the other hand, advocated some sort of protectorate on the part of the United States, either singly, or, in a few cases, jointly with other nations. Significantly, none whatever approved of giving the islands back to Spain, and only three still desired to sell them to another power, though earlier this had been a common suggestion.[33]

As the poll indicated, there was a significant shift of opinion from distrust to acceptance of the Philippine venture during the summer and autumn of 1898. An important factor in this shift was the general belief that the United States had effectively conquered the archipelago, and was now in virtual control there. Even if one had not wished American control of the islands, many came to feel, the question had suddenly become academic. The only relevant issue was what to do now that such control existed. This view rested in part upon a gross oversimplification of the real situation. In fact, United States forces occupied only the City and Bay of Manila when the peace conference opened, and the Spanish government pointed out then that the city had surrendered after the signing of the armistice which ended hostilities, and was therefore not a legitimate capture. Elsewhere, Spanish troops held many strategic posts, while much larger areas were controlled by the Filipino insurgents, who moved rapidly to consolidate their control and organize a native republic. Most of the American public, however, seemed curiously indifferent to these facts, though the anti-imperialists repeatedly pointed them out.[34]

Thus it was widely argued that the fortunes of war had made the United States solely responsible for deciding the fate of the Philippines, and that no withdrawal was possible until provision had been made for their future. The majority believed so from early in the discussion, which moved debate at once to the question of specific alternatives, and accomplished by far the longest and most difficult step in the novel process of fastening American rule upon an oriental land. "There is a very general feeling that the United States, whatever it might prefer as to the Philippines, is in a situation where it can not let go," President McKinley wrote in October to the head of his peace commission. Elsewhere, the President implied that it was Providence which guided the matter. "Congress can declare war," he said, "but a higher Power decrees its bounds and fixes its relations and responsibilities."[35]

The feeling that the United States could "not let go" in the Philippines flowed in part from a profound fear of international complications, and particularly of German ambitions. The German government had hoped to acquire bases in the islands if Spain should be ousted by the Filipino insurgents. Knowledge of these aspirations, coupled with exaggerated alarm at the presence and actions of a German squadron in Manila Bay, led the State Department to suspect the Germans of the most sinister designs.[36] In support of such fears, disquieting reports poured into Washington during the summer of 1898. Ambassador Andrew Dickson White warned from Berlin that, should the United States allow the establishment of a Philippine Republic, the Germans meant to exploit the resulting political instability in order to gain a foothold for themselves. White incautiously allowed German officials to discuss with him the possibility of Germany receiving some Philippine territory, and was sharply reprimanded for it by the secretary of state. John Hay heard from a friend in the British embassy in

Berlin that Germany would strongly oppose any transfer of Philippine territory to England or France. Hay himself wrote that the British government desired permanent United States ownership of the islands, which would effectively block the Germans, but that the British would insist upon an option to buy them should they be put up for sale. An American businessman reported from the German capitol that "all Europe believes that future war can only be prevented" by the United States holding on in the Philippines.[37]

Under the circumstances, it appeared that sharing the archipelago with other powers could lead to endless complications, while any plan to transfer it entire would set off a scramble which might have dangerous consequences. Furthermore, fears of European intervention furnished another argument against Philippine independence. There was grave doubt in America about the Filipinos' readiness for self-government: they had been in a colonial status for three centuries; the Spanish had done little to prepare them for responsibility; they were non-white and "backward"; the islands contained too great a diversity of cultures and languages to make a nation — the arguments were legion. But the conviction that disorder in the islands would entail international dangers made American policy-makers even less ready to take a chance on Filipino self-rule. An American protectorate, they thought, would be even worse, for it would bring responsibility without authority, and involve the nation in Philippine crises which it would not have sufficient power to prevent.[38]

A third set of reasons for remaining in the Philippines grew from economic considerations. The depression of the 'nineties led to a cry for increased export markets for American goods, and China, with its great population, was most frequently singled out as a promising field of enterprise. The Philippines offered commercial bases in the Orient, and these, it was held, would be vital in gaining an enlarged China trade. This view was characteristically expressed in a Chicago *Inter-Ocean* editorial which called the islands "the key to the wealth of the Orient," and proclaimed that "we need only the advantages abroad which the Philippines would give us to become the greatest commercial power on earth." Many of these commercial expansionists desired only Manila, which they hoped to make into "the new Hong Kong," but if, as came to be asserted, the archipelago must be kept or rejected as a unit, then they most assuredly favored keeping it all.[39]

All of these factors together, however, do not entirely explain how so many Americans could adjust their thinking so quickly to a venture which, everyone agreed, lay outside the traditional limits of national policy, and which to many violated the national spirit. In musing upon this question, Captain Mahan found the answer in that "sentiment that has swept over the whole civilized European world," and which was embodied in the imperialist tide. "Habit had already familiarized men's minds with the idea of national power spreading beyond the bounds of this continent, and with the reasons that made it advisable, if not imperative." Therefore, "though staggered for an instant by a proposition so entirely unexpected and novel as Asiatic dominion," most of the public accepted the annexation of the Philippines. To Mahan, "the result has the special interest of showing the almost instantaneous readiness with which a seed of thought germinates when it falls upon mental soil prepared already to receive it."[40]

4 James Harrison Wilson: A Transitional Expansionist

THE INTERACTIONS between the various expansionist themes of late-nineteenth-century America — traditional expansion, business expansion, and imperialism — are complex and difficult to pin down. At a time when the old frontier movement was still fresh in the national consciousness, and when the impact of the new business expansion was just beginning to be understood, many a man thought in terms which differed sharply from the norms since created by historians to typify the period's thought. One such man was James Harrison Wilson, whose career and ideas illustrate in miniature some of the relationships between the larger currents of his day.

James Harrison Wilson was once a name well known to the American public. He was at various times a successful military commander, a railroad executive, an international promoter, an influential lobbyist, and a civil administrator. He wrote frequently for publication, and was personally acquainted with most of the national political figures for two generations. Active, versatile, and articulate, Wilson was one of those men whose position never quite reaches the first rank, but who often seems on the brink of real eminence. A man of large ambitions, he was never reconciled to the persistence with which greatness eluded his grasp.

Like many of his contemporaries, Wilson was a product of the Civil War, for it was the war which raised him to a high position early in life and threw him into personal contact with many of the men who were to dominate the American scene for the remainder of the century. Few officers in the Union army had a more meteoric rise than Wilson, who was a West Point cadet in 1860 and a major general with an independent command in 1865. Joining the staff of General Ulysses S. Grant as an engineering officer at the beginning of the Vicksburg campaign, he soon won Grant's confidence, and his career prospered with that of his superior. He was a general at the unlikely age of twenty-six, making the transition from staff officer to cavalry commander, and ended the war in charge of the Cavalry Corps of the Military Division of the Mississippi.

Wilson became a brilliant combat commander, and is remembered by military historians as a significant innovator in the use of cavalry forces. He played a conspicuous part in crushing the Confederate army under General John B. Hood at the Battle of Nashville, and by the spring of 1865 he headed the largest single cavalry command in America. In the closing days of the war, Wilson led over 12,000 mounted men on a spectacular raid deep into Confederate territory, decisively defeating the defending forces of the redoubtable General Nathan Bedford Forrest and destroying one of the South's last industrial complexes at Selma, Alabama. These feats, however, were overshadowed by the general collapse of the Confederacy and by the surrender of Robert E. Lee's army at Appomattox, so that they brought the youthful general less attention than would otherwise have been the case. Nevertheless, when the war ended Wilson was fast emerging as one of the leading younger commanders on the Union side.[1]

Wilson stayed on in the army for several more years, though at much reduced rank, occupied mostly in engineering duties on the western waterways. There seemed little future for him, however, in a shrunken military establishment overloaded with leftover generals, and in 1870 he resigned to enter the business world. He came from a prosperous Illinois farming family, and a wealthy uncle there had decided to become a railroad promoter. The latter desired the benefit of his nephew's engineering experience, and his equally useful connections with the Grant administration. Wilson spent most of his time during the 1870s working on his uncle's project, the St. Louis and Southeastern Railroad, in capacities ranging from general manager to receiver, for like many another speculation the company fell prey to the Panic of 1873. During the early 1880s, the General participated in the bitter and intricate struggle for control of the New England trunk lines which was then underway, becoming president of the New York and New England Railroad in 1881. Like most of the roads involved, Wilson's was eventually swallowed up by a merger in 1883, and its erstwhile president found himself squeezed out. Though he continued to hold positions as director or receiver of various roads, Wilson's career of active railroad management was ended. Henceforth he would be a promoter, lobbyist, salesman, and go-between, always well-to-do but never the tycoon he incessantly schemed to become.[2]

He was also something of an author and traveller. He travelled in Europe in 1872, Mexico in 1884, China in 1885–86, and Russia in 1891. As an author, Wilson was to publish eight books, mostly biographies of Civil War generals. His life of Grant, written in collaboration with Charles A. Dana, was probably the best known of these. The General was also an occasional contributor to the periodical press, writing articles on a number of subjects, and entering into those endless controversies over the military operations of the late war which were so popular for thirty years or more after its close.[3]

To his later career, General Wilson brought these varied experiences plus the qualities he had acquired as a soldier. He was intelligent, aggressive, quick at making decisions. Increasingly talkative as he grew older, he spoke fluently and convincingly, but was capable of wearying his companions by his garrulity. He possessed absolute self-confidence, manifested at times by a kind of naive boastfulness. His penchant for scheming, and for seeing plots about him, ripened with age. In other respects the years touched him lightly, however. Though portly in later life, he was always soldierly and erect, with a sweeping white cavalry mustache, and a soldier's wide-eyed and alert glance. A fine horseman, he rode regularly until old age. Even in later life his vitality and enthusiasm were notable; in 1902, when he was sixty-four years old, an acquaintance described him as being "still as fresh and youthful as a boy." And always he displayed the bold imagination and the romantic optimism of the true promoter. From the 1880s on, Wilson's business activities had a distinctly international flavor, and he thought increasingly about foreign affairs. By the Spanish War period, he was identified with the expansionist movement in a variety of ways, some of them traditional and some new.[4]

According to his own account, Wilson acquired the gospel of Canadian annexation from General Grant himself. Late in 1865, the two men met in Atlanta, Georgia, for the first time since Grant had sent Wilson west the previous year. During the long talk that ensued, the rest of those present went off to bed one by one, until only Grant and Wilson remained in the room. As Wilson told it, the talk turned at length toward Canada, and Grant stated his desire to march an army into that country to even the score for the *Alabama* claims and expel the British flag from North America. He could, he said, mobilize an army of five hundred thousand men, containing the best infantry and artillery in the world. Grant thought that the ex-Confederate leaders would be eager to join in this great national project, and that it would go far toward healing the divisions caused by the late war. Heard in this highly colored form, the idea must have made a deep impression on Wilson, and he was still beguiled by it a quarter of a century later.[5] Nevertheless, it was not until the late 1880s that he became an active annexationist, and then his interest appeared to spring more from business considerations than from abstract patriotism. The General emerged at this time as a foe of the movement for "commercial union," or free trade, between the United States and Canada, and he justified his opposition by annexationist arguments.

A small but persistent group of men in both countries had long urged commercial union. In the United States, they were largely tariff reformers, free traders, and manufacturers who wanted a Canadian market. Their leader was a Canadian-born New York businessman named Erastus Wiman, who had large interests on both sides of the border which would be benefited by the removal of the tariff wall dividing them. In Canada the leading spokesman was Goldwin Smith, a former Oxford history professor and anti-imperialist who had settled in Toronto in 1871, and who eventually became a leading advocate of union with the United States. According to some of its disciples, commercial union would be a step toward annexation, as closer economic ties led toward political connections. Wilson's position was that such a policy would in fact delay annexation rather than hasten it.[6]

In 1889, Wilson and Wiman, the high priest of commercial union, participated in a public debate on the question in Wilmington, Delaware, where Wilson had moved after the close of his New England railroading years. Wilson began by sounding a blast for manifest destiny, a force "as immutable and constant as the law of gravitation." It was inevitable that the United States should some day absorb Canada. But a customs union would only serve to delay matters; by giving the Canadians what they most needed from the United States, it would deprive the latter of a potent weapon with which to coerce Canada into a real political union. The true policy of the United States lay in giving Canada a choice: enter the union as so many states and territories, or see the Great Republic declare commercial war and bar its trade to Canada, seize its rights in the Newfoundland fisheries, and insist upon the uncontrolled navigation of the St. Lawrence River. Then, Wilson concluded ominously, let the Canadians beware of our national growth.[7]

The real point of all this was that in the previous year Wilson had become a lobbyist for the eastern trunk line railroads, and was battling on their behalf to limit Canadian competition. One of his major goals was the abolition of transit-in-bond, a practice by which the governments of Canada and the United States had agreed that a shipper in either country, shipping goods to a destination within his own country, could send them across a portion of the other nation's territory without paying duty. The practice enabled Canadian railroads to compete for a portion of the United States' domestic carrying trade, and by the late 1880s they were pressing their rivals hard, especially after the completion of the Canadian Pacific.[8] Testifying before the Senate Interstate Commerce Committee in 1888, Wilson argued that the railroads were as much entitled to protection from foreign competition as the shipping industry, which was by law guaranteed a monopoly of the American coastwise trade. His peroration, however, stressed annexation: ending the transit trade would threaten Canadian railroads with bankruptcy, and thus put further pressure on the Canadian government to seek annexation in order to regain national prosperity.[9]

Wilson's legislative campaign ultimately failed, largely because of the opposition of Midwesterners, who benefited from international railroad competition through lower freight rates.[10] As the General's ulterior motives receded into the past, he remained eager for continental union, but gradually moved away from his earlier crudely coercive approach. The influence of Goldwin Smith, with whom he became acquainted, helped to lead him to a new perspective, and by 1896 the General favored tariff reciprocity or commercial union as a move toward the eventual absorption of Canada. This conversion to the support of a gradual union through a series of intermediate steps indicates that in time, at least, his primary interest lay in union itself, rather than in vanquishing the Canadian railroads, but vestiges of the older view still cropped out in moments of irritation.

A prominent Delaware Republican, Wilson became a national committeeman, and served on the 1896 platform committee. He afterward claimed that it was at his suggestion that the plank calling for "the ultimate union of all English-speaking parts of the continent by the free consent of its inhabitants" was inserted in the national platform. He also visited William McKinley, the Republican presidential candidate of that year, during the campaign to sound him out on the subject of closer trade relations with Canada. The expansionist wave which ended the 'nineties would still see Wilson more firmly committed to continental union than to any overseas acquisitions.[11]

A more exotic phase of the General's foreign activities centered about his railroad schemes in China, which extended over more than a decade. In the year 1885 he became interested in a project which was to occupy his attention for most of the next two years, and which marked the beginning of a new and broader phase of his railroad career. This first project was an attempt to secure a Chinese railroad-building contract, and it launched the General on an unsuccessful but interesting course of international promoting.

The news in the mid-1880s that the Chinese government was contemplating the construction of a national railroad system set off a worldwide race for contracts and concessions. In the United States one immediate result was the appointment by the new Cleveland administration of Colonel Charles Denby of Indiana as United States Minister to China. Denby was a well-connected Midwestern lawyer and railroad director, and it was understood that one of his major interests in China should be to aid United States interests in securing a share of the prospective railroad contracts.[12] At the same time that the government became interested in possible Chinese contracts for American business, General Wilson turned a searching gaze in the same direction. Although he had moved to Delaware, Wilson kept in close touch with his old associates in New York. Some of them were anxious to investigate the China prospect, as was Wilson himself, and he soon emerged as the field representative of a loose, tentative syndicate. He arrived in China in October of 1885, soon after Denby got there to assume the post of United States Minister, and immediately saw the principal Chinese officials to offer them the services of his group. Wilson spent the winter travelling about China, talking to prominent Chinese and examining with an engineer's eye the terrain over which the new roads would presumably be built.[13]

By the spring of 1886 it was apparent that things were going badly, and Wilson's difficulties multiplied rapidly thereafter. In the first place, the Chinese themselves were deeply divided over the desirability of railroad building. While one faction in the government expected railroads to add greatly to China's military and economic strength, another regarded them with suspicion as an avenue to increased foreign influence and further weakening of the ancient fabric of Chinese society. There was also the problem of financing. The Chinese lacked money, but feared loans which would make the government even more vulnerable to western coercion and intervention. Furthermore, the competition was intense for any business opportunities which should develop in spite of these obstacles. English, French, and German syndicates were especially active, and when Wilson's prospects for securing a construction contract seemed brightest, the German Minister even brought diplomatic pressure on the Chinese government in an attempt to blight them. Nevertheless the General persevered, presenting plan after plan to overcome the barriers in his way.[14]

It was the financial problem that was the most intractable. The Chinese held fast to three conditions for any government railroad loan: the foreign lender must have no voice in the management of the project; foreigners must be excluded from owning any interest in the railroad; and the loan could not be secured by customs revenues, which were already over-pledged, but must be separately funded, perhaps from the profits of the railroad itself. These terms were sufficient to frighten away American bankers, and Wilson's backers found themselves unable to make headway on either a loan or a construction contract. At one point the resourceful General wrote Secretary of State Thomas Bayard, presenting an audacious scheme to get his project financed by the United States Treasury. Why not lend the Treasury's silver surplus to China for railroad building? he asked. Such a loan would enable the idle surplus to earn interest, open great opportunities for American business interests (his own included), and help to build new markets for American products. The idea failed to commend itself in Washington.[15]

It was Minister Denby, with whom Wilson worked closely, who seemed at last to provide the solution. Since it appeared impossible to obtain a loan to the Chinese government, Denby proposed that the Chinese should organize a private corporation to build the railroad, in which the government could hold a controlling interest.

THE WHITE MAN'S BURDEN.
— *The Ram's Horn,* Chicago.
Reprinted in the *Literary Digest,* May 27, 1899.

Such an alternative would escape the rigid limitations placed upon government borrowing, and for a time things seemed to go forward again. General Wilson was to become chief engineer for the projected Chinese corporation, and to take charge of arrangements for constructing the first section of the line. "The Viceroy has assured me . . . that my assistance will be required in all they do . . . ," Wilson wrote Denby, and he returned to the United States in August, 1886, to recruit engineers and investigate sources of supply, but before he had accomplished much, the situation had changed again. Upon reflection, the Chinese soon saw other and more attractive possibilities in the device of a Chinese corporation. If such a corporation organized by foreigners was a good thing, one organized by Chinese would be an even better one. It was a simple matter to form the new company about the existing, and genuinely Chinese, Kaiping Railway Company, bypassing Wilson's organization altogether. In spite of the best efforts of Wilson and Denby, the Wilson group found itself ousted entirely from the railroad enterprise after nearly two years' effort on the part of the General.[16]

Wilson failed for a number of reasons. For one thing, both he and Denby were new to China, and lacked insight into the complexities of Chinese affairs. Furthermore, large-scale American finance capital was not yet available in the 1880s for such exotic enterprises as Chinese railroads. The Chinese themselves were not yet ready for major railroad-building; they did not in fact build most of their much-heralded national railroad system until after the turn of the century. Few of the other foreign promoters did much better than Wilson, and as usual the indefatigable Wilson salvaged something from the wreck. In 1887 he published a book entitled *China, Travels and Investigations in the Middle Kingdom,* which gave a partial account of his recent travels and activities, and publicized the opportunities for American enterprise which he still believed to exist in that country.

That the General retained his faith in oriental opportunity was proven by his originating a new Chinese railroad scheme in the 1890s. This project, inaugurated in 1896, saw Wilson working with a prominent New York attorney named John J. McCook. Even younger than Wilson, McCook was also a Civil War prodigy, having been mustered out as a brevet colonel at the age of twenty. He had been counsel, and later receiver, for the Atchison, Topeka and Santa Fe Railroad, and was a director of such large concerns as the Equitable Life Assurance Society and the Mercantile Trust Company. A leading Presbyterian layman, a trustee of Princeton University, and a New York Republican party stalwart, McCook was a well-known figure, and as a schemer he was equal to Wilson himself.[17]

After his previous Chinese adventure, Wilson was skeptical of getting firm commitments from the Chinese without being able to coerce their government. It was his old collaborator, Charles Denby, who suggested a way to achieve this coercion. Denby, still Minister to China, thought that Russia now exercised the greatest foreign influence in that country. This being the case, the proper approach might be to make an arrangement in partnership with the Russians, and leave it to them to force it on the Chinese. Eager to promote American business interests in China, Denby first sounded out the Russian Minister in Peking, and then recruited Wilson as the moving spirit of the proposed venture. The General enlisted McCook's support, and the result was a plan for an "American Syndicate," drawn up in October, 1896. According to its draft charter, the purpose of the syndicate was to "secure contracts and concessions and to engage in the location, construction and equipment of railroads, and other public works, and to undertake other business for both Russia and China . . . . " In essence, the plan called for an interlocking system of American railroads in China and Russian railroads in Manchuria, to be tied in with the nearly completed Trans-Siberian Railway on one side, and by steamship links to North America on the other.[18]

The partners plunged into a fury of activity, talking to prominent Russian and Chinese officials who visited the United States and besieging the nabobs of the day for financial support. McCook went to the top in his quest for money, appealing to J. P. Morgan, Andrew Carnegie, and H. M. Flagler of the Standard Oil Company. The pair would also need political influence, and their attempt to insure this was in some ways the most daring aspect of their plan. What they proposed was nothing less than to place themselves and their confederates in key diplomatic positions, and in the Cabinet itself. Wilson was to become Ambassador to Russia, McCook Secretary of War, and Assistant Secretary of State W. W. Rockhill, a well-known orientalist with diplomatic experience in China, was enlisted and designated as prospective Minister to China in place of the Democratic Denby. The election of William McKinley in 1896 meant that the federal offices were to be reassigned to Republicans, and the partners organized a barrage of letters from influential supporters to support their collective aspirations.[19]

On the political side, this improbable scheme came surprisingly close to success. Wilson received serious consideration for the Russian post, backed by important business figures and such expansionists as Senators Cushman Davis of Minnesota and William E. Frye of Maine. Hearty support came from Theodore Roosevelt, whom Wilson had known for some years, and Senator Henry Cabot Lodge, whose personal acquaintance with the General ran back to 1876, when they had briefly been political confederates. And Charles A. Dana, one of Wilson's oldest friends, was editor of the New York *Sun*. Nevertheless, Wilson was hampered in his pursuit of office by the fact that the Republican party in Delaware had just fallen into a bitter and prolonged factional fight, with Wilson prominently identified with one faction. McKinley, fearing to appear partial to one side, ended by refusing to give appointments to the leaders of either. To Wilson's disappointment, the Russian post went to another man. The other arrangements also went awry. McCook mobilized solid New York backing in his quest for a cabinet position, and McKinley was disposed to give him one. The President-elect ultimately offered him not the War Department, however, but the Interior, a department which dealt so exclusively with internal affairs that McCook declined it. Nor did Rockhill get the Chinese ministry, though he soon became Minister to Greece.[20]

The failure in Washington was paralleled on Wall Street. None of the tycoons wanted to risk large sums until tangible progress was in sight, and the progress was impossible of achievement without command of the money. Not surprisingly, the scheme died in 1897. Unlikely as the Wilson-McCook project appeared, however, it foreshadowed a similar and better known plan which the railroad king, Edward H. Harriman, initiated with as little success in 1909, although his resources in money and influence were far superior to those of the Wilson group.[21]

Once again disappointed in his personal ambitions, General Wilson continued to believe in the economic importance of China to the United States. Early in 1898 he published an article in which he repeated his faith in China's imminent "awakening," and described glowingly the new markets for American products which would accompany the westernization of China. The great danger lay in China's partition by the great powers, which then seemed likely, and which would leave United States interests there at a decisive disadvantage. Instead of working with Russia, therefore, Wilson now favored a silent partnership with Great Britain. Since American and British interests were parallel in the Orient, Wilson thought, and since both nations opposed Chinese partition, he called for vigorous cooperation with Great Britain in keeping the trade of China open to all nations on equal terms, thus stating the object of the later Open Door Policy. He also urged the immediate annexation of Hawaii, in order to enhance American power in the Pacific.[22]

The onset of the Spanish-American War diverted the General from business affairs and marked a renewal of his army career. Although he had been out of the service for twenty-eight years when the war began, he was barely sixty years old and still vigorous. As one of the few important Civil War commanders from either side who was still available for duty, he looked forward with confidence to a high command in the new volunteer army, and he was not in error; the President appointed him major general of volunteers almost at once. The war proved to be brief, however, and the fighting in Cuba fell largely to the regulars. For a time it seemed that Wilson's role would be confined to the training of recruits, but a hastily organized invasion of Puerto Rico, which perforce depended upon volunteer troops, provided the opportunity for active service. Although only a subordinate commander in the relatively bloodless campaign, the General did lead his own column against the Spaniards in some skirmishes, and heard once more the sound of bullets in the air. It was in Puerto Rico that the armistice found him, advancing against light opposition through the mountains in the central part of the island.[23]

The three months' war ended in August, and the General decided that henceforth the big jobs in the army would be administrative: someone must head the military regimes in the newly occupied areas. He soon set his sights on becoming the first military governor of Cuba, and again mobilized a lobby to influence the President in his favor. As before, it included Theodore Roosevelt, who at one time had considered going to the war as a member of Wilson's staff, and Senator Lodge, whose son-in-law had actually done so as the result of an arrangement between the General and the Senator. In addition there were several more senators, the editor Paul Dana, who took over the management of the New York *Sun* upon his father's death, and many others. Even the Secretary of War, Russell A. Alger, recommended Wilson for the post, but McKinley gave it to John R. Brooke, one of the senior regular army generals who had stayed in the service during all the lean years after the Civil War, and under whom Wilson had served in the Puerto Rican campaign. General Wilson again became a subordinate commander, this time in the Cuban occupation which began on January 1, 1899.[24]

The General's old business associate, Colonel McCook, had already been active on the Cuban front. Shortly before the war, he had formed a secret Wall Street syndicate to fund Cuban independence at a profit. A confidential agreement with the Cuban revolutionary authorities in August, 1897, provided for the syndicate to induce Spain to give Cuba her freedom in return for the repayment to Spain of a portion of the enormous insular debt. Large Spanish forces had been bogged down in Cuba for more than two years, fighting against a rebellion which they were unable to quell, while the Spanish treasury was in a desperate condition. It seemed to the promoters that the time had come when the Spanish government might be willing to get out of Cuba, if only it could recover some of the money which it had poured into the island. The syndicate would receive interest-bearing bonds of the Cuban Republic to the amount of one hundred and fifty million Cuban dollars, secured by the island's customs revenues. It would in turn pay to the Spaniards an amount to be determined by negotiation with them; a good bargain could mean a large profit for the syndicate.

The group was ostensibly headed by Samuel M. Janney, of the New York banking firm of Christy and Janney, but McCook was named in the contract as the central agent. His function was to enlist the support of the McKinley administration, securing its aid in pushing the Spanish into an agreement and getting the United States government to act as guarantor for the resulting financial arrangements. This first contract was soon supplemented by another, which simply provided for a lesser payment in bonds to the syndicate for securing the evacuation of Cuba by Spain and recognition of its independence by both Spain and the United States. This cryptic arrangement implied the purchase of influence in Washington rather than Madrid.[25] The disclosure several years later that in May, 1898, the Cubans gave two million dollars in bonds to "influential Americans" under the terms of this second contract supports the contention that the McCook syndicate claimed credit for the passage of the Teller Resolution, which pledged the independence of Cuba, and profited largely by it. While Cuban President Tomás Estrada Palma promptly denied the whole thing, the United States Minister to Cuba investigated the story in 1904 and concluded that it was true.[26]

There is no evidence that General Wilson was a party to these machinations, but he did play a significant role in the next chapter of the Cuban story. Although a large cut in the size of the army resulted in Wilson's reduction in rank to brigadier general, he went about his new duties with undiminished energy, for the situation was one which challenged his fertile mind. The Teller Amendment to Congress's war resolutions of April, 1898, had pledged that the United States would not annex Cuba, nor "exercise sovereignty, jurisdiction, or control over said island except for the pacification thereof," after which Cuba's government was to be vested in her own people. Yet the McKinley administration was extremely vague about its plans for Cuba during the first year of the United States occupation, and annexation sentiment was rising in the United

States. There was a general feeling that Cuba's future was still undecided, and in the absence of any clearly expressed central policy, Wilson formulated and began to recommend a Cuban policy of his own.[27]

General Wilson's ideas about Cuba took shape in a letter he wrote in May to Senator Joseph B. Foraker of Ohio, with whom he corresponded regularly throughout 1899. To begin with, Wilson expressed his regret at the adoption of the Teller Resolution. It would have been better, he thought, if Congress had openly declared an intention to annex Cuba. But instead it had promised not to do so, and, once made, the promise must be kept. Before the island was turned over to the Cubans, however, the United States must negotiate a treaty with the incoming Cuban regime which would leave it under an effective protectorate. Wilson thought that the United States should furnish Cuba with military protection, and maintain common diplomatic, customs, and postal services with the Cubans, but "leave them free to manage their internal affairs in their own way." The treaty should also tie the Cuban economy to that of the mainland through a customs union, which the Cubans needed at any rate to insure the marketing of their sugar under favorable conditions. A later draft of Wilson's proposed treaty included a provision that made the United States responsible for peace and stability in Cuba, and suggested giving the United States the right of intervention there when such a state was endangered. These arrangements would tie the Cuban government and economy closely to the United States, while internal self-rule would give the Cubans experience in democracy. In a few years, Wilson thought, these factors, working together with Cuban self-interest, would draw the Cubans steadily toward their powerful neighbor until annexation could be easily and peacefully achieved.[28]

During his remaining year in Cuba, Wilson persistently advocated this same general policy, and attempted to put himself in a position to implement it. When the office of Secretary of War became vacant, Wilson lobbied for it, and he made strenuous attempts to replace Brooke as military governor when the latter departed. At first he had the aid of Theodore Roosevelt, whose star was rising fast, and who urged Wilson also for military governor of the Philippines. But Roosevelt's patronage was soon transferred to his old commander and Wilson's rival, Leonard Wood, and Roosevelt began to become irritated at Wilson's importunities. In August, 1899, he wrote Wilson that "when one's original recommendations are not taken, or when one is informed that certain arrangements are impossible, and yet is asked to make suggestions, it is not possible to make the same suggestions over again."[29]

While the General's attempts to secure promotion failed, his efforts to influence the new Secretary of War, Elihu Root, in favor of his policy were more successful. The new military governor, Leonard Wood, advocated simply staying on in Cuba and ignoring the Teller Resolution, while saying as little as possible about the whole thing. Wilson strove through official reports and private letters to Root and others to persuade the administration of the advantages of his own more subtle plan. For a time, the normally ebullient General despaired for his policy; his repeated failure to gain promotion had shaken even his supreme confidence. A last desperate letter to Root in November, 1899, pointed out that "such a treaty as I have proposed would practically bind Cuba, hand and foot, and put her destinies absolutely within our control." Yet it would also comply technically with the Teller Resolution, for "we have made no promises either to the Cubans or to the world at large" about the terms which might be exacted in a treaty with an independent Cuba. Best of all, Wilson's plan would save face for the Cubans, and give them at least home rule; anything less risked armed rebellion. Root's failure to reply to this letter, and Wood's appointment to replace Brooke, convinced Wilson that his ideas were to be rejected along with himself.[30]

In fact, Wilson's recommendations foreshadowed the protectorate actually established by the Platt Amendment of 1901 and the Cuban Reciprocity Treaty of 1902. While the final provisions differed from Wilson's in important particulars, and were the fruit of many men's thinking, the General must be numbered among those who shaped the course of Cuban-American relations in the period after the Spanish-American War. He was among the first Americans to see the possibilities of indirect rule rather than outright annexation, though in his thinking the former was merely a transitional stage leading to the latter rather than a separate and permanent alternative.[31]

The Spanish-American War also gave new impetus to Wilson's continental expansionism, and led him to join forces again with Colonel McCook in an attempt to push President McKinley toward a scheme of Canadian annexation. It was the Colonel who made the opening moves. In May, 1898, McCook wrote McKinley his views of United States expansion. He was principally interested in annexing Canada, and was convinced that the Canadians were rapidly moving toward voluntary acceptance of the idea, but he also looked to the building of a Nicaraguan canal. Conceding that "our possessions should not extend south of the Rio Grande," McCook felt that the protection of the proposed canal "may compel us to have a friendly guardianship, if not a more complete control, of the Central American Territory." But North America took first priority. "Let us heed the advice of Washington and confine our ambitions and territory to this continent," McCook advised. "That will surely be enough, if we have it all, or as much as comes to us voluntarily . . . ."[32]

In November, McCook wrote the President again, this time to propose a plan for taking all of the Philippine Islands and trading them to the British for the right to annex Canada, and perhaps Bermuda and Jamaica as well. Confident that recent developments had "strengthened the existing feeling for closer relations between Canada and the other British North American provinces and the United States," McCook believed that the Canadians would assent to annexation if the British gave the union their blessing. "At the end of your second administration our Government should control a compact domain, practically covering this continent . . . ," he assured McKinley. "If this is accomplished you will go down in history as the President whose administration . . . solidified and enlarged its possessions upon this continent, to an extent, and in a way, which our early Presidents hardly dared dream of."[33]

At this point General Wilson took a hand in the game. In the following month, December, 1898, the President toured the South, and in the course of his tour he reviewed an army corps then commanded by Wilson, at Macon, Georgia. After the review came speeches by the President and several of his generals. Wilson's speech was the most startling of the day, for he echoed McCook's aspirations for expansion, while saying nothing of the means by which they would be achieved. Wilson shared McCook's hope of trading the Philippines for Canada, but on this occasion he said nothing about that possibility. He merely repeated McKinley's theme that the war had reunited the nation, and went on to urge that this new national strength should now be turned to an even larger task: "I hope to see the day when our starry flag shall float everywhere, from the frozen north to the sunny clime of Central America. We are too big and powerful and progressive to have neighbors on this continent, and I trust that before the next administration of the President closes, the flag will fly over every foot of the continent from the northern extremity of the Dominion of Canada to the Gulf of Mexico."[34]

As an attempt to mobilize opinion for contiguous rather than distant expansion, the speech was a failure. It had sounded like an invitation to conquest, and was widely regarded as unfortunate. In a scathing editorial, the New York *Times* pointed out that Wilson had made it while sharing the platform with the President of the United States. "At best it is a silly dream, but in the circumstances the proclamation of it verged on the offensive," the editorial said, and suggested that henceforth McKinley should have Wilson's speeches censored in advance. Nevertheless, the General continued to advocate the scheme which McCook had outlined, although he was henceforth careful to disavow military aggression as a means to achieve it.[35]

By the spring of 1900, Wilson was discouraged with his status in Cuba, and in April he was further depressed by the shocking death of his wife, who was fatally burned in a freak accident. The outbreak of the Boxer Rebellion in China crystallized the General's determination to leave the island, and he applied for a transfer to Chinese duty on the basis of his previous experience there. The request granted, he hastened to the Orient, arriving in Peking in September. The Boxers had attacked foreigners throughout northern China and besieged the foreign quarter of Peking, and in response the Western powers raised an international army, which fought its way into the capital and raised the siege during the summer of 1900. When Wilson arrived the fighting was virtually over, but during the winter he served as second in command of the United States forces in China, and supervised the administration of the American-occupied zone of Peking. This was his last significant military duty, and in March, 1901, the General left the army and returned to civil life and his former business pursuits.[36]

By this time Wilson had long since arrived at a general philosophy of American expansion, as well as detailed plans for its achievement. In speeches, articles, and private correspondence, he had advocated and publicized his views for many years. Altogether they made up a complex but coherent whole, mixing the traditional themes of manifest destiny with elements of a newer commercial imperialism. The assumptions upon which Wilson's outlook rested had three chief characteristics. First, Wilson always saw the territorial growth of the United States in terms of traditional expansion, the expansion of his own youth, almost unaffected by some of the newer concepts of imperialism. Second, his thinking about international relationships showed a strong current of economic determinism, which grew progressively stronger as the years passed. Third, his concepts were largely derivative rather than original, and the most important addition to the point of view which he had acquired in his youth was the assimilation of some of the ideas of Professor Goldwin Smith.

All of his life, General Wilson possessed an unwavering faith in manifest destiny. The United States, he believed, was irrevocably fated to keep expanding until her destiny should be fulfilled. This

was inevitable and would take place regardless of the actions of
men or nations, but since it "lies at the very base of our progress"
it was everyone's duty to facilitate the process. But unlike some
of the exponents of manifest destiny, Wilson thought he knew in
advance the limits which destiny had set for American growth. The
ultimate boundaries of the United States were the boundaries of
the North American continent. The West Indies were included as
natural geographic and economic appendages of North America,
but, except for Hawaii, Wilson's vision of expansion never went
beyond these bounds. The only growth that he envisaged was the
addition of neighboring territory to the central block: he was unmoved by the imperialist notion of scattered and non-contiguous
possessions. "Our own national expansion," he wrote, "should be
continental, like that of Russia, rather than across sea, as that of
Great Britain, France, and Germany has been of late years."[37]

This was in part a consequence of a second and vitally important
conviction: that the only legitimate purpose of acquiring new territory was to bring it into the union, erected in time into new self-
governing commonwealths which would take their proper place in
the councils of the central government. "The law of our national
growth," he said in 1889, "is by accretion, not colonization . . . , "
and some years later he thanked God that "the Great Republic
has nowhere under the sun any subjects," but only citizens.[38] He
had formed his own dream, and repeated it often:

> I think I see clearly the road on which we are compelled, per-
> haps all unconsciously, to travel. It lies fair and broad before
> us, and leads straight forward . . . to a continental republic,
> extending from the tropics to the north polar sea, and bounded
> on all sides by the ocean which encircles the world. The people
> within it, as well as the separate states which govern their local
> affairs are free and equal, and subject only to that written
> Constitution, which the wisest of English Statesmen has pro-
> nounced to be the grandest instrument of Government ever
> framed at a single epoch by a single set of men.[39]

It is no surprise that Wilson made frequent references to Professor
Goldwin Smith, for this picture was essentially Smith's plan.

Goldwin Smith had been a history professor at Oxford, and was a prominent Victorian intellectual. He first attained note as an educational reformer and an anti-clerical. Also a pacifist, an anti-imperialist and a free-trader, he called himself, late in life, "the very last survivor of the Manchester school." During the American Civil War he was active in England in publicizing the Northern cause, which he favored because of his disapproval of Southern slavery. Also at this time he published his first book on the contemporary affairs of the British Empire, advocating the conversion of the self-governing colonies into independent states and the abandonment of some of the subject territories. Smith came to live in the United States in 1868, teaching history at the newly founded Cornell University. Three years later he moved to Toronto, Canada, where he agitated for the "emancipation" of Canada from Great Britain. At first he called for independence, but in time he came to favor a commercial union with the United States, and finally proposed outright annexation.[40]

In his book, *Canada and the Canadian Question*, published in 1891, Smith presented his matured thinking on the subject. He argued that Canada was divided by natural barriers into mutually isolated segments, each of which was closely connected by its physical or economic nature with the adjoining section of the United States. There was little commerce between these component parts of Canada, even though the Canadian government had erected tariff barriers to block the natural flow of commerce and force it into artificial channels within Canada. The various segments of the country had common institutions and language with their common neighbor to the south, and the "primary forces" at work tended to drive these areas into union with the United States. The real Canadian question, according to Smith, was how long this artificial Dominion could be kept united by purely political agencies, and separated from the continent of which it was naturally a part.[41]

Smith went further, and foresaw a United Continent of North America. This idea, Smith said, was both grand and practical, far

more so than the often discussed plan for imperial federation of the
British Empire. Opposed to the visionary and arbitrary federation
plan was "the idea, which can hardly fail to make way, of a great
continent with an almost unlimited range of production forming
the home of a united people, shutting out war and presenting the
field for a new and happier development of humanity."[42] This concept fitted in well with General Wilson's notions of manifest destiny
and expansion by accretion. He liked not only the plan but the
predominantly economic cast of the reasoning behind it, and the
whole fabric went intact into his own thinking.

Wilson's insistence on accretion and assimilation placed necessary limits on the methods of expansion which the United States
could successfully use. If a new area was destined to become a part
of the union, it must be populated by a people who were both
capable of sharing the nation's institutions and willing to do so.
It was clearly impossible to erect new states out of already populated areas seized by conquest and annexed against their will.
Wilson saw this from the first in regard to Cuba, and he realized
that the principle applied to Canada as well, but on the latter subject his logic sometimes broke down. To him the union with Canada
seemed patently beneficial to both parties, and was inevitable at
any rate. Therefore the subborn refusal of the Canadians to be
annexed appeared to him mere petty obstructionism, and his irritation at their seemingly irrational behavior sometimes boiled
over into demands for some sort of coercion. This was particularly
true in the period of his lobbying activities against the Canadian
railroads, when ulterior motives loomed large in his thinking. But
in his later and more sober statements he usually renounced the
idea of coercion and spoke of a free and voluntary union. Nevertheless, the General's addiction to purely economic factors, and his
ignorance of the birth and growth of Canadian nationalism, insured
that he would never really understand Canada and its people.

The second great necessity, that the annexed population be capable of sharing the nation's institutions, brought racial considerations
into play. Racism was rampant at the close of the nineteenth century, and Wilson was not immune to it. Before the beginning of the

Cuban occupation he had recommended the discharge of all Negro volunteers from his First Army Corps, which was slated for occupation duty, declaring that they were "in no way fit exemplars of the American Army." Much to Wilson's relief this was done, and he could write that "none but white Americans of the best type" were left to carry on the work of occupation.[43] During the occupation Wilson, who hoped for the eventual annexation of Cuba, kept pointing out the essentially white nature of Cuban society. In reports, interviews, and speeches he repeated the theme that white Cubans outnumbered the colored part of the population two to one, and that white domination was as solidly established in Cuba as in the Southern states of the United States.[44]

While Cuba was basically white, Wilson thought, and thus fit for annexation, this was not the case with the Philippines, a fact which provided one more of the many reasons why he always regarded those islands with a skeptical eye. To him they had no place in the American system. They possessed alien institutions and a distant location, they belonged to another economic system than the American, and finally, "When it is remembered that the whites are to the colored in Cuba as two to one, while in the Philippines they are not more than one to fifty, the political and sociological inferiority of the Filipinos will be apparent to all."[45]

Such factors made up the framework of United States expansion as Wilson saw it: a United States embracing most of the North American continent, Hawaii, and parts of the West Indies, all included in states of the union or in territories destined in time to become states, populated by white or white-dominated societies, and under Anglo-Saxon political institutions. This scheme had in it no place for far-flung overseas possessions, territorial conquests, rule by force, or "inferior" peoples. The General did not deny the existence of the White Man's Burden, but he left it to those whose political institutions were capable of assuming it, on the belief that those of the United States could not. The Constitution provided only for citizens, not subjects; its terms debarred a true colonial empire.

While uniting political and economic factors in his schemes of

North American expansion, Wilson separated them when thinking
of regions outside the proper American sphere. Interested as he
was in overseas business expansion, the General refused to mingle
what he regarded as incompatible elements in his plans for the
future. Thus he attached great importance to winning a share of
the China trade for the United States, and thought it proper to
support the quest by diplomatic means, but would not espouse
annexations in the Far East.

Wilson held these views before the United States entered her
imperialist period, and kept them largely unchanged while it lasted.
What changed in his thinking was his plan of action, the method of
achieving the goals of expansion. Always inclined toward economic
determinism, he turned more and more to economic factors as time
taught him the practical difficulties in the way of speedy annexations. As he had become a convert to commercial union with Canada in place of the old headlong annexation by coercion, so he
extended the idea of a customs union further and further as his
experience widened. The customs union idea sprang from a conviction that the affairs of the world were regulated by forces primarily
economic in nature: "To thinking men it is evident that with the
best we can do the larger questions of our day and generation, are
settled by what Professor Goldwin Smith calls 'the greater forces,'
which work silently and out of sight, but irresistibly . . . . most of
these questions are in the last analysis, questions of economics,
rather than morals, of plain business and good administration,
rather than of abstract principles and forms of government."[46] But
while political events tended to be shaped by economic conditions,
the flow of commerce could be affected by political regulation,
particularly by tariffs.

It was necessary to regulate the flow of commerce in some way
because the United States was faced with the necessity of finding
new markets for her surplus products, new sources of raw materials,
and new investment opportunities. The nation had an expanding
economy: "If it is true that the time has come when we must find
new markets for the products of our industry, or obtain cheaper

raw materials of any kind, obviously we should look to the nearby countries."[47] In spite of his long interest in Chinese business opportunities, and perhaps because of his lack of success with them, the General emphasized the Americas as the region where economic salvation was mainly to be sought. Like Blaine before him, he foresaw a Pan-American economic system dominated by the United States, which would benefit by the extension of its free trade area, as long as that extension was confined to regions whose economies were complementary to its own. Analyzing the sources of United States prosperity, Wilson found one of the primary factors to be a large internal free trade area with external protection against outside competitors. All this led him directly to the idea of a great American customs union.[48]

The idea was not new to American diplomacy. In the mid-nineteenth century it had appeared as an accompaniment to the low tariff policies of the Democratic party. In the later 1840s a North American "commercial union" emerged as a definite program, and had actually gone one long step toward realization with the ratification of the Canadian Reciprocity Treaty of 1854, which was in effect from 1855 to 1866. A treaty containing a similar reciprocity provision was negotiated with Mexico in 1859, but rejected by the Senate. The plan reappeared in a different form at the first Pan-American Conference in 1889, to which Blaine proposed a general American customs union. The majority report of the delegates declared the plan to be impractical at the time, but recommended the negotiation of reciprocity treaties as a step toward it.[49]

Wilson's thinking along these lines was probably stimulated also by the discussion in England of similar ideas. Joseph Chamberlain, the Secretary of State for Colonies, proposed an "Imperial Zollverein," or customs union of the Empire, in 1896. When the idea found little favor among the colonies, he watered it down to "imperial preference," and made this one of the chief issues in English politics by 1903. In short, there was little original in the General's basic scheme, for something like it had been widely discussed in both England and the United States.[50]

Wilson called himself a "free-trade protectionist," meaning that he favored free trade within the largest practical area, but that this entire area should be protected against outsiders by a common tariff barrier. For the present the goal should be a customs union covering North America and the West Indies. This area of mutual free trade would bring immediate economic benefits to all concerned; it would tie the other regions more closely to the United States, while at the same time "it would effectually keep them out of our political system, till they had shown themselves worthy or desirable parties to be invited into it." According to Wilson, the scheme would yield most of the benefits of territorial expansion, while eliminating many of the political difficulties involved. It was a compromise between the expansionist urge and the practical problems of extending the union.[51]

This program, the General thought, should have begun by negotiating a customs union with Cuba at the end of the occupation period. A similar agreement would be reached with Canada as soon as possible, and the arrangement would already be nearly continental in scope. In time Mexico and other countries could be induced to join the system. If the results were favorable, perhaps South America could some day be included, but this was a speculation for the remote future. The first treaties should provide for complete free trade within the union and a uniform tariff schedule against all others, while the United States should promise to respect the independence and integrity of all other member states.[52]

Once his customs union was achieved, Wilson was convinced that it would give the United States economic hegemony over an area so vast and rich that the nation would experience an unparalleled prosperity. At the same time, the more backward members of the customs union would also benefit. As time passed they too would grow more prosperous and progressive, while, linked economically to the United States and in the shadow of her growing power, they would inevitably be drawn into her orbit. As they developed economically they would begin to seek membership in the United States' political system, Wilson thought, as always underestimating cultural and ideological factors, and when ready they would be granted it. According to the General, Canada and Cuba were already qualified for admission; other areas might need a long preparatory period. But in the long run, there could be but one result: a continental republic.

General Wilson once summed up his program in a discussion of the Cuban question. Rather than annex Cuba at once, he said, the United States should keep the door always open, tie the Cuban economy to its own, cultivate her friendship and make her prosperous, until she came into the union of her own accord, with a full realization of the benefits. "Let us take this course," the General declared impressively, "because it is noble and just and right, and besides because it will pay."[53]

PART II
The Matrices

5 The Tone of Society

AS AMERICANS excitedly discussed their victorious little war with Spain, they found many reasons for self-congratulation. In the first flush of success, they boasted of martial prowess, gloried in new prestige, and calculated possible cash benefits. A surprising number of them also believed that the war had improved the quality of American society in intangible but significant ways. For an editorialist of the Portland *Oregonian*, its most important effect had been to "elevate the tone of our national life," not only in politics, but in every other field of human activity: "Trade ought to be fairer, education more honest, society purer, and religion more sincere for this baptism of blood and fire, with its lessons of unselfish sacrifice and high-minded endeavor."[1]

Nor was this an isolated reaction. A Denver newspaper announced that the rate of crime in American cities had fallen off sharply since the outbreak of the war, for "the war has turned into patriotic and nobler channels the minds of men heretofore engaged in the ignoble and the inglorious." War, it developed, "propagates a higher plane of thought and action." It also turned men's minds from narrow to broad interests, others contended. "If there are difficulties in the policy of expansion there are dangers in the policy of isolation and contraction," one writer declared, tracing the decline of American oratory and statesmanship to provincialism and "an absence of public issues appealing to men's imaginations and patriotic impulses." At a touch of these broader issues, sectional animosities

99

had evaporated and Americans had acquired a world perspective. Another writer concluded that the years of peace had encouraged a narrow individualism which subordinated large affairs to personal greed, and led to interest-group politics. The war would create a "new civic spirit," inspire true statesmanship, and shift attention to international issues, eclipsing what was petty and parochial in politics. Miss Charlotte Perkins Stetson, the "poetess laureate of American Socialism," worked a variation on the theme. Not only did war bring the noblest emotions and the highest virtues, Miss Stetson believed, but it also taught obedience, the conquest of individual selfishness, and respect for the "prior claims of the greatest number." It was, she declared, the one greatest "socializer"![2]

That a nation so purified and ennobled could produce numerous bids, after the capture in 1901 of the Filipino leader Emilio Aguinaldo, to rent him from the War Department and exhibit him for a fee,[3] proved only what many Americans had long suspected: that society was in need of all the uplift it could get. From the 1880s on, a rising volume of criticism had gathered about the uglier aspects of the nation's life. What was the future of a political system in which elections were controlled by city "machines" manipulating illiterate aliens, and public offices had become the spoils of victory at the polls? The ruthless quest of wealth, the crudeness and ostentation of the Gilded Age, the appearance of a new plutocracy, had drawn the attack of both new reformers and traditional elite. To many anxious observers a golden age seemed to have passed, in which the mass of Americans had sprung from a rugged, honest, native yeomanry, close to the soil and to their Maker, preserving the sturdy integrity of the Founders.

Whether or not this had been true in the past, it fitted ill with a present in which Americans increasingly left the soil for cities, to become wage-earners and adapt to an indoor life of softer living and modern convenience. The myth of the Jeffersonian past was further weakened by mass immigration, labor strife, periodic depressions, and talk of socialism and anarchism. The frontier mystique was fading as the age of pioneering drew to a close. Even the remaining yeomanry, it appeared, had been corrupted, nurturing every fresh heresy that came along. Had not farmers supported populist nostrums and free silver, and cheered the class-oriented appeals of William Jennings Bryan? To men of education and substance, the prospects were alarming. As the fiery young Beveridge proclaimed in 1896: "The intense materialism of the time is palsying manhood, poisoning justice, driving faith from its throne." Epicureanism, corruption, and dollar-chasing were the order of the day. "We measure careers by dollars. We measure political questions by our pocket-books. We are losing sight of the eternal."[4]

There was also an external dimension to the problem. In a world of intensifying struggle and bitter rivalry, how long could a nation survive the decline of its fighting qualities? A soft, self-indulgent society of mollycoddles and money-grubbers would be short work for a warlike foe. The richer the United States grew, the more essential it became for it to be formidable as well, and this depended upon the toughness and moral strength of the people. To the extent that contemporary forces tended to weaken these qualities, the nation was endangered.

There was much agreement, in a general sort of way, that contemporary trends *were* endangering the moral fibre of the nation, but it remained for Brooks Adams, younger brother of Henry Adams and unorthodox theorist of contemporary trends, to discern a cosmic inevitability in the process. With characteristic gloom and self-assurance, Adams announced in 1896 his discovery of a new "law" governing social development. Disclaiming authorship of this natural phenomenon, which according to him had simply unfolded from the facts of the case, he forestalled debate with the observation that "to approve or disapprove" of such a law "would be as futile as to discuss the moral bearings of gravitation." Adams' "law of civilization and decay" held that each successive stage in the development of any civilization was marked by certain intellectual, moral, and physical changes. The earlier phases favored the imaginative and individualistic qualities, and produced an abundance of religious, military, and artistic minds. As people multiplied and consolidated, created complex institutions, and became economically competitive, however, the "economic organism" tended to replace the "emotional and martial." In the last stage, the capitalist-industrial, "the economic, and, perhaps, the scientific intellect is propagated, while the imagination fades, and the emotional, the martial, and the artistic types of manhood decay." Fierce economic competition would in time weed out the "non-economic" men, and leave society largely composed of two extreme classes, "the usurer in his most formidable aspect, and the peasant whose nervous system is best adapted to thrive on scanty nutriment." At this point, disintegration would set in, and the society would perish at the hands of more virile peoples, or from internal decay, bringing a reversion to primitivism. In time a new civilization would begin to develop.[5]

Further than this pessimism could not go, and even among viewers-with-alarm Adams' forecast had only a limited popularity. He had, nevertheless, articulated a general concern, even if in terms too extreme for wide acceptance, and his concept of an "economic man" became part of the thinking of his contemporaries. The problem was clear enough: how to conserve the sturdy virtues and higher ideals amid the changing conditions of an urban-industrial society.

To a few iron souls, there was an obvious answer. The martial virtues came, they held, from Mars alone; a nation kept its "fighting edge" only by fighting. While this view never commanded majority support, it received considerable attention during the 1890s, and there resulted a rather startling glorification of war. Not surprisingly, career officers of the armed forces contributed copiously to the literature of uplift through combat; curiously, the navy led in these expressions.

In an 1891 article, Admiral Stephen B. Luce made a vigorous case for war as a positive good. "War," he announced, "is one of the great agencies by which human progress is effected." Scourge though it might be, and accompanied by unquestionable horrors, it was a necessary condition of social health. "It stimulates national growth, solves otherwise insoluble problems of domestic and political economy, and purges a nation of its humors." There was wisdom that came only from suffering, and a strength tempered in adversity; man was perfected through pain. Conversely, "riches and easily-acquired success enervate the strongest character and unfit it for protracted effort." The real advances of civilization, Luce argued, were frequently gained only through fighting. Democracy and freedom had often been advanced by war; the English civil wars of the seventeenth century produced a constitutionally limited monarchy, and the American Civil War destroyed chattel slavery. "Strife in one form or another in the organic world seems to be a law of nature," and was a tool of evolutionary progress. Without it, the "active forces" would atrophy, and luxury would become "more destructive than the sword." The proof could be seen in China, where the absence of conflict with superior races brought stagnation, and where the rights of man were unknown. "China, to-day, presents a picture of what the modern world would have been without war," Luce claimed.[6]

Luce's better-known protege, Alfred Thayer Mahan, held similar views. Scorning "ease unbroken, trade uninterrupted, hardship done away with," he pointed to the foreign dangers which threatened the nation, and which could be held at bay only as long as Americans retained the "masculine combative virtues." At the same time, internal ills could also overwhelm a society not firmly buttressed by the sturdy virtues, and united by a vigorous patriotism. Thus peace, "that alluring, albeit somewhat ignoble, ideal," must not be allowed to sap Americans of their manhood, "from fighting animals becoming fattened cattle fit only for slaughter." Named a member of the American delegation to the Hague Peace Conference in 1899, Mahan proved a great embarrassment to the delegation's chairman, Andrew Dickson White. His consistent opposition to the limitation of armaments and general arbitration agreements justified White's private complaints that the Admiral had little sympathy with the purposes of the conference.[7]

It was not only professional fighting men who thought in this way. "We hearken not to rhymers on universal peace . . . , " cried the militant Albert J. Beveridge in 1892. "I subscribe to the doctrine of war. It is the divine instrument of progress."[8] And the claims of the battlefield received consideration from men far more thoughtful than the boyish Indiana orator. After long pondering the issue, no less a philosopher than William James was eventually to admit much of the martial case. In "The Moral Equivalent of War," James agreed that militarism was the "great preserver of our ideals of hardihood," and opined that "life with no use for hardihood would be contemptible." Mankind must preserve some of its military character, if only to insure that "weaklings and molly-coddles" did not inherit the earth. For a pacifist, James' statement that "the martial virtues . . . are absolute and permanent human goods" was a substantial concession to the war party.

Given these convictions, the problem for James was how a society could preserve the necessary military qualities of mind and character without suffering the otherwise useless horrors of war. He suggested that a substitute might be found in a carefully fostered "civic passion" which would lead men to risk and to sacrifice for their country in the conquest of their environment. In place of military conscription, young men might be conscripted for a fixed term into a national service force, in which they would work in the mines, man the fishing fleets, build skyscrapers, and assume the other hard and dangerous tasks of society. This experience would inculcate the military ideals of hardihood and discipline, acquaint gilded youth with a knowledge of how the other half lived, knock the childishness out of the next generation, and teach it to respect the needs of the whole society. Heretofore, James said, only war had disciplined the community in such a fashion. Before man could dispense with war, therefore, he would have to create some such "moral equivalent" to assume its vital social role.[9]

Although James did not publish his article until 1910, some Americans were seeking such a "moral equivalent of war" in the 1890s. Influenced by numerous English writers, many of them came to find it in imperialism. Imperialism, after all, served the purposes of progress. Its agents, soldiers of the light, went out to obscure corners of the globe and braved danger and disease to bring civilization, order, knowledge, tangible achievement. At times, the process was even accompanied by actual wars, but these tended to be limited, not very bloody (at least for the conquerors), and fought for the highest of motives. For a generation, a column headed "Our Little Wars" was a fixture in the London *Times*, bringing daily reports of the fighting which was always in progress somewhere within the broad expanse of the empire. Its title betrayed the rather light-hearted attitude toward such conflicts which made them seem, somehow, less serious than "real" wars. And, once the fighting stage was over, the whole business became akin to James' service corps, transplanted to a foreign land.

The resulting benefits had long since been described by some of England's best-known authors. Sir Charles Dilke had concluded in 1896 that colonial dependencies formed a "nursery of statesmen, of warriors," and warned that his countrymen "should irresistibly fall into national sluggishness of thought were it not for the worldwide interests" provided by the empire. In the 1880s, James Anthony Froude found that men whose horizons were bounded by their personal interests had small aims and narrow thoughts; the citizen of an imperial power, however, escaped these limitations, lifted above himself by the grander scope of the organism of which he was a part. "His thoughts are wider, his interests less selfish, his ambitions ampler and nobler," Froude declared, concluding that "a great nation makes great men; a small nation makes little men."[10]

It had even been pointed out that America showed the lack of such influences. James Bryce's famous examination of American political life, *The American Commonwealth*, attempted to explain why so few really prominent Americans sought public careers in the 1880s. While acknowledging the existence of some genuine political talents, Bryce concluded that the proportion of men of "intellectual and social eminence" who entered public life was smaller in the United States than in the free countries of contempo-

rary Europe. Among the factors which he believed to account for
this was the pure dullness of American politics; not one of the really
interesting issues was present. Without any great questions of foreign policy or constitutional change, and with religious affairs
wholly outside of politics, legislative debate centered on financial
and economic matters which were doubtless important, but of limited appeal. "How few people in the English or French legislatures
have mastered them, or would relish political life if it dealt with
little else!" Although Bryce offered no remedy for what he described, and clearly disapproved of the adoption of imperialist
policies by the United States, his readers could and sometimes did
infer from his analysis that a colonial policy would raise just the
type of issues needed to regenerate American public life.[11]

In 1898, the London *Spectator* urged Americans to appropriate
the advantages of empire to themselves. If the United States faced
up to its duties to humanity and accepted the rule of colonies, it
would find its own government improved as its statesmen were
tempered by responsibility in large affairs. Patronage and paro-
chialism would retreat before a heightened idealism and enhanced
vision, and the development of an honest, efficient colonial civil
service would end in the reform of the civil service at home.[12]
American interest in these ideas quickened during the Spanish-
American War, and they became popular themes with the authors
and orators of the day. "Nations, like families, need to look outside
themselves," wrote Admiral Mahan, "if they would escape, on the
one hand, narrow self-satisfaction, or, on the other, pitiful internal
dissensions." The real gain from the war, the Admiral later decided,
had not been territorial, for the added areas were "trivial" compared
to the previous national domain, or with recent European annexations. Neither had it been principally material or commercial.
"What the nation has gained in expansion is a regenerating idea, an
uplifting of the heart . . . ," he declared.[13]

Another writer was sure that governing colonies would build a
new class of American leaders. On a sea voyage, he had met and
been impressed by a quiet young Englishman who proved to be a

district commissioner in Burma, ruling millions of people by his own personal authority. There was no such class of young Americans as this, the author mourned, for the opportunity to develop it had been lacking. The "best class" of American youth was therefore tending to become idle dawdlers and socialites, but now the remedy was at hand. The United States, too, could send the flower of its youth out to the colonies to dare and to sacrifice, and they would return home to leaven the entire mass. "They will be the means of introducing into our national life . . . an element of unselfishness, of conscientiousness, of dignified and earnest manhood, which has been but sparingly represented of late," the author believed.[14] He had put his finger upon a sore spot that distressed many of the "best class," and which had been noted by their idol and chief spokesman, E. L. Godkin, editor of the New York *Evening Post* and of its weekly cousin, *The Nation*. A peculiarity of American democracy, Godkin believed, was that it had produced a state in which the poor ruled the rich. The jealousy of the masses had gone far to drive the wealthy and educated out of public office, thus depriving them of a sense of responsibility for the rest of society. As the wealthy, leisured class grew, the prevalence of idleness, vice, and amusement became more noticeable, and to the nation's loss in leadership was added the bad effects on the masses of the pernicious example presented by society's natural leaders.[15]

Although Godkin was strongly anti-imperialist, like most of his fellow political independents of the "mugwump" persuasion, he campaigned for a career colonial service once the Spanish War annexations were an accomplished fact. The British model was the best, of course, and the Indian Civil Service the pinnacle of public administration. There was no possibility, Godkin thought, that the United States could create anything comparable to that august institution, but there was benefit even in trying: "It shows us, not what we can accomplish, but what we ought to aim at." Once such a service was created, it must be staffed by the best type of young men, representatives of the very class about whom the author had been so concerned. And, as long-time civil service reformers, God-

kin and his fellows undoubtedly hoped that the example of a really
honest and efficient career service in the Philippines and elsewhere
would bring the end of the spoils system at home, as the *Spectator*
had predicted. "The one thing which will prevent expansion being
a disgrace, is a permanent colonial civil service . . . . " the editor
wrote in 1899.[16]

Some theorists hoped to find employment in the new empire, not
merely for the nation's gilded youth, but for all of its excess energies.
Franklin H. Giddings, a professor of sociology at Columbia University, found "no population on the face of the earth . . . so largely
descended from daring adventurers" as that of the United States.
Settled by a self-selected portion of Europe's most restless types,
Americans were an unusually active and warlike people, Giddings
declared. They were, in fact, "the most stupendous reservoir of
seething energy to be found on any continent." Far from needing
inculcation in the virile qualities, they needed an outlet for those
which they already possessed. Usefully employed in such pursuits
as colonial development, the nation's energies could "do more for
the advancement of the human race than imagination can now
conceive," but denied such outlets, this volatile force might "discharge itself in anarchistic, socialistic, and other destructive modes
that are likely to work incalculable mischief." Colonial rule thus
became a lightning rod for social tensions, and imperialism a force
for conservatism, in Giddings' scheme.[17]

There was at least a superficial resemblance to this view in Senator Lodge's wartime comment that "this new foreign policy will
knock on the head silver and the matters which have embarrassed
us at home." In addition, the Senator ranged himself beside the
other advocates of a regenerative imperialism, and by 1900, he
could summarize his entire argument in a single paragraph. As he
told the Senate:

> The athlete does not win his race by sitting habitually in an
> armchair. The pioneer does not open up new regions to his
> fellow men by staying in warm shelter behind the city walls . . . .
> If a man has the right qualities in him, responsibility sobers,

strengthens, and develops him. The same is true of nations. The nation which fearlessly meets its responsibilities rises to the task when the pressure is upon it. I believe that these new possessions and these new questions, this necessity for watching over the welfare of another people, will improve our civil service, raise the tone of public life, and make broader and better all our politics.[18]

The prospect gave hope even to so confirmed a pessimist as Brooks Adams. While convinced that the march of civilization toward ultimate decline and destruction was irrevocable, Adams began to think that it could at least be appreciably delayed. To accomplish this, the nation must adopt measures to reverse the "consolidating" tendencies in society, and to encourage those martial and imaginative qualities which were so gravely threatened with extinction. To Adams, as to many others, the answer was to be found in empire, the modern equivalent of the old frontier. Dispersion was salvation, for "as masses solidify, the qualities of the pioneer will cease to be those that command success! Imperialism would grant a reprieve for individualism by continuing the frontier conditions that made it possible."[19]

All of these men found in imperialism a relevance which went beyond considerations of foreign policy, and which could not be understood in either economic or strategic terms. They saw it in direct relation to the central problems of their own society: how to protect traditional values in a period of metamorphosis, how to offset class struggles with a unifying nationalism, how to reintegrate the upper class into the main currents of public life, how to combat a sordid and pervasive materialism. Ultimately, they regarded it as a way to preserve the American character.

6 Theodore Roosevelt and the Sturdy Virtues

IT IS DIFFICULT, if not impossible, to write dispassionately of Theodore Roosevelt. Larger than life, full of gusto, moralistic, shrewd, learned, yet sometimes juvenile, he was a bundle of contradictions. He was also a human dynamo, and a political genius who virtually created the modern American presidency. He is remembered more vividly, perhaps, for his legend than for his very real achievements. Cowboy, crime-fighter, soldier, and explorer, it has often been noted that he fulfilled as an adult the ambitions of every small boy. Yet his blatant romanticism and shrill moralizing were wedded to an underlying realism that made him, in the end, an extremely effective national leader. The personality of Theodore Roosevelt has so gripped the public imagination, in his own time and since, that he has become the popular personification of the American imperialist. Colorful and flamboyant, with a knack for attracting publicity, he made his short-lived role as commander of the "Rough Riders" volunteer cavalry regiment the best-remembered service of the Spanish-American War. Since he had previously been one of the most forceful advocates of an expansionist foreign policy, and was soon to become President of the United States, it is natural to see Roosevelt as a central actor in the stirring events of the later 1890s.

Yet it would be erroneous to read back into the 'nineties the enormous influence which the dashing colonel would achieve as President. While an interesting and significant figure, Roosevelt played only a secondary part in shaping the great decisions of the McKinley era. William McKinley was the master of his own administration, and Roosevelt's letters contain abundant evidence of his many failures to win over the President to his point of view. Congress was similarly run from the top, the greatest weight in congressional councils belonging, as usual, to those senior Senators and Representatives who constituted the inner circles, held the committee chairmanships, and had formed numerous personal bonds with their fellows. If Roosevelt's influence was very limited within the executive branch, it was even smaller among the legislators, to whom he was a mere outsider. It is true that the young Assistant Secretary of the Navy did much to help the fleet prepare for war, but he neither initiated nor carried out any important step without the knowledge and approval of his superiors. In particular, the Far Eastern Squadron's attack on Manila Bay was a part of the war plans for a conflict with Spain before Roosevelt went to the Navy Department, and neither it nor any other large movement was undertaken without McKinley's consent. The widespread impression to the contrary was fostered by Roosevelt himself, and persisted long after his death.[1]

In the era of the 'nineties, Roosevelt's importance was rather as a publicist than as a policy-maker. As Federal Civil Service Commissioner, New York Police Commissioner, Assistant Secretary of the Navy, and volunteer army officer, he attracted the attention of the press and public to an extent far beyond the normal impact of such relatively obscure posts. This was partly owing to a prolific pen, which poured out books, articles, and reviews in variegated profusion. A man of unusually wide interests, Roosevelt was taken seriously as both a naturalist and a historian. He also had vigorous theories of public policy and international relations. While neither strikingly original nor distinct from the currents of contemporary opinion, these views were frequently and forcefully expressed, formed a coherent whole, and suited the temper of the times. In

America, they eventually became more closely identified with Theodore Roosevelt, who knew how to lend them a special glamor, than with any other man.

Roosevelt was a conscious expansionist by the mid-'nineties: in 1894 he favored the annexation of Hawaii and the construction of an isthmian canal. Late in 1895, he published a full-scale evaluation of foreign policy in a piece written for *Century Magazine*. In addition to annexing Hawaii and digging a canal, this manifesto called for the construction of a first-class navy, based upon a heavy battleship force rather than a mere collection of light commerce-raiders. As to international relations, the author praised the aggressiveness of the Harrison administration, while condemning what he viewed as the weakness of the Cleveland foreign policies. An intimate of Henry Cabot Lodge and a regular correspondent of A. T. Mahan, he closely paralleled their views and reasoning.[2]

As the Cuban situation worsened, Roosevelt became a leading warhawk, advocating the forcible ejection of Spain from the West Indies a year before war broke out between Spain and the United States. In September, 1897, he was urging the President to prepare for military action in Cuba: "I gave him a paper showing exactly where all our ships are, and I also sketched in outline what I thought ought to be done if things looked menacing about Spain, urging the necessity for taking an immediate and prompt initiative. . . . " He also warned the President of the possibility of "the Japs chipping in," but concluded, wistfully if incongruously, that "I haven't the slightest idea that there will be a war."[3]

When war did come, Roosevelt soon saw it as a golden opportunity for expansion. " You must get Manila and Hawaii," he wrote Lodge, "you must prevent any talk of peace until we get Porto Rico and the Philippines as well as secure the independence of Cuba." The reasons he gave for desiring these annexations were numerous, varying somewhat with time and occasion. He wished to drive out European influence from the western hemisphere, to insure a share for America in the future commerce of the Orient, to forward world peace and order by extending the area of civilization. World peace was only possible, he insisted, when the whole world was ruled by civilized masters, through "the expansion of the great, orderly, peace-loving powers."[4]

He also wished to increase American power. Inevitably, his life-long preoccupation with power made Roosevelt a "realist" rather than a "legalist" in his views of international relations. He tended to think in military-strategic terms, and to worry a great deal about the national security. With no strong neighbors in the hemisphere, it was clear that aggression could come only from Europe or Asia. As early as 1897, Roosevelt defined the immediate threat as emanating from Germany and Japan, and the passage of time strengthened this conviction. A war with Japan was most likely to arise from a clash of interests in the Far East, or over Hawaii, he thought, but a war with Germany would probably come from an actual German attempt to penetrate the western hemisphere. In either case, it was essential that the United States have a powerful navy, and strategically placed bases from which it could operate. American domination of the Caribbean and Hawaii would make it possible to secure most of these bases, while denying them to the potential enemy. In addition to other considerations, therefore, some expansion was necessary to the nation's safety.[5]

Historians have tended to make light of Roosevelt's fear of a German incursion into the hemisphere, but recent evidence has made the possibility more credible. The Kaiser at least toyed with the idea of an active American policy in the period just after the Spanish-American War. These ambitions became overt in December, 1899, when he ordered the general staffs of the German army and navy to prepare a plan for a war against the United States, in which the first move would be a German invasion of Cuba. The general staffs substituted Puerto Rico for Cuba and completed the plan, but warned that its implementation would require the use of so much of Germany's naval strength as to leave the homeland unprotected, besides committing a large portion of the army. In the uneasy state of Europe, they regarded it as prohibitively risky to strip Germany of her strength at home for distant adventures in the New World. While the Kaiser was probably only indulging his fondness for grandiose dreams, Roosevelt heard of these discussions, coupled them with previous alarms over the Philippines, and allowed them to confirm his earlier fears.[6]

In spite of his own military romanticism, Roosevelt's obsession with tangible power often made him a shrewd judge of international realities, and as President he was frequently more cautious and realistic about foreign affairs than the majority of the American public. He distrusted commitments that went beyond the available power to fulfill them; on the other hand, he always strove to maximize that power in areas where he considered the United States necessarily committed, such as the Caribbean. To that extent, Rooseveltian jingoism reflected the spirit of *realpolitik*.

Important as it was, however, the strategic factor alone is insufficient to explain Roosevelt's expansionism, which was also based upon considerations which transcended material national interests. Once the Philippine Islands were securely annexed, Roosevelt frequently spoke as though the tangible advantages which they brought to the United States were doubtful or non-existent. "While I have never varied in my feeling that we had to hold the Philippines, I have varied very much in my feelings whether we were to be considered fortunate or unfortunate in having to hold them...," he wrote in 1901. He had earlier recorded his belief that settlement colonies like Australia or New Zealand, rather than mere conquest colonies like India or, presumably, the Philippines, were the ones which most genuinely extended the power of a race, and left its mark on history. Strategically, he soon came to see the Philippines as a liability rather than an asset. Yet the task of ruling the archipelago, in Roosevelt's opinion, would in itself be good for the United States. He put the matter succinctly in 1899: "I believe in the expansion of great nations. India has done an incalculable amount for the English character. If we do our work well in the Philippines and the West Indies, it will do a great deal for our character."[7]

The Philippine issue therefore illustrated both continuity and change in Roosevelt's thinking. Although his views of expansion were remarkably consistent over the years, he did make a substantial alteration in his scheme when he enlarged it to include the annexation of those islands. Even after he had done so, they never really fit comfortably into his conception of American foreign policy. What they did fit was his idea of what the country needed to restore its moral fiber and to retain its social vigor, a subject upon which his thoughts changed very little between 1895 and 1901.

Like so many of his contemporaries, Roosevelt was keenly concerned about the state of the national character, and before the war with Spain he had catalogued the qualities to be fostered in it: "Love of order, ability to fight well and breed well, capacity to subordinate the interests of the individual to the interests of the community, these and similar rather humdrum qualities go to make up the sum of social efficiency. The race that has them is sure to overturn the race whose members have brilliant intellects, but who are cold and selfish and timid . . . . In other words, character is far more important than intellect to the race as to the individual."[8]

Character, in fact, was everything, and Roosevelt repeatedly showed uneasiness about the future of the American character in the years from 1895 to 1901. He saw "grave signs of deterioration" in the English-speaking peoples — the diminishing birth rate in North America, the excessive growth of cities, an increasing love of luxury, the "lack of fighting edge" shown by the British soldier in the Boer War, were omens of danger. There seemed to be a "gradual failure of vitality in the qualities . . . that make men fight well and write well," which gave Roosevelt "a very uneasy feeling that this may mean some permanent deterioration." The whole spirit of the times was unhealthy. "Oversentimentality, oversoftness, in fact, washiness and mushiness are the great dangers of this age and this people. Unless we keep the barbarian virtues, gaining the civilized ones will be of little avail."[9]

Reviewing Brooks Adams' *The Law of Civilization and Decay* for the *Forum* in 1897, Roosevelt rejected the most extreme predictions of that gloomy prophet. Yet he acknowledged the dangers of a sharpening separation of classes, as the rich grew richer, and the poor more concentrated in cities and more self-conscious. There was, undeniably, "a certain softness of fibre" becoming visible, too, while the "deification" of the stock market and the trading-counter was contemptible. "That there is grave reason for some of Mr. Adams melancholy forebodings, no serious student of the times . . . will deny," he asserted.[10]

The cultured young scion of inherited wealth reserved a special loathing for the new American plutocracy. There was not in the world "a more ignoble character than the mere money-getting American, insensible to every duty, regardless of every principle, bent only on amassing a fortune . . . . " Such men were all the more dangerous if they occasionally put their money to good use in supporting a college or a church, for these actions disguised their real iniquity and made it easier for humbler people to take them as models. The widespread worship of wealth and emulation of the rich served to generalize the evil influence of a sordid and morally slack plutocracy. Nor were the wealthy any better when they turned from money-getting to money-spending. "I have a feeling of contempt and anger for our socially leading people on this side . . . , " Roosevelt wrote an English friend; living lives of frivolity and vice, they exercised an unwholesome influence on the community at large by the false and unworthy standards which they established.[11]

After his presidency had ended, Roosevelt recorded his surprise and amusement, while on a tour of European capitals, at being welcomed by the Austrian nobility as a fellow defender of the traditional upper classes. The socialites of Vienna had heard of his enmity for the business tycoons of his own country; instead of viewing this, as Roosevelt did, as a democratic resistance to the tyranny of wealth, they looked upon it as "fundamentally in the interests of the right kind of aristocracy" as against the wrong kind.[12] There was truth in both views, for Roosevelt believed in a natural aristocracy of merit, and tended to find its criteria in the values of the old elite from which he had sprung.

Thus to Theodore Roosevelt a central problem of American society was to find ways of counteracting the physical softness and moral slackness which appeared to accompany the change from a pioneering country to a wealthy and developed one. For a portion of this problem he had a ready-made response. Sickly and asthmatic as a child, Roosevelt early became a devotee of physical fitness, and for the rest of his life he both pursued it and prescribed it for others with an enthusiasm bordering on fanaticism. He eagerly took up boxing, riding, hiking, and hunting. After purchasing a Dakota ranch in 1883, he spent several interludes as an amateur cowboy, and grew to think of himself as a man of the open. Famous for his presidential hiking and hunting trips, he advocated vigorous sports as a physical and moral tonic for the softening influence of city life. "It is a good thing for a man to be forced to show self-reliance, resourcefulness in emergency, willingness to endure fatigue and hunger, and at need to face risk." A speech in 1899 produced a phrase that became famous: " . . . I wish to preach, not the doctrine of ignoble ease, but the doctrine of the strenuous life . . . . " A new leadership was needed to spread this doctrine.[13]

It was vital that the mass of the people should adopt the proper kind of leaders, admiring and imitating men whose influence upon them would be healthy rather than vicious. A society was molded by its heroes, Roosevelt believed, and by its conception of its own past. "In the same way that we are the better for the deeds of the mighty men who have served the nation well, so we are the worse for the deeds and words of those who have striven to bring evil on the land." The authentic hero served his nation doubly, for his example helped to produce new heroes as the years passed. Conversely, the ruthless speculator who used evil means to become immensely rich "exerts over the minds of the rising generation an influence worse than that of the average murderer or bandit, because his career is even more dazzling in its success, and even more dangerous in its effects upon the community."[14]

In 1895, Roosevelt and his close friend, Senator Lodge, wrote a collection of stories entitled *Hero Tales from American History,* in a direct attempt to provide the next generation with proper models for their aspirations. "It is . . . an especially good thing for young Americans, to remember the men who have given their lives in war and peace to the service of their fellow-countrymen . . . , " said the authors in their preface; the heroic virtues were needed in peace as well as in war. This literary venture had its model in the works of Thomas Carlyle, and in a mid-century series of sketches by the English writer James Anthony Froude. Adopting hero-worship as a weapon with which to attack the commercial spirit, Froude had sought modern examples of the kind of men whose stories should inspire the young with higher ideals. Well acquainted with the leading English writers, Lodge and Roosevelt attempted in their book to do the same thing with the American past that Froude had done with that of England, and for identical purposes.[15]

In the summer of 1897, the new Assistant Secretary of the Navy explored these themes in a speech delivered at the Naval War College. "Much of that which is best and highest in national character is made up of glorious memories and traditions. The fight well fought, the life honorably lived, the death bravely met — those count far more in building a high and fine type of temper in a nation than any possible success in the stock-market, than any possible prosperity in commerce or manufactures." The speaker left no doubt as to where inspiration was most often to be found: it was the battlefield which produced the most heroes, and the best. In widely quoted and much-criticized words, he asserted: "No triumph of peace is quite so great as the supreme triumphs of war. The courage of the soldier . . . stands higher than any quality called out merely in time of peace." War was not the only source of the manly qualities, of course, but "if the peace we enjoy is of such a kind that it causes their loss, then it is far too dearly purchased . . . . "[16]

The fact was that Roosevelt had always had a romantic infatuation with war, and longed to sample its intoxications for himself. As early as 1886, he had hoped to raise a force of cowboys to participate in a war with Mexico which he believed to be imminent. In 1889 he declared his willingness to "see a bit of a spar with Germany" over the Samoan controversy; the Germans might burn New York, but this in turn would persuade the nation to build adequate coast defenses! The Venezuelan crisis of 1895 again found him ready for combat, this time with England: "The clamor of the peace faction has convinced me that this country needs a war." In the following year, Roosevelt wrote his sister that "it is very difficult for me not to wish for a war with Spain." His eagerness for war became notorious, one prominent New Yorker referring disgustedly to "those jingling jingoes, Cabot Lodge and Theodore Roosevelt."[17]

To Roosevelt, pacifism was identical with softness and cowardice, and pacifists virtual traitors. "If we ever come to nothing as a nation," he wrote Lodge in 1896, "it will be because the teaching of Carl Schurz, President Eliot, the *Evening Post* and the futile sentimentalists of the international arbitration type, bears its legitimate fruit in producing a flabby, timid type of character, which eats away the great fighting features of our race." By 1898 he was linking pacifism and materialism; in both the Venezuelan and the Cuban crises, he thought, it was the representatives of big business who took the lead in attempting to avoid war, and who were willing "to court any infamy if only peace can be obtained and the business situation be not disturbed." All of the influences which Roosevelt feared and hated seemed to draw together into a single enemy: over-civilized softness, sordid materialism, the new plutocracy, all made common cause for inglorious peace. The more reason, then, for war, which would smite them all equally, and open the way for national regeneration. He wished a war with Spain, Roosevelt declared, not only to drive the Spanish out of Cuba, but also for "the benefit done our people by giving them something to think of which isn't material gain."[18]

In retrospect, Roosevelt also viewed war as a unifying and democratizing force. While modern urban life tended to accentuate the diversity of individual interests, he claimed, war emphasized the great common interests which overshadowed all others. It brought together men of all classes, sections, and professions, and led them to respect one another. "It was a good thing, a very good thing, to have a great mass of our people learn what it was to face death and endure trial together, and all on an exact level," whether in great struggles like the Civil War or lesser one such as the recent war with Spain. The Spanish War had seen "scores" of rich men serving in the ranks under officers whose only income was what they earned, and as comrades of the workingmen of America. It could only benefit the country when men were brought together on such terms.[19]

Beneath all reasoned justifications for war, however sincere, rested Roosevelt's childlike delight in war for its own sake. "Did I tell you that I killed a Spaniard with my own hand . . . ?" he asked Lodge excitedly in 1898. To another friend, who had been wounded in Cuba, he unburdened himself at length: "And now, you old hypocrite, don't ever pretend to me that you are not as proud as a peacock at having been wounded in action in the late war! I should be, if I were in your place; and as a matter of fact, I am as proud as I can be now. It was a great thing! . . . we have both cause to feel profoundly satisfied that . . . we . . . had the luck to get into the fighting." In addition to his combat experience, Roosevelt was eager for the traditional martial honors. Deeply disappointed at not being promoted to the rank of general before his discharge, the demobilized warrior decided that he must at least have the nation's highest military decoration, the Congressional Medal of Honor. Senator Lodge obediently visited the War Department, but found the officials there cool to the project. The Senator then mustered further support and went to work in earnest, while Roosevelt bombarded him with affidavits and encouragement. "I am entitled to the Medal of Honor, and I want it," the erstwhile Colonel wrote modestly, but this ambition was never to be gratified.[20]

At times, the warlike Rooseveltian image threatened to become a political liability. He denied in 1899 that he was an advocate of bloodshed: "I very earnestly desire peace, but I think that peace often comes only as the result of labor and strife," he declared somewhat paradoxically. Both before and after the Spanish War, he was consistent in arguing that to be prepared for war was the most effective means of avoiding it. "An unmanly desire to avoid a quarrel is often the surest way to precipitate one; and utter un-readiness to fight is even surer." Thus pacifism invited aggression and humiliation, while his own insistence upon the martial activi-ties was the truest road to peace. By so arguing, Roosevelt managed to play simultaneously the roles of hawk and dove, with just enough truth in his reasoning and skill in his practice to make the position viable.[21]

He also coupled martial preparation with doing good. Wherever righteousness was at stake, Roosevelt held, it was impossible to separate virtue and strength, for each was essential to the other. By strength, of course, he meant power. The lesser nations of Europe, even the most civilized and "self-respecting" of them, could accomplish no great good in international affairs, because they lacked the power; there was no force behind their good wishes. A newly emergent United States, on the other hand, had demon-strated what strength and virtue could accomplish together. While president, Roosevelt totted up the recent achievements of his na-tion, which he credited with advancing the cause of international arbitration, and which had been able "to keep the peace in the waters south of us; to put an end to bloody misrule and bloody civil strife in Cuba, in the Philippines, and at Panama; and . . . to exercise a pacific influence in China," all because it possessed a powerful navy and was prepared to use it. He had taught his son, he once said, that "he could be just as virtuous as he wished if only he was prepared to fight." Only the strong could do good.[22]

While he attempted to overcome resistance to his naval building program by depicting it as a means of preserving peace, and while he became deeply and honestly involved in arbitration plans and peace activities, Roosevelt never overcame his ambivalence about war. If war alone produced the highest human qualities, if there was no real substitute for actual combat, then mere martial exer-cises or power potential would not suffice. It is difficult to believe that Theodore Roosevelt ever wished to see the total triumph of peace, however he rationalized his position.

On the other hand, even Roosevelt had no thought of continuous

warfare for his country, although he believed that periodic wars
were necessary. In the meantime the nation, like its citizens, must
seek to lead the strenuous life: "if a nation is great, as we claim
that ours is, it can remain so only by doing a great work and achieving dangerous and difficult tasks." Normally the individual rose to
greatness only through struggle. "As we all know this is invariably
the case with the species. In the great majority of cases it is also
true of the nation. If we lead soft and easy lives, concerning ourselves with little things only, we shall occupy but an ignoble
place in the great world drama of the centuries that are opening."[23]

The nation needed hard work, according to the familiar biological analogy, and the acquisition of colonies would provide work of
just the proper kind. There could be no doubt, Roosevelt thought,
as to "the excellent effect upon the national character" of colonial
expansion. No sensible American, it was true, wished to plunge into
a course of "international knight-errantry," or to attempt the construction of a great colonial empire like the British or French. But
such colonies as came along in the natural course of events represented duties and opportunities which must not be ignored.[24]

That rejection of such duties would be a fatal sign of decadence,
Roosevelt never doubted. A failure to annex Hawaii, he told Mahan
in 1897, would "show that we either have lost, or else wholly lack,
the masterful instinct which alone can make a race great." Similarly, the victories at Manila and Santiago had left an inescapable
legacy of duty. An American withdrawal from Cuba and the Philippines would be followed at once by chaos in the wretched islands
themselves. "Some stronger, manlier power would have to step in
and do the work, and we would have shown ourselves weaklings,
unable to carry to successful completion the labors that great and
high-spirited nations are eager to undertake." The country had
emerged into manhood; if it would avoid disgrace and degradation,
it must accept man's work, and for the strong, virile nations, this
included sharing in the policing and uplift of the backward peoples
of the globe.[25]

That there were backward peoples who required the guidance of the superior races seemed so clear as to need no debate. Roosevelt believed firmly in the inequality of peoples and often used the word "race" in expressing the idea, though he was sophisticated enough to recognize that the usage was unscientific. He hailed the exclusion of Chinese immigrants from the United States as the deepest kind of racial wisdom: the "clear instinct" of democracy had perceived the "race foe" and barred him out. As president, he charged that American Negroes had suffered more from their own "laziness and shiftlessness," "vice and criminality," than from "all acts of oppression of white men put together." Yet his was no simple creed of white superiority. Although he despised the Chinese for their alleged lack of fighting qualities, he felt similarly, though less intensely, about the Mediterranean Europeans. On the other hand, he respected the Japanese as a "wonderful and civilized people" who could fight with the best of them, and he expressly rejected the view that progress was only for Teutons or Aryans.[26]

But whatever the basis of judgment, the fact remained that some peoples were superior to others, and Roosevelt concluded in his later years that democracy was "an ideal for which only the very highest races are fit." A failure to recognize that fact in portions of Latin America had led to endless trouble, while it was "a fact obvious to any sane man" that the presence of a large Negro electorate in the southern United States had "rendered it practically impossible to apply the Democratic principle in the South." In short, some peoples were so inferior as to require a long term of rule by their betters, who alone could inculcate sounder values and higher ideals. To the end of his life, Theodore Roosevelt never doubted that imperialism was a good thing for the subject peoples as well as the dominant ones. White European expansion had been "fraught with lasting benefit to most of the peoples already dwelling in the lands over which the expansion took place." Whether one spoke of the English in India or Egypt, the French in Algiers, or the Germans in East Africa, the conclusion must be the same: the expansion of their rule had been to the advantage of mankind.[27]

In this great movement, however, the "English-speaking race" held an especially important place. "The day of the Latin races is over . . . ," Roosevelt had decided. While the Germans were "a good people," and one to be feared, in the long run the real contest would lie between the Anglo-Americans and the Russians. It must be the English-speakers who put their stamp upon the world of the future, and they must not become "effete" lest they fall prey to the advancing and absolutist Slavic hordes. As the United States had become the greatest branch of the English-speaking race, it was essential that it be the dominant power in the western hemisphere, and assume its proper role elsewhere.[28]

Although Roosevelt had not contemplated American rule in the Philippines, and was at first doubtful of the wisdom of such a distant and exotic enterprise, he was soon convinced that duty left no choice in the matter. The Filipinos could neither be handed back to Spain, abandoned to the mercy of the European powers, nor left to "sink into a condition of squalid and savage anarchy." They were clearly unfit for self-government, he declared, and fate had made the United States inescapably responsible for them. In Roosevelt's eyes, those Americans who shrank from the task were, in most cases, simply afraid of it, and were guilty of using moral arguments to justify an immoral abdication of responsibility.[29]

If they were to play their part in the improvement of the nation's character, then obviously the only possible justification for keeping the new acquisitions was a fixed intention to do them good. If this were lacking, "then for Heaven's sake let them go . . . ! " The time had passed, Roosevelt said, when any civilized nation was content merely to exploit its colonial populations for selfish purposes; the problem was to govern each colony in its own interest without falling into over-permissiveness and "mawkish sentimentality." He was soon convinced that the United States had succeeded in finding this golden mean in its own colonies. "I question if any three peoples have ever owed more to another nation than the Filipinos, Cubans and Porto Ricans owe us for what we have done during the last three years," he wrote in 1901. A few years later, he said of the Philippines: "It has been everything for the islands and every-

thing for our own national character that we should have taken
them and have administered them with the really lofty and dis-
interested efficiency that has been shown."[30]

While he believed that empire would improve the tone of American society, Roosevelt never saw foreign adventure as a total
solution for the nation's problems. Regeneration through overseas
action must be matched by reconstruction through domestic reform, and even in 1899, Roosevelt attached the greater importance
to the latter. Expansionist though he was, he told a friend, he
believed that coping with the "evil forces at work" in the nation
would require paying even more attention to affairs at home than
to international activities, for at least fifty years to come. Rooseveltian expansion was intended, not to avoid domestic problems by
shifting attention overseas, but to play a complementary role in a
program of general uplift at home and abroad.[31]

Roosevelt's world view is best understood, perhaps, in terms of
his view of himself. Nowhere is this self-image more clearly revealed
than in his reply to a solicitous friend shortly after Theodore had
been wounded by a would-be assassin in 1912. Shot while cam-
paigning for the presidency on the Bull Moose ticket, the aroused
ex-president had gone on to make his scheduled speech with the
attacker's bullet still in his body. Afterward, he explained rather
elaborately to his correspondent that such a course should be regarded as no more than natural, at least for himself. Modern civilization, it was true, was undoubtedly somewhat soft, and the typical
political leader or business executive reflected this softness. "Such
a man accepts being shot as a frightful and unheard-of calamity,
and feels very sorry for himself and thinks only of himself and not
of the work on which he is engaged or his duty to others . . . . "
But the good soldier or sailor, or such civilians as were deep-sea
fishermen, miners, cowboys, lumberjacks, and the like, "would
normally act as I acted without thinking anything about it." So,
naturally, would at least half of the men of the Colonel's old Rough
Rider regiment. "Now I wish to be ranked with such men . . . , and I
expect to be judged by their standards and not by the standards of

that particular kind of money-maker whose soul has grown hard while his body has grown soft . . . . " In short, Roosevelt saw himself as having personally preserved the pioneering virtues, while most of the leaders of his society had not; what he had done for himself, he wished to do for the nation as a whole.[32]

7 Civilization, Barbarism, and Christianity

"THERE ARE three popular arguments for a colonial policy," said an editorial in the *Outlook* magazine's 1898 Christmas number. One, prevalent west of the Rockies, was commercial, resting on hopes for a large Far Eastern trade. A second, centered in the Midwest, expressed "the spirit of enthusiastic Americanism," and held that the extension of American institutions abroad would serve the national mission and uplift alien peoples. The third argument, said the *Outlook*, dominated the Atlantic states, where there was alleged to be less popular excitement about Asian commercial prospects, and where "the passion of Americanism" was "very considerably modified by conservative instincts." This argument emphasized the inescapable duties imposed by the late war, particularly toward the Filipinos, who must be saved from Spanish despotism, foreign aggression, and domestic anarchy. The "united demand of the Eastern conscience, the Western enthusiasm, and the Pacific self-interest," declared the editorial, would prove irresistible.[1]

However questionable this neat sectional analysis may have been, appeals to the sense of national mission and the spirit of altruism were certainly important in securing popular support for expansion. They served to legitimize the more practical aspirations of the "large policy" group, to equate national self-interest and philanthropy, and to win over many who had little other interest in colonies. Many of the expansionist leaders themselves believed deeply in the righteousness of their actions, whether or not they

127

were primarily moved by that belief. It was comforting to conclude that the nation was doing God's work as well as its own. As one editorialist declared, Americans "may well believe that Manila and Santiago have emphasized divine approval of America's mission by the preternatural victory of America's arms."[2]

In an often-used phrase, Assistant Secretary of State David J. Hill described American expansion as "the extension of civilization." Federal Judge Peter S. Grosscup of Chicago announced the "breaking up of Asia" to be imminent, exposing the Asians at last to a western influence which would "undoubtedly cleanse and advance them as only a clean, wholesome civilization can." It was a task, he declared, in which Anglo-Saxons were bound to labor, and the United States must play its part. Another observer, the aged politician and ex-diplomat Cortlandt Parker, wrote the President that Providence had imposed upon the nation responsibility for the extension of Christian civilization, and for teaching the Cubans and Filipinos about "that progress in all good things, of which our nation is an example." By 1901, the historian Albert Bushnell Hart could ask rhetorically: "Who can doubt that the purpose of the American people is not only to make the nation felt as a world power, but also to spread Western civilization eastward?"[3]

William McKinley, too, reiterated his belief that the nation acted from duty as well as interest. In the autumn of 1898 he toured the Midwest and South, both judging and molding public opinion on expansion, and everywhere he touched upon the subject of mission. He told an Iowa audience that "wherever our flag floats . . . , it is always for the sake of humanity and the advancement of civilization." Chicagoans learned that "duty determines destiny." In Indiana, the President appealed to his listeners to "help the oppressed people who have by the war been brought within the sphere of our influence," and in Ohio he spoke of "the trust which civilization puts upon us." A few months later, in Boston, McKinley made mission his central theme: "Our concern was not for territory or trade or empire, but for the people whose interests and destiny, without our willing it, had been put in our hands." In short, the civilized peoples had a duty toward the uncivilized.[4]

The concept of a world divided between civilized and barbarous peoples had never been stronger, and it was accompanied by a conviction that the time was at hand when the advanced nations must begin the final assault on barbarism. No one was more strongly moved by this vision than Alfred Thayer Mahan, who revealed it repeatedly in his writings between 1893 and 1897. Mahan described western civilization as "an oasis set in the midst of a desert of barbarism." Outnumbered by the numerically overwhelming but inadequately organized hordes of the uncivilized, the West survived only because it was stronger, "diked off," in a new metaphor, from the human sea around it by "the magnificent military organizations of Europe." Mahan was certain that the fate of the rival cultures must be finally settled in the era just opening. The challenge to Christian civilization, which it must meet or perish, was to "receive into its own bosom and raise to its own ideals those ancient and different civilizations by which it is surrounded and outnumbered." As the older races of Asia roused from the sleep of centuries, they must be taught true enlightenment and the Christian spirit, or, gradually assimilating material progress, they would become merely more efficient barbarians, able to crush the West with their weight. When the fate of Hawaii was debated in 1893, Mahan wondered aloud whether the archipelago was to be an outpost of European civilization, or of a Chinese barbarism which might soon burst the barriers which contained it, and bury civilization under a wave of invasion.[5]

On the other hand, the nation faced duties and opportunities as well as threats, and after the war with Spain Mahan emphasized these. The United States could help to bring backward peoples forward, and thus alleviate the barbarian threat. Interest and altruism ran together, he wrote in 1899, but duty must be in the forefront: "if the ideas get inverted, and the nation sees in its new responsibilities, first of all, markets and profits, with incidental resultant benefit to the natives, it will go wrong." The primary aim must be to "regenerate" the "stagnant societies." Only an impulse from without could begin the regenerative process, and the source of that impulse might well determine the nature of the new society which was to arise from the old. A crucial question, then, was "under the genius of what race or what institutions, is the movement to arise and to progress?" Superimposed upon the "yellow peril," Mahan foresaw a struggle, peaceful or otherwise, between rival western societies, to shape the world in their own image. He predicted in 1900 that this contest would lie between the "Slavonic" and the "Teutonic" peoples, and that China would provide its main arena, for China's millions could tilt the world balance toward one side or the other. Thus the land-power of the Slav faced the sea-power of the Teuton, and the outcome would bring the world liberty or autocracy, freedom or serfdom, in the generations to come.[6]

To many besides Mahan, the times were pregnant with a special meaning. The realization that the impact of the West was destroying the traditional cultures of half the world's population was a valid insight, however dimly perceived or distorted by prejudice it might have been. The modernization of Japan, the disintegration of China, the decline of the Ottoman world, the constant extension of European rule, and the far-reaching changes wrought by these events, all portended a new epoch, and evoked statements of confidence or concern from the spokesmen of the white man's world.

There were certain "focal points" observable in history, Josiah Strong had asserted in *Our Country,* and he believed that the close of the nineteenth century would bring one of them, second in importance only to the birth of Christ. The coming generation would shape the destinies of mankind for centuries. The pace of events was speeding to a crisis, in which twenty years of the new century might "outmeasure a millenium of older time." Strong's view was echoed in the slogan of the college-based Student Volunteers for Foreign Missions during the 1890s: "The evangelization of the world in this generation." The thought reflected the special urgency with which many contemporaries endowed their own era.[7]

Orville H. Platt of Connecticut, one of the Senate's most influential Republicans, drew a connection between these ideas and the movement to annex tropical peoples. Many of his constituents, he said, saw these annexations as a God-directed duty, and felt it sinful to withhold support. "Among Christian, thoughtful people the sentiment is akin to that which has maintained the missionary work of the last century in foreign lands." Platt himself, a dignified seventy-three-year-old who vigorously opposed the drift into war over Cuba, soon became an enthusiastic convert to the doctrine of providential guidance.

> Does not Providence, does not the finger of God unmistakably point to the civilization and uplifting of the Orient, to the development of its people, to the spread of liberty, education, social order, and Christianity there through the agency of American influence [Platt asked a correspondent in 1898]? Can any man, even the least thoughtful, fail to see that the next great world wave of civilization is to overspread China, and how much that means? What kind of civilization is it to be, Russian, German, French? Or shall it be the civilization of the English-speaking people, led indeed by the United States? . . . Can you fail to see that in the Providence of God the time has come when the institutions of the English-speaking peoples are in final conflict with the institutions of despotism and irreligion, and that China is the battleground? . . . We are first in the family of nations; the head of the family has no right to disclaim an interest in the welfare of the other members.

Pointing out the harmony of duty and self-interest that marked the American initiative in the Far East, Platt grew almost poetic, likening each of Dewey's warships in Manila Bay to "a new Mayflower steering boldly through the wintry sea, the harbinger and agent of a new civilization . . . . " "Pardon my enthusiasm," he begged at last. "I am so full of the idea that I cannot write or look upon the situation tamely."[8]

If large portions of the earth were teetering on the brink of a new era, other areas contained people who were regarded as simply unequal to the task of regulating their own affairs. Approaching no visible regeneration, these people's very ineptitude made them fit wards for the abler, advanced societies. As the eminent English writer James Anthony Froude explained in the 1880s, "the sections of men on this globe" were unequally gifted. Some were strong, and capable of self-government; others were weak, and subject to external aggression and internal anarchy. Freedom, Froude said, "which all desire, is only attainable by weak nations when they are subject to the rule of others who are at once powerful and just." The Roman empire had extended the necessary trusteeship in one age, the British empire in another. In any age, it was a vital function.[9]

While Froude had been writing specifically of the West Indies, all of the non-white peoples of the tropics were thought to pose a problem of world order. This special problem was defined by Benjamin Kidd, an Englishman who gained a considerable reputation in the 1890s for his works on social issues. In *The Control of the Tropics*, published in 1898, Kidd elaborated his earlier views into a completed system, inspired in part by the prospect that the United States was about to join Great Britain in taking on major tropical commitments.

The great international rivalry of the past, Kidd asserted, had been over those parts of the earth suitable for the white race. That phase was over, and the rivalry of the future would be for the control of the tropics. This contest had an important economic aspect: the last great field for the extension of trade lay in the exchange of goods between the temperate and tropical zones, which produced unlike and complementary products. The central issue, however, was more sociological than economic. At its core lay the fact, according to Kidd, that tropical peoples were incapable of self-government: "there never has been, and there never will be, within any time with which we are practically concerned, such a thing as good government, in the European sense, of the tropics by the natives of these regions." The tropical peoples were as children; they could neither govern themselves nor develop their lands, and non-colonial tropical societies could be characterized by the words "anarchy and bankruptcy." As a final complication, Kidd declared, the white man could not successfully transplant himself to tropical areas. Physically degenerating in a hostile climate, cut off from his own society and its sources of vitality, surrounded by alien races at a lower stage of development and tempted by their slacker and easier standards of conduct, the white man invariably proved unable to raise the level of "the races amongst whom he has made his unnatural home," and tended rather "himself to sink slowly to the level around him." The writer likened the white resident of the tropics to a diver working underwater: he must keep in close contact with his own civilization, and return to it at regular intervals; he would suffer grave harm if he stayed too long submerged in the alien culture around him.[10]

Given these assumptions, Kidd's conclusion followed plausibly: the tropical zone must be administered by agents of the western nations, as trustees of mankind. Ruled by career civil servants who were sent out in their youth from the European homeland, were regularly reinvigorated by home leave, and who returned home when their work was done, the original inhabitants would remain in physical possession of the land and gain the benefits of western supervision. In the West, "the inexpediency of allowing a great extent of territory in the richest region of the globe . . . to remain undeveloped, with its resources running largely to waste under the management of races of low social efficiency" would become increasingly obvious. In a separate article, Kidd applied his thesis to the United States, which as a rising leader of the "vigorous races" must participate fully in the work of tropical development.[11]

Kidd's book was reviewed and discussed everywhere in the United States. The New York industrialist, politician, and philanthropist Abram Hewitt sent a copy to President McKinley and urged him to read it, although Hewitt was not yet certain that he totally agreed with the book "except so far as he stands upon the ground that the control of the tropics must necessarily be assumed by white people, and possibly by the Anglo-Saxon race." Debate turned most hotly upon Kidd's allegation that white men could never successfully colonize the tropics, critics pointing to contrary examples from the past, or to modern medicine, the infant art of air-conditioning, and other innovations as future solutions of the problem. But whether they favored white settlement in the tropics or merely white control, few challenged Kidd's evaluation of the indigenous peoples as collectively incompetent. "It is better for all mankind that territory should be in the hands of those who can best govern it," proclaimed an editorial in the Detroit *Tribune,* "and as a rule, those can best govern who are capable of conquering. That is the reason that conquest is moral enough for all practical purposes."[12]

Conquest was even more moral, of course, if its object was to conquer souls for God, and to much of the Protestant religious press in America, it appeared that the Spanish War would ultimately serve just that purpose. The churches had been slow to obey God's command to preach the gospel to the heathen, said the *Congregationalist* in the summer of 1898: "And now our Father is taking matters into his own hands, and is forcing the nation to pay its hundreds of millions and to give up its tens of thousands of sons to spread the gospel. For this war is to be God's means of hastening the time when all shall know him." The *Christian Herald* found that "it is in no sense man's war at all . . . . The God of Battles called us to arms . . . ."[13]

Even before the war, this sense of divine destiny had frequently found expression. Doctor Richard S. Storrs, upon leaving the presidency of the (Congregational) American Board of Commissioners for Foreign Missions in 1897, declared that the duty of spreading Christianity now rested preeminently upon the American people. "Every time this thought has come before me," he said, "it has grasped me with a more prodigious power. This nation, the great minister of God for doing this, his transcendent work, in these tremendous times!" Storrs voiced an attitude which was rapidly emerging across the nation in the decade of the 1890s. Late-nineteenth-century revivalism in America had merged with a new sense of national power to produce in Protestant circles the spirit of crusade. The ferment was particularly noticeable on college campuses, where the Student Volunteer Movement for Foreign Missions publicized the missionary appeal and recruited young people to engage in the work abroad. Volunteer groups travelled from campus to campus, holding indoctrination classes that often ran for weeks and used regular textbooks. They worked also with local church groups and with the Young Men's and Young Women's Christian Associations, which had originally sponsored the Student Volunteers. In the years before 1898, hundreds of Volunteers went overseas, and tens of thousands who stayed home became interested in their work.[14]

John R. Mott, a Y.M.C.A. official and long-time head of the Student Volunteers, made a world organizing tour between 1895 and 1897. Upon his return he published his official report as a book, under the title, *Strategic Points in the World's Conquest*. Aspiring to "the evangelization of the whole world in this generation," Mott discussed the prospects of mass conversions in India, China, and elsewhere, and found them good. Undaunted by the admittedly serious obstacles to this goal, he overflowed with an astonishing faith and energy, maintaining a brutal, killing pace of travel and exhortation for twenty consecutive months. Travelling 60,000 miles, visiting 144 campuses in 22 countries, arranging almost two dozen conferences and conventions, and personally meeting 1300 missionaries, the conviction that the Lord was literally and personally beside him drove him on. "Time after time have we stood before walls of difficulty, opposition, and peril," he recalled, "which were, so far as man could judge, insurmountable, and have seen them fall to the ground in such a marvellous manner as would be totally inexplicable apart from the almighty unseen forces of the prayer kingdom which were being wielded on our behalf."[15]

In the light of such faith, it is not surprising that missionaries, even more than other apostles of western civilization, took for granted the superiority of western values over indigenous ones. To the missionaries, they were superior precisely because they were Christian; Christianity was the essential condition for creating any truly advanced society, anywhere. Western, Christian civilization had therefore not only the right but the duty to attack the very foundations of the non-Christian societies. Robert E. Speer, Secretary of the Board of Foreign Missions of the Presbyterian Church in the United States, brusquely disposed of the contention that missions were a disturbing and revolutionary force in traditional societies like China. The whole western movement upon Asia was revolutionary and subversive, he declared bluntly. "In comparison with territorial seizures which shake national pride to its foundations, and trade development which destroys the institutions and vested interests of centuries, and wars which lay waste great areas and arouse the deepest passions of mankind," it was "puerile" to talk of the revolutionary influence of the missionaries. The "tremendous subversive power of our western movement" was directed against the non-Christian religions; even without Christian missionary activity, those religions were doomed, but without it there would be nothing to replace them. Speer found it, however, "scarcely possible to deny" that in time, the missionary movement would produce "one of the most magnificent and most colossal revolutions that human history contains."[16]

While remaining a distinct current within the imperialist tide, the missionary urge touched the other main streams at several points. It added emotional intensity to the idea of national mission, and gave it a higher-than-human sanction. In addition, supporters of missionaries regularly pointed out the relation between missionary activity and the quest for new markets. By spreading western concepts and increasing western influence, the bearers of the Word opened a path for the salesmen of western products. This theme was explored in a spate of magazine articles with such titles as "Do Foreign Missions Pay?", "The Secular Value of Foreign Missions," and "The Influence of Mission Work on Commerce," and helped to weld religious and commercial activists into a mutually useful alliance. Finally, missionary organizations became powerful political lobbies, able to mobilize significant segments of public opinion. Politicians learned to handle them cautiously, the veteran editor Whitelaw Reid warning John Hay that: "I am as much afraid of the political effect of offending the missionaries as of offending the Irish!"[17]

Significant as the missionary movement undoubtedly was in affecting the general outlook of American expansionism, however, its application to specific colonial areas and issues was handicapped by grave obstacles. For one thing, it was the hordes of mainland Asia that seemed to offer the grandest harvest of souls, and the American Protestant missionary movement gave more of its attention to China than to the rest of the world combined. It was in China that most American missionaries worked, and of China that the greatest things were expected.[18] But the new areas which came under American control in 1898 lay elsewhere, and, most unsettling of all, they had all been Christianized long before. Hawaii, an example of an earlier American Protestant incursion, was less difficult to deal with religiously than were Cuba, Puerto Rico, and the Philippines, all of which had for centuries belonged to the Roman Catholic world. Collectively, the new acquisitions raised the delicate question of Protestant-Catholic relations, an issue at least as explosive at home as abroad.

American Catholics, already troubled by such recent manifestations as the national rise of the shrilly anti-Catholic American Protective Association, and seriously divided by ethnic rivalries and internecine quarrels within the Church, faced additional problems with the confrontation of the United States and Spain. Conspicuously Catholic and traditionally influential with the papacy, Spain's religion was to many Protestant Americans inseparable from her nationality, and the war with Spain seemed to some a new campaign in the continuing struggle against Romanism. Furthermore, the annexation of lands where the separation of church and state had never been known posed painful problems for even the most tolerant of non-Catholics. The direct participation of the church in government and in economic areas such as lending and land ownership, not to mention the church's domination of public education in the former Spanish colonies, were incompatible with American ideas and institutions. The resulting complications taxed the wisdom and ingenuity of the Catholic hierarchy in America.[19]

One leading churchman who grappled with these problems was

Archbishop John Ireland of St. Paul. Unlike most Catholic leaders, Ireland was a Republican. An ex-Civil War army chaplain, he was a member of a politically active veterans' group, the Grand Army of the Republic, and had campaigned for McKinley in 1896. Because of his friendships with Republican bigwigs, the Vatican selected Ireland to work for a peaceful settlement of the Spanish-American crisis, and just prior to the outbreak of war the Archbishop obediently went to Washington to lobby unsuccessfully for papal mediation. Seeing the risk of a popular identification of the Vatican as pro-Spanish, Ireland repeatedly urged that the Pope recognize the new power of the United States and adopt a friendlier attitude toward it. "I am not much of an Anglo-Saxon," he wrote early in the war, "but, Anglo-Saxonism is to reign, and, if there is wisdom in the Vatican, it will at once seek influence with English-speaking countries, especially America." Ireland soon became an advocate of expansion, partly because he hoped that the new world role of the United States would increase the importance in the eyes of Rome of the American church and portions of its leadership. As a prominent member of the "American" faction, which advocated a closer assimilation of the church into all phases of American life and played down the "old country" appeal to immigrant groups, the Archbishop had long been involved in bitter feuding with church conservatives and supporters of foreign-language churches in the United States; by associating himself with the new nationalism, he hoped to score a decisive victory over his enemies. Furthermore, the American church, though containing only a minority of the population and lacking state support, was still one of the largest and richest in the world, and well able to take up the colonial pastorates from the failing grasp of Spain. By June, Ireland favored retaining the Philippines, Cuba, and Puerto Rico, writing that "this war is Providence's opportunity to make a new world . . . . So, let us go in for New America: I will preach the New Gospel." It was not only Protestants who supported manifest destiny.[20]

In general, American Catholics loyally supported their government in the war with Spain, and accepted the necessity for the separation of church and state in the annexed territories. It was the declaration of some Protestants that these new territories must be protestantized which upset them. An article in the *Christian Herald*, written shortly after Dewey's victory at Manila Bay, illustrated the danger. Noting that the Philippine population was largely Roman Catholic, the article matter-of-factly declared that, should the United States retain the islands, "it will be our task to . . . Christianize their population" through Protestant missionary work, in order to "redeem" them from their present "moral degradation." The Presbyterian *Evangelist* recalled Rome's policy of barring Protestant activity in Catholic countries. The tables were now turned, it exulted, and the former Spanish islands were ripe for the harvest: "Where war has opened the door the church may enter." Baptist and Methodist journals expressed similar sentiments, and there was soon a cry for "religious reconstruction" in the new possessions.[21]

Catholic spokesmen fought back stoutly, defending the Philippine friars' orders against charges of tyranny and corruption, and assailing Protestant critics. Rejecting an appeal for Catholic-Protestant cooperation in the new territories, Archbishop Ireland suggested further considerations; Protestantism, he said, could never replace Catholicism in the hearts of pious islanders, it could only undermine their present faith, and "to take from them their faith is to throw them into absolute religious indifference." More probably, Protestant activity would only irritate good Catholics, further complicating the transition to United States rule. "In the name of religion, of civilization, of common sense," pleaded Ireland, "give the Catholic Filipinos at least a chance to know us as we really are, that we are not out there to stir up religious as well as political hate."[22]

Protestants themselves were by no means united on these prickly issues, as the division within the Protestant Episcopal Church demonstrated. This body had traditionally refrained from sending missionaries to Roman Catholic countries, and one of its organs, *The Living Church*, favored continuing that policy; since missionary work was already underfinanced and spread too thin, it should be

concentrated upon the out-and-out heathen. *The Church Eclectic,*
on the other hand, called for seizing the unique opportunity to
bring the new colonial peoples to a "higher" form of Christianity,
regardless of former policies.[23]

President Jacob Schurman of Cornell University, head of McKinley's first Philippine Commission, attempted to find some middle
ground in the dispute. Rather than subjecting the Filipinos to a
babble of voices from a dozen competing sects, he suggested publicly, one form of Protestantism should be selected to represent
them all, giving the Filipinos a simple choice between the two competing forms of the Christian religion. This suggestion affronted
virtually everyone, bringing angry comment from Protestants and
Catholics alike. "Is McKinley's Philippine commission empowered
to recognize and name this new state church of imperialism . . . ?"
inquired the *Catholic Universe* acidly. "If it is, what are the leading
features to be? . . . The immersion tub of the Baptists, the amen
corner of the Methodists, the rationalistic tendency of the Presby-
terians, or that composite entity called Episcopalism?" As the *Literary Digest* declared editorially, the only point of general agreement was that the religious problem in the Philippines was fully as
puzzling as the military and civil issues, and required still greater
care in handling.[24]

Just how to civilize the nation's new wards soon appeared almost
as difficult a question as how to Christianize them. At first, it was
widely assumed that the "subject peoples" would be overjoyed to
come under the beneficent influence of the United States, and
would adopt American methods and institutions as rapidly as these
could be explained to them. A brief experience sufficed to dispell
these illusions, and the savage and frustrating struggle with Aguinaldo's Philippine independence movement made it all the more
difficult to ignore colonial realities. Believing the colonial populations unready for self-government, and finding them unexpectedly
resistant to imposed social change, expansionists began to recognize that they faced serious problems in governing the recent
acquisitions. While never doubting their civilizing mission, they

came to define its secular side as the bringing of honest government, sanitation, education, and public works. The humdrum
routines of administration inevitably replaced the glamor of conquest, with a corresponding decline in popular interest in the
United States. In addition, many Americans were puzzled and
frustrated by the stubborn refusal of affairs in the new regions to
conform to their preconceptions. "There are multitudes of Americans who say now that if they had known what a sorry lot the
Cubans are, we would never have gone to war on their behalf,"
Carl Schurz noted in 1898.[25] The remark reflected the irritation of
a nation which had projected upon the outer world a picture fash-
ioned from its own imagination, only to find the vision and the
reality literally worlds apart. Automatically, if not always consciously, it blamed the islanders for the difference.

On rare occasions, a voice from the backward regions penetrated
vast physical and psychological distances to be dimly heard by a
startled American public. Thus, in the spring of 1899, the Chinese
Minister to the United States made a speech in Philadelphia which
was notable for its direct challenge to prevalent western thinking.
"Some people," he said, "call themselves highly civilized, and stig-
matize others as uncivilized. What is civilization? Does it mean
solely the possession of superior force and ample supplies of offensive and defensive weapons?" The mandarin took it to mean something more: a truly civilized nation should respect the rights of
other societies, and refrain from stealing other men's property, or
imposing upon others unwelcome beliefs. But the voice of Wu
Ting-Fang, though it aroused a ripple of comment in the press,
failed to shake the more popular faith that western values were
the soundest, and must prevail.[26]

Indeed, this faith remained so general and so deep as to become
one of those ultimate sanctions which are used as advertising appeals. Also in 1899, a full-page magazine advertisement for Pears'
Soap pictured Admiral Dewey himself washing his hands on ship-
board with a plainly marked bar of the sponsor's product. Among
the surrounding lesser scenes in the layout was a vignette of a

The first step towards lightening

The White Man's Burden

is through teaching the virtues of cleanliness.

Pears' Soap

is a potent factor in brightening the dark corners of the earth as civilization advances, while amongst the cultured of all nations it holds the highest place—it is the ideal toilet soap.

missionary presenting a bar of soap to a semi-naked and kneeling savage on a tropic strand. The text below this moving scene supplied the following message: "The first step toward lightening the White Man's Burden is through teaching the virtues of cleanliness. PEARS' SOAP is a potent factor in brightening the dark corners of the earth as civilization advances, while amongst the cultured of all nations it holds the highest place—it is the ideal toilet soap."[27] (See p. 142.)

8 Elihu Root: A World of Order and Progress

WHILE THE concept of a world divided between civilization and barbarism had a widespread appeal, not everyone equated civilization with Christianity quite so directly as did the missionaries. To Elihu Root, for example, the civilized and the uncivilized societies could best be differentiated by their attitudes, not toward religion, but toward orderly procedure and the law. Divided on this basis, the world's peoples fell, not into two clear-cut groups, but along a wide range of gradations from the highest civilization to the lowest savagery. Yet Root, too, saw significance in the co-existence of the enlightened and the backward, and believed that the former must be responsible for the tutelage of the latter. What was equally significant, he saw a role for American influence and leadership in dealing with the "semi-civilized" peoples who occupied the spectrum's middle ranges.

It was the nation's new colonies which first brought Elihu Root into public life, launching him upon a belated career that in time made him Secretary of State, United States Senator, and Republican elder statesman. Previously little known outside of New York City, his appointment to the post of Secretary of War in 1899 made him responsible for the military governments currently ruling Cuba, Puerto Rico, and the Philippines, and a central figure in the formulation of colonial policy. It was specifically for that purpose that McKinley chose the new secretary, in a move which surprised the latter as much as it did the political world of Washington. When

notified of McKinley's offer, Root protested that he knew nothing
about the Army, but was told by his informant that the President
needed "a lawyer to direct the government of these Spanish islands,
and you are the lawyer he wants."[1]

At first sight, it seemed a curious choice. By the late 1890s, Elihu
Root was one of the country's leading corporation lawyers, earning
from his practice the then immense sum of over $100,000 a year.
Already in his middle fifties, he had held no previous office except
for a two-year stint, years earlier, as a Federal District Attorney,
nor had he sought any other. He had shown no particular interest
either in military affairs or in foreign policy, and, although long
active in Republican affairs, his activity had been largely confined
to the politics of his own city. In New York, however, his judgment
and ability increasingly impressed the local political elite. Back in
1886, Root had served as chairman of the Republican county committee, and worked closely with Theodore Roosevelt in the latter's
unsuccessful campaign for the office of mayor of New York. After
that Root continued active in various reform movements, citizens'
committees, and party battles, keeping his close ties with Roosevelt
and others. When the McKinley administration took up the reins
of power, one of Root's friends, New York merchant Cornelius N.
Bliss, became Secretary of the Interior, and the new President
heard favorable reports of Root from others among his advisers
as well.[2]

Shortly after his inauguration, McKinley privately asked Root to
accept an appointment as United States Minister to Spain, a particularly sensitive post because of the growing possibility of war
over Cuba. After some hesitation, Root declined on the ground that
his ignorance of the Spanish language would be a fatal handicap in
any really serious negotiations. With this decision, he seemed to
have chosen to stay in private life for the remainder of his career.[3]

When the threatened war with Spain was actually imminent in
the spring of 1898, Root wrote Bliss an evaluation of the situation
which the latter showed McKinley, who was much impressed by it.
On the one hand, Root declared, he was as much opposed to going

to war as was McKinley, and thoroughly approved of the President's efforts to avoid the conflict. In Root's view, the United States owed no obligation to Cuba commensurate with the costs of a war. "I deplore war," he wrote. "I have earnestly hoped that it might not come . . . . I agree with the President that it is not his duty to sacrifice his own people for the benefit of others . . . . " Nevertheless, if the American people insisted upon fighting over Cuba, they had a right to do so. The Cuban cause was just, and Spain's position was untenable on either legal or moral grounds. The chain of events since the destruction of the battleship *Maine* had ended, he thought, by making war unavoidable. "Fruitless attempts to hold back or retard the enormous momentum of the people bent upon war would result in the destruction of the President's power and influence, in depriving the country of its natural leader, in the destruction of the President's party, in the elevation of the Silver Democracy to power," Root prophesied. It was on such grounds, rather than for moral or expansionist reasons, that Root originally came to accept the great crusade of 1898.[4]

As to the territorial acquisitions to which that crusade led, Root had mixed feelings. He had no part in the decisions which settled their fate, being still merely a private citizen engaged in the practice of law. "McKinley never discussed with me his reasons for taking the Philippines," Root recalled many years later. And he confessed, perhaps with the wisdom of hindsight, to "a subconscious feeling of gratitude that I didn't have to decide the thing." Thus, when the new Secretary of War began his duties on August 1, 1899, it was to deal with a *fait accompli*. The question of whether to take the new territories and commitments belonged to the past; what was now relevant was how to manage them. That it was a question, not merely of administration, but of the lives and welfare of people, Root recognized from the first. On the day he was sworn into office, he revealed his feelings in a letter to his wife: "When I consider the power now placed in my hands & its tremendous effect on the lives of millions of poor creatures who are looking to this country for civilization & freedom & the blessings of law and order, the little sacrifices I am making seem very small indeed."[5]

The circumstances under which Root took office made it difficult to sustain this lofty note. With a new war raging in the Philippines, and domestic opinion critical of the War Department's record during the recent conflict with Spain, Root had his work cut out for him. His predecessor, Russell A. Alger, had been judged incompetent by most of the press and public, and the remaining leadership of the department was badly demoralized by the charges, investigations, and feuds which plagued the army after the making of peace with Spain. It took all of Root's toughness and ability to control the situation, restore confidence in his department, and provide a new army for the prolonged struggle in the Philippines, while at the same time beginning to establish a sense of direction in what had been a sorely confused Cuban policy. Able, self-contained, austere, and sometimes ruthless, Root soon emerged as a major power in the McKinley administration, and his views on colonial affairs came to have a weight equal to any in the government.[6]

These views were shaped by Root's firsthand experiences in coping with his many problems, by his natural conservatism, and by the strongly legal cast of his thinking. If he had not been notably expansionistic before, he rapidly became so in the course of implementing expansionist policies. As the man in ultimate charge of the Philippine war, it was perhaps inevitable that Root would see in Aguinaldo's movement, not a people's legitimate aspirations for liberty, but the spurious facade of a turbulent barbarism. There was no such thing as a Philippine "nation," he declared shortly after taking office; merely hundreds of islands, inhabited by dozens of distinct tribes, speaking many different languages and at varying levels of civilization. Aguinaldo represented only one tribe, the Tagalogs, who occupied a portion of the single island of Luzon. Not even all of this tribe supported the fight against American authority, and at any rate the Filipinos collectively were incapable of self-government. To Root, the issue was a simple one: "We are fighting against the selfish ambition of a military dictator."[7]

From the first, Root drew a sharp distinction between those peoples which were capable of self-government and those which were not, and he was therefore unmoved by appeals to the consent of the governed. "Government does not depend on consent," he declared with finality. What was essential was that each society should have an adequate government, whether or not it was capable of providing it for itself; it was necessary "that the weak shall be protected, that cruelty and lust shall be restrained, whether there be consent or not." He refused to believe, he said, that it could be a violation of Jeffersonian principles "for the external forces of civilization to replace brutal and oppressive government, with which . . . people in ignorance are content, by ordered liberty and individual freedom . . . . " The ability to govern was unequally distributed over the globe, and those who possessed it must rule the rest. "We, of America, have discovered that we, too, possess the supreme governing capacity," Root announced several years later, "capacity not merely to govern ourselves at home, but that great power that in all ages has made the difference between the great and the small nations, the capacity to govern men wherever they were found."[8]

As often as he attempted to analyze the nature of this special gift, the lawyer-turned-statesman came to the same conclusion: its essence lay in a long conditioning which ultimately inculcated a popular respect for the law. The Puerto Ricans, he explained in 1899, lacked precisely this attribute. In all their previous experience under Spanish rule, law and freedom had been ideas which were not associated with each other, but mutually opposed. Furthermore, the Puerto Ricans had never learned "the fundamental and essential lesson of obedience to the decision of the majority." In recent municipal elections there, the defeated minority had withdrawn from all participation in public affairs, and boycotted politics. Just such an attitude, Root said, lay behind the continual revolutions in the West Indies and Central America, and marked a merely rudimentary stage of political development. A long "course of tuition under a strong and guiding hand" would be needed to improve the islanders' political skills enough to justify entrusting them with self-government. The process would necessarily be very slow, because it was a matter "not of intellectual apprehension, but of character and of acquired habits of thought and feeling." In the meantime, even the most perfect of constitutions would be useless until the new habits had been acquired.[9]

The case of the United States, Root believed, was exactly the opposite. There, respect for constitutional methods and principles had become a tradition, continuing through centuries and universally felt. "These traditions with us amount to a kind of unwritten constitution," he claimed, "which the most illiterate man has taken in through the pores of his skin." In the United States, Root once observed, "every citizen has learned that obedience to law, and respect for the results of popular elections, is a part of the order of nature." That Root himself could remember his country's convulsion in one of the most terrible of modern civil wars, that hundreds of Negroes were annually lynched in the United States, that Western gunmen flouted the law while Eastern politicos stole elections, had little apparent effect upon Root's view of his own society. In the United States, orderly legal procedures were "a part of the order of nature"; in Cuba, Puerto Rico, and the Philippines, they were not, nor would they be soon. The difference was fundamental, and not subject to debate.[10]

These reflections led Root to a paternalistic attitude toward colonial areas. As a part of this paternalism, he felt deeply the responsibility of the United States toward the subject peoples. He fought hard for tariff concessions for Cuba and Puerto Rico which would open to them markets under favorable conditions in the United States. Strong congressional opposition to a Cuban reciprocity treaty moved the normally cool Root to an unaccustomed show of feeling. He was willing, he wrote Cuba's Governor General, Leonard Wood, to hold on in Cuba despite all attacks as long as he was free to do what was best for the Cubans, "but if we once get into a position where we are retaining our hold in Cuba, to the injury of the Cuban people, doing them an injustice, refusing to properly care for them while we prevent them from caring for themselves, the position will be untenable, and I am not willing to occupy it." Similarly, when Wood uncovered postal scandals in Cuba in which a protegé of the powerful Mark Hanna was implicated, Root ordered Wood to "scrape to the bone, no matter whose nerves are hurt by it," for "the first essential of administration in this Island is that we shall be perfectly honest with ourselves."[11]

Furthermore, in his first annual report the new Secretary of War proclaimed the right of the people of the ceded islands to the essential safeguards of the individual against governmental power, "not because these provisions were enacted for them, but because they are essential limitations inherent in the very existence of the American government." Lawyerlike, Root discerned an "implied contract" on the part of the American people which provided that the principles of individual liberty must be applied to every man who submitted to United States rule. Individual rights, as opposed to political rights, automatically accompanied the flag. A conservative who believed in a government of limited powers at home as well as in the colonies, Root wished to establish a rule of laws and not of men.[12]

Nevertheless, ultimate authority must belong to the ruling power, to be delegated to the natives cautiously if at all. Barred from annexing Cuba by the formal and specific pledge of his government, Root led the way toward the creation of a United States protectorate over the island. This protectorate, embodied in the Platt Amendment of 1901, provided for a United States right of intervention in Cuba, thus assuring the larger nation's dominance at will in Cuban affairs. For Puerto Rico, which had been made United States territory, Root favored a minimum of self-government, fruitlessly opposing as premature the grant of an elective legislative assembly which came in the Organic Act of 1900. In the Philippines, he worked relentlessly to crush resistance to American authority, rejecting any compromise short of total submission on the part of the Filipinos. When that end had at last been achieved by force of arms, Root expressed faith that the Filipinos would "follow in the footsteps of the people of Cuba," though more slowly, because they were less advanced. At last, in the dim future, they would "come to bear substantially the same relations to the people of the United States as do now the people of Cuba"; that is, even when the long years of tutelage had wrought their utmost, the Philippines would achieve, not full independence, but self-government under an American protectorate. He later expressed a similar view of the future of Puerto Rico. Full, unabridged sovereignty for the "backward peoples" was evidently too utopian a consummation for even the longest-range projections.[13]

Nevertheless, an impressive amount could be accomplished, and Root spoke glowingly of the work of his Cuban occupation commanders in 1899: "I am prouder of Wood in Santiago and Wilson in Matanzas and Ludlow in Havana, cleaning the streets and disinfecting the pest holes and teaching the Cubans how to live clean and orderly lives, teaching them the simple elements of civil government; teaching them how to go back to work, to earn their living; teaching them how to become self-governing citizens of a free state, than I ever could be of a hero on the ramparts amid the hail of shot."[14]

The sentiment directly contradicted Theodore Roosevelt's famous dictum that "no triumph of peace is quite so great as the supreme triumphs of war." Elihu Root had no love for war, even as a war leader, and there was an intimate relationship between his advocacy of imperialism and his hopes for world peace. In addition to all other considerations, Root thought that the continued existence of uncontrolled barbaric or semi-civilized societies constituted a serious obstacle to the abolition of war.

Root's generation was intensely interested in the future prospects for major world conflict. In turn-of-the-century discussions of the question, two views were particularly common in the United States. One, which had been expounded in the 1880s by the English historian John R. Seeley, held that the size of the world's national units would grow, and their number diminish, with time. A few imperial agglomerations would become so large and powerful as to overshadow the lesser nations, the weaker of which would be absorbed further to swell the giants. As the empty places and uncivilized peoples of the earth fell under the control of one or another of the super-powers, the rivalry between them would intensify, ending perhaps in a final titanic struggle to determine which power should be supreme on earth.[15]

To many, the events of the 1890s lent credence to this view. One imperial "scramble" was drawing to a close in Africa just as another seemed to be starting in the Far East, while the United States, latest arrival among the great powers, stripped defeated Spain of her colonies and embarked upon her own career of expansion. To Lord Salisbury, the British Prime Minister, it was clear that the future held only struggle. "You may roughly divide the nations of the world as the living and the dying . . . . The weak States are becoming weaker and the strong States are becoming stronger . . . , " he said in May, 1898, as the news of Dewey's victory at Manila Bay reverberated around the globe. This, Salisbury thought, inevitably led to the further aggrandizement of the strong, which in turn spread the seeds of future conflict among the civilized, or superior, nations.[16]

While so many American editors and orators quoted or paraphrased Salisbury's words that they became a cliché to rival Kipling's "white man's burden," a different and opposed view of the future continued to maintain a wide currency. The 1890s saw the development of a very general optimism that war between nations was fast becoming an anachronism, and that the twentieth century might well see the end of it. The increased use of arbitration and the development and acceptance of international law would eventually make war not merely unpalatable, but unnecessary, many thought. The civilized nations would be forced less and less often to resort to arms to protect their rights, while the growth of a hostile world opinion would be a further deterrent to militaristic policies.[17]

It was, of course, the *un*civilized nations which would continue to pose a threat to peace. As Theodore Roosevelt explained in 1900, wars between the civilized nations were dreadful things, and as these nations grew even more civilized "we have every reason, not merely to hope, but to believe that they [the wars] will grow rarer and rarer." But this tendency was limited strictly to the genuinely civilized societies; with barbarous nations, war was a normal condition, and fighting must always be expected upon the borders between civilization and barbarism. "In the long run civilized man finds he can keep the peace only by subduing his barbarian neighbor . . . ." Roosevelt but restated the familiar; John Fiske had said the same thing back in 1880.[18]

While these two views, the one of a continuing international struggle bringing forth a few rival titans and the other foreseeing the spread of peace through the extension of civilization and of civilized controls, were in many respects mutually opposed, they were not in practice irreconcilable. They both demanded foreign policies based on imperialism, for example, whether as the price of surviving the conflicts to come, or as the means of preventing them. That the two views might even be integrated was demonstrated by the nation's leading international lawyer, Columbia University's Professor John Bassett Moore. "Multitudes of petty states, with diverse interests and claims to distinction, have been absorbed into great national organizations" by the current process of consolidation, Moore pointed out. One effect of this, however, was greatly to simplify international relations; many issues formerly between states had now become issues within states. As a result, the possibilities of international cooperation and harmony had increased, Moore hopefully concluded.[19]

Elihu Root, too, was hopeful of future world peace; predictably, he found its seeds in the development of international law. That same instinct which, in Root's opinion, made obedience to law "a part of the order of nature" in the United States, was also evolving in the other advanced nations, he thought, and would increasingly become the basis of relations between the major powers. Discussing the Platt Amendment in 1901, Root made a characteristic definition: "Good diplomacy consists in getting in such a position that upon a conflict's flaming up between two nations the adversary will be the one which has violated the law."[20] Those societies which lacked respect for law simply must be brought under the control of the more advanced peoples, if an orderly system of international relations were ever to become a reality. The same tutelage that made men fit for self-government would prepare them to become good citizens in the world of nations as well.

A few months after taking office, Root made a speech proclaiming "a new dispensation of American progress" which would work for "the spread and establishment of liberty and law and justice throughout the globe . . . . " The extension of direct colonial rule over backward regions was only one hue of a wider spectrum which opened before Root's gaze in the years after 1900. During his tenure as Secretary of War from 1899 to 1904, and as Secretary of State from 1905 to 1909, Elihu Root helped to evolve a Caribbean policy which attempted to impose stability upon a troubled area through the combined use of United States power and international law. The Platt Amendment, which the Cubans were forced to accept both as a part of their constitution and as a treaty with the United States, was the first stone in this edifice. Root described Article Three, which granted the United States the right of intervention in Cuba, as "the Monroe Doctrine, but with international force"; putting it into the form of an international treaty raised the doctrine, at least as it applied to Cuba, from a mere national policy to a covenant sanctioned by the law of nations. Furthermore, the Platt Amendment would effectively outlaw internal warfare in Cuba. No revolutions such as plagued the neighboring states could disrupt Cuba, "because it is known to all men that an attempt to overturn the foundations of that government will be confronted by the overwhelming power of the United States."[21]

From this it was merely a step to the famous Roosevelt Corollary to the Monroe Doctrine, expounded by the President in 1904. As Roosevelt then said: "Chronic wrongdoing, or an impotence which results in a general loosening of the ties of civilized society, may . . . ultimately require intervention by some civilized nation, and in the Western Hemisphere the adherence of the United States to the

Monroe Doctrine may force the United States . . . to the exercise of an international police power." Root expressed his complete sympathy with the President's announcement. The construction of the Panama Canal alone, he thought, was enough to require the United States to "police the surrounding premises"; the situation created an obligation on the part of the United States to keep order.[22]

Not every Caribbean nation, however, could be transformed, like Cuba, into a formal protectorate. What could be done about Central America, embroiled in chronic turmoil and significantly near to the precious canal? An outbreak of war between Honduras and Nicaragua threatened to draw in the neighboring countries, and made necessary a major effort to solve the Central American conundrum. With the cooperation of the Mexican government, Root arranged for a conference of the five republics concerned, which convened in Washington in November, 1907. Under Root's quiet but firm guidance, the conference fathered a number of treaties and conventions, some of which perfectly exemplified his vision of peace through law. There was, for example, a solemn agreement that none of the signatories would accord recognition to regimes which came to power through *coups d'etat*; this, presumably, would penalize revolutionary methods and thus help to insure legitimate electoral succession in the area. Closest to Root's heart, however, was a treaty which created the Central American Court of Justice, a unique international court to which all controversies between the member nations were to be submitted. Independent of national control, the court's decisions were to be binding, and its jurisdiction was made amply broad to support its function of supplanting war in the area. This new legal machinery, operated by the Central Americans themselves and backed by the power and influence of the United States, was Root's response to the isthmian problem.[23]

The same year, 1907, saw the meeting of the Second Hague Conference and Root seized the occasion to attempt to translate his Central American scheme into global terms. The First Hague Conference in 1899 had provided for the convening of an international court of arbitration upon the request of the parties to a dispute. In 1907, Root proposed to strengthen and reorganize this court, making it a principal means of resolving conflicts between nations. Nations were reluctant to submit important issues to arbitration, he declared, because of the tendency of arbitral commissions to "split the difference," rather than impartially to establish the law and facts of the case. As a result, any government which felt itself to be in the right hesitated to adopt a process of settlement which would automatically grant its adversary at least some of the points at issue. What was needed, Root thought, was to replace the essentially diplomatic process of arbitration with a genuinely judicial form of decision which would provide, not compromise, but justice. To do this, a permanent and supra-national body, staffed by authorities in international law, was required. In time, the slow growth of usage and precedent would make the machinery effective, and bring general acceptance of its decisions. Root's proposed new court was intended to make all this possible.[24]

The rejection of his court plan by the Hague Conference, and the failure of the new devices to keep the peace in Central America, failed to dampen Root's hopes for the future. Doggedly he worked on, negotiating twenty-four bilateral arbitration treaties as Secretary of State, and serving for years as president of the Carnegie Endowment for International Peace. A firm believer in the inevitability of progress, he declared late in life that "in public affairs every good idea if worked out and definitely recorded can be trusted to take care of itself and command acceptance in the course of time . . . ."[25] After the Hague Conference, Root expressed this idea in a striking metaphor:

> Not only the conventions signed and ratified, but the steps taken toward conclusions which may not reach practical and effective form for many years to come, are of value. Some of the resolutions . . . do not seem to amount to very much by themselves, but each one marks on some line of progress the farthest point to which the world is yet willing to go. They are like cable ends buoyed in mid-ocean, to be picked up hereafter

by some other steamer, spliced, and continued to shore . . . .
Each necessary step in the process is as useful as the final act
which crowns the work and is received with public celebration.[26]

Full of faith in the ultimate future, Root could accept patiently the
slow and fumbling pace at which the world moved toward its goals.
In spite of constant irritations and conflicts of interest, he insisted,
"the general trend of international relations is a trend towards mutual respect, mutual consideration, and substantial good understanding."[27]

Elihu Root was no exalted idealist. He put first priority on the
national interests of the United States, for which he desired peace,
prosperity, and security. As Secretary of State, he took a vigorous
and continuing interest in efforts to expand the sale of United
States products in Latin America.[28] He was fully susceptible to the
urgings and passions of partisan politics. He had close and sympa-
thetic contact with big business leaders and, after 1899, with the
military establishment, and he reflected much of the outlook of
both. And he firmly believed that large portions of the earth's population were inferior in significant ways to the people of the United
States, whom he clearly idealized.

Nevertheless, Root did have an underlying ideology: the lawyer's
vision of the majesty of the law. To him, civilization and law—his
kind of law, law as embodied in American institutions—were as
inseparable as were civilization and Christianity to the missionary.
From this flowed one of the main organizing principles of Root's
foreign policy. The United States, first of all, would do its share in
bringing order to the turbulent and backward regions, and would
work to inculcate a respect for law and constitutionality in the
colonial peoples whose government it had directly assumed. In the
non-colonial areas of the Caribbean, American influence, wielded
through the establishment of protectorates or the exercise of a regional "police power," would bear heavily against internal anarchy
and international conflict, moving the region toward the same goals
of law and constitutionality. In the world at large, the nation would

inspire, exhort, and set an example, while the inexorable march of civilization insured that the other really civilized powers would take up the work and help to bring it to fruition. The means must be varied with the circumstances, but the goal was fixed: a world of law and progress, of order and stability, of peace and economic growth. Such a goal, surely, was worth a little imperialism.

In 1915, faced with the horrors of the first World War, Root was forced to abandon his more optimistic assumptions about the coming of international order. If the timetable of progress seemed slower than ever, however, its vehicle remained much the same. "The more I reflect upon the possibilities of the future . . . , the more certain I become that the establishment of adequate law is the essential of every proposal for a new condition of international affairs better than the old," Root wrote. "At the basis of all reform... lies an agreement upon certain, definite, specific rules of national conduct, very general and very rudimentary at first but capable of being enlarged by continual additions." With a court to apply these rules in specific cases, backed by adequate power to enforce its judgments, "we may get away from the . . . present dreadful condition."[29]

9 Commercial Domination

THE SENSE of economic crisis which constituted so notable a feature of American attitudes in the 1890s was reflected in almost every major aspect of public policy. In domestic political affairs, it appeared most prominently in the form of a great debate over monetary policy. The supporters of an inflationary "free silver" currency plan which was calculated to help debtors and farmers fought bitter battles with the deflationary "gold-bugs," in a struggle which brought a partial realignment of party lines and culminated in the hard-fought presidential campaign of 1896. Besides the monetary issue, which was accompanied by a sharpening of class consciousness, the insecurity resulting from hard times produced a confusion of theories and panaceas, movements and unrest. Labor leaders, socialists, bimetallists, Populists, social gospelers, nativists, anarchists, all vied for the public's attention. But amid this welter of argument, diagnosis, and prophecy, a measure of common agreement about the economic problem had appeared by the later 1890s: most business spokesmen and politicians came to accept, in some degree, the validity of the so-called glut theory. Publicized in America by steelmaker Andrew Carnegie and by David A. Wells, economist and adviser to the Cleveland administration, it became one of the standard explanations of the disastrous depression which began in 1893.

Proponents of the glut theory held that the national productive capacity had permanently outrun consumption levels, and that this

159

fact lay at the bottom of the boom-bust cycle of the later nineteenth century. The full production of the boom years led to the creation of unsalable surpluses, which were slowly absorbed during the following period of depression. With the surplus finally liquidated, the market grew livelier and prices rose, leading to a new boom and another spate of over-production. Since full production was a condition of economic health, the problem must be attacked by attempts to dispose of the surplus. And if this surplus was, by definition, that which could not be sold at home, then it must be sold abroad. The nation could save itself only by increasing its exports; the traditional preoccupation of American manufacturers with the home market alone had become obsolete, the experts announced.[1]

"We cannot remain wholly dependent for an active industrial life upon the home demand," wrote Charles R. Flint in 1897, "and the markets of the world are open to us, ready to absorb the surplus products of our utmost manufacturing capacity." Flint, known as "the rubber king of America," headed a large New York mercantile concern, and played a leading part in the formation of the United States Rubber Company in 1892. He had formerly been a United States consul in Chile in the 1870s, a partner in W. R. Grace and Company, which traded with the west coast of South America, and president of an early electrical manufacturing company which was absorbed by Westinghouse in the 1880s. Once an intimate of James G. Blaine, Flint represented those business leaders most interested in overseas opportunity, particularly in Latin America, but by 1897 his views were shared by many of his fellow executives.

It was exports alone, Flint maintained, which had enabled the nation to survive the disastrous depression which began in 1893: "if it had not been for the sustaining power of foreign orders, many factories would have been forced to close; thus breaking up organizations which it had required years to perfect, and throwing laborers out of work at a time when they would have been unable to obtain other employment." The lesson was clear; in the future, exports must be increased to a level which would prevent, rather than merely alleviate, depressions. The first priority must go to the

increase of manufactured exports, for they brought a higher per-
centage of profit than did raw materials. Furthermore, the American economy was steadily becoming more industry based, and at
any rate raw materials needed less aid in finding foreign markets.
A number of measures were necessary, Flint thought, to aid industrial exports. The establishment of international banking facilities
by the American financial community would ease credit and exchange problems. The federal government must help to revive the
moribund shipping industry and thus create needed transportation
facilities to connect United States ports to important overseas trading areas. The State Department should be instructed to negotiate
more commercial treaties with other countries, and to reform and
improve its diplomatic and consular services. American industry
must strive for maximum efficiency, and begin to tailor some of
its production to the demands and preferences of specific foreign
markets.[2]

That these views were widely held had been demonstrated by
the formation in 1895 of the National Association of Manufacturers.
Essentially a movement of hundreds of smaller companies to combine for more effective action in the face of hard times, the group's
initial program concentrated upon the expansion of exports. Like
Flint, it hoped to do so through such measures as the rehabilitation
of the American merchant marine, the negotiation of reciprocity
treaties with other countries, and the establishment of permanent
exhibition warehouses in selected foreign cities to show the products of member companies. The first such warehouse opened in
Caracas, Venezuela, in 1898, while the group sent agents to study
the market situation in Argentine and Brazil in 1896, and in Japan
the following year. An American-controlled isthmian canal was
another goal of the Association, whose members hoped by this
means to lower their shipping costs to Pacific markets.[3]

The quest for exports soon acquired general support. By 1898,
even the staunchly anti-expansionist Senator Stephen M. White of
California found that "it must be conceded" that the needs of foreign trade called for "increased attention and better treatment,"

since the home market could no longer satisfy the nation.⁴ But in spite of a near consensus on the glut theory, there remained those problems of application which accompany any theory, however widely held. What, for example, of the politically potent tariff issue? According to the new view, that inflexible protectionism so long championed by the Republican party and so dear to American industrialists actually inhibited foreign trade and encouraged retaliatory tariffs on the part of foreign countries.

It was easy enough for the Atlanta *Constitution* to welcome the new attitude as presaging a change in the kind of tariff policy which had "made it possible for the specially protected interests to continue their robbery of the people." More novel was a statement in the conservative *Bankers' Magazine* that "the doctrine of the protection of home industries can not be accepted in too narrow a sense." Properly construed, it developed, real protection now involved "a consideration of chances of competition not only in domestic but also in foreign markets"; in short, some measure of tariff reciprocity was needed. Yet there remained formidable forces ready to resist with all their strength any attempt to break holes in the protectionist wall that insured domestic producers the domination of the home market. Moderates took a middle position, recommending reciprocity arrangements with "complementary" economies which produced raw materials needed in the United States, but not with economies which produced competing manufactured goods. Popular in business circles, this approach came under fire from farm groups, which demanded the same kind of protection for natural products that industry received for its finished goods. Reflecting the clash of many interest groups, the tariff issue survived the end of the century still unresolved. Every tariff act from 1890 on exhibited some attempt to embody the principle of reciprocity, but in each case the result was too limited and contradictory to be effective.⁵

Less directly political but just as important was the question of where to cultivate the desired new markets. Since Europe traditionally took the bulk of United States exports—almost 80 per cent in 1898—it would seem logical to have concentrated new sales efforts there. Surprisingly few contemporary observers, however, took this position. Europe too was rapidly industrializing; Western Europe and the United States were the world's principal industrial areas. Would it not be bringing coals to Newcastle to send more manufactured goods across the Atlantic? In spite of the consistent record of success there, theorists regarded the European market, important as it obviously was, as precarious and transient.

"In Europe our manufacturers can win but limited success, owing to hereditary skill and keen competition" on the part of the Europeans, one writer concluded. Another, Whitelaw Reid, found the long-standing and enormous American commerce with Europe "an artificial trade." Western Europe, after all, was occupied by "people as advanced as ourselves," who could produce at home most of what American manufacturers sold them, just as Americans could produce locally most of what they bought from Europe. In a nationalistic age, why should they not begin to do so? was the question implied by Reid's statements.[6]

Thus it was not to industrially advanced Europe that the new economic prophets looked for expanding markets, but to the non-industrialized areas of the globe. Furthermore, their aspirations were limited to regions not already incorporated into the European colonial system. Colonial areas, they argued, were closely controlled by the mother countries, which would discriminate against foreign competition whenever it grew serious. The action of the French government in 1897 in closing off Madagascar to a growing American trade tended to confirm this view.[7] The result was the virtual elimination of Africa and southern Asia from American commercial calculations and the emergence of Latin America and eastern Asia as the chief target areas of the new export drive.

Latin America was a traditional area of United States interest, and the Yankees' conviction that hegemony of the hemisphere should be theirs made commercial domination seem a natural goal. Interest in economic ties with the countries to the south reached a peak at the end of the 1880s, under the electric leadership of James

G. Blaine. This interest long survived Blaine's death in 1893, however, and was expressed in later projects like that of James Harrison Wilson for a great customs union of the United States and her neighbors. Congressman Sereno Payne, Chairman of the House Ways and Means Committee, typified one view of Latin American opportunities when he supported a Cuban reciprocity treaty in 1903. Properly nurtured, Payne predicted, United States exports to Cuba would soar from the current sixty million dollars per year to a glittering three hundred million. "Why," he cried enthusiastically, "there are millions in this bill to the farmers and manufacturers of the United States."[8] While the Congressman's optimism was generally regarded as excessive, many men believed that the United States must replace Europe as Latin America's chief provider of finished goods, and that, once achieved, this change must substantially swell the nation's exports.

By 1898, however, public interest in Latin American markets had become secondary to a growing preoccupation with the markets of the Far East, and particularly of China. This fascination with China was based upon future possibilities, not present realities; in 1898 all of Asia took less than 4 per cent of United States exports, and China alone barely 3 per cent. Small as it was, the total had grown rapidly during the past decade, a fact which supported speculation that the real growth was yet to come. Confidence in the future of the China market rested chiefly upon two considerations. First, China's population was huge—the generally accepted figure was four hundred million people, though this was merely a guess. So many people must be capable of buying enormous quantities of goods, once they developed a taste for western products. Second, the westernization of China was thought to be imminent, and would surely kindle the desire for new products among the countless Chinese. The Japanese were rapidly taking on western ways, and, with the rising tempo of European penetration in China, it could not be long before the mainland did the same. Since China seemed on the very threshold of becoming the world's greatest export market, "getting in on the ground floor" became a matter of urgency to a public deeply concerned about the health of its economy.[9]

The attractions of the Chinese market, moreover, gained piquancy from the imminent possibility of its being lost to the United States through a European partition of the country into exclusive spheres of influence. Not only was the opportunity great, but immediate action was essential, ran a popular argument. Thus in 1899 Robert T. Hill admitted that there were "other and perhaps as important fields of trade nearer home" in the Latin American countries, which might even be "more worthy of our attention" than China, but they could wait, he insisted. They were, after all, "dormant fields," which were "not threatened with cloture" as China was. "Nowhere else in the world is there such a reservoir of untouched wealth as in China . . . , " John Foord added. "The great nations of the world are pressing forward to get their share of the rich returns which will attend the opening up of the resources of China." Clearly, the United States could not afford to be left out of an arena which Whitelaw Reid pronounced "the best hope of American commerce."[10]

The same message came from across the Atlantic. Rear Admiral Charles Beresford, who toured China in 1898 on behalf of England's Associated Chambers of Commerce, returned by way of the United States in the following year and publicized his conclusions from coast to coast. Beresford proposed an agreement between the United States, Great Britain, Germany, and Japan to "maintain free and equal commercial relations for all time in the Orient," by formal pledges among themselves and by imposing on China what amounted to a joint protectorate. The powers should take over and reorganize the Chinese army, placing it entirely under European officers at all ranks. This force could open up and police the interior, as well as insure that the Chinese government did as it was ordered. Failure to adopt this plan, or a similar one, would mean the partition of China, with Russia seizing the northern portion and France the southern. England and Germany would then have to scramble for what they could get, while the United States would find itself left out altogether. Yet the United States, the Admiral asserted, probably had more at stake in the future of China than any other major power, for it might find a potentially enormous market there.[11]

An occasional skeptic, it was true, raised doubts about the entire concept of a Far Eastern bonanza. Worthington Chauncey Ford, former chief of the Treasury Department's Bureau of Statistics, argued before a meeting of the American Academy of Political and Social Science in 1899 that just as China currently provided no great market for United States products, neither would it do so in the future. Most of China's masses, he pointed out, lived in the interior, which totally lacked modern transport facilities, and access to which was hampered by an elaborate system of internal customs duties and other local taxes. The Chinese themselves, suspicious of foreign penetration, had become expert obstructionists and raised a subtle but effective opposition to western enterprise which added to the difficulty and expense of reaching the consumer in the hinterland. Ford's most crushing argument was that the extreme poverty of the Chinese masses, and their resulting low standard of living, insured that they could never be very effective consumers of foreign goods. It was buying power, not mere numbers, which made a market, and the Chinese lacked it. Finally, Ford suggested, if China did westernize, she might well develop her own industries, taking advantage of the country's abundant cheap labor, and become a competitor rather than a customer of the west.[12]

While Ford's fellow speakers at the meeting disagreed with him, they also diverged considerably in their own views. Robert T. Hill, of the United States Geological Survey, was sure that the China market had an enormous potential, but thought that its realization was dependent upon China's being "Europeanized." "No great benefit to our trade in the East may be expected should Asia be permitted to remain Asiatic," he declared. If, on the other hand, Chinese society was westernized, then the result would be favorable to American business interests even if European partition took place, though admittedly this would present difficulties. After all, he argued, " 'closed doors' can sometimes be opened, while Chinese walls have no doors at all." The important thing was the opening of China to western influence, which would expand the country's productivity and create a demand for western goods.[13]

Another panelist disagreed with both Ford's pessimism about the China market and Hill's minimizing of the results of European partition. John Foord was Secretary of the American Asiatic Association, a business group organized in 1898 to promote government support of American business interests in China, and editor of the New York *Journal of Commerce,* which vigorously seconded the group's activities. Foord held that the Chinese opportunity was unquestionably a great one, but that it would be utterly lost to Americans if the European powers achieved political control there. A fourth speaker, Professor E. R. Johnson of the University of Pennsylvania, agreed with Ford's suggestion that the Chinese might themselves industrialize, but was undismayed by the prospect. In that case, he explained, the population would urbanize, leading to a decline in agricultural productivity. Since China's food supply was already barely adequate for her population, any decrease in it would force importation of vast quantities of foodstuffs, creating a bonanza, not for American industry, but for American farmers.[14]

This kind of disagreement was bound to create uncertainties, and they were voiced on occasion even by men like Clarence Cary, a leading publicist for Chinese enterprises and counsel for the American-China Development Company, a syndicate seeking Chinese railroad concessions. Cary once ironically pictured the perennial American concession-hunter in China as "chasing rainbows" and "cabling home, 'Prospects better, remit funds,'" amid the "wreck and chaos of a crashing and dismembered empire." Nevertheless, Cary took the future of the Chinese economy very seriously, and so did most of his contemporaries.[15]

Besides the perennial search for railroad concessions, the chief American interest in China lay in the sale of cotton textiles and kerosene. Between them, these two items accounted for fully 87 per cent of all United States exports to China in the years just prior to the Spanish-American War, and they remained the leading categories after it. In 1903, Senator Lodge noted: "I have had letters from Lawrence, where some of the mills make cotton goods which go to Manchuria, urging the strongest possible action" to protect the American market there. Lodge got similar letters from outside his own state, including a number from Northwestern flour interests and Southern cotton mills. The Southerners were particularly excited by Asian market possibilities, since the period was one of rapid expansion for the Southern textile industry, which needed outlets for its burgeoning production.[16]

Seized with the vision of a "New South" which would balance its traditional agricultural economy with a new industrial development, some Southern leaders had long seen a connection between the success of their development schemes and the directions taken by American foreign policy. Senator John T. Morgan of Alabama, an early and prominent member of this group, wished to create close ties between foreign policy, regional aspirations, and the search for foreign markets. One of the many "Confederate Brigadiers" sent to Congress from the post-war South, General Morgan entered the Senate in 1877 and remained there until his death in 1907. He was soon appointed to membership on the Senate Foreign Relations Committee, and his twenty-nine consecutive years of service upon it gave him, in time, an almost unique position in Democratic councils on matters pertaining to foreign policy. A maverick, he supported Presidents from either party in expansionist schemes, and deserted his fellow Democrats if they failed to do likewise. "He did not have the faculty of seeing both sides of a question, and once he made up his mind, it was impossible to change him," a colleague recalled after his death. Gruff, irascible, and formidable, the grim old general fought hard for the interests of his beloved South.[17]

Senator Morgan had declared as early as 1883 that the United States must "have the same control over the commerce of the Pacific Ocean that Great Britain now has over the commerce of the Atlantic Ocean," and he never ceased to believe it. As a step toward achieving this goal, he advocated the construction of a modern navy; for a generation he was to be found on the side of naval

expansion, even when a sizable fleet had already been created. He
also supported reciprocity treaties with Hawaii, Mexico, and other
countries, and approved the pan-American programs of James G.
Blaine. Always a commercial expansionist, he favored Hawaiian
annexation, and broke with President Cleveland on that issue in
1893. Most of all, however, he desired the construction and American control of an isthmian canal, which would cut the transportation costs for Southern goods going to Pacific markets.[18]

He considered it his duty, Morgan told the Senate in 1888, "to
advocate any and every scheme" that might succeed in "furnishing
to the Gulf States and the South Atlantic States this coveted outlet
to the Pacific Ocean." Years later, he wrote that a Nicaraguan Canal
seemed to him "the only real and beneficial work of 'public improvement' that is open to the South in respect of our relations to the
outer world." The undisputed leader of pro-canal forces in the Senate, Morgan became so dogmatically committed to the Nicaraguan
route that, paradoxically, he went into opposition when the Panama
canal project was adopted, although he eventually became reconciled to it.[19]

While long suspicious of large annexations outside the region of
North America, Morgan desired a network of Pacific naval stations,
and looked forward to United States hegemony in the West Indies.
By 1898, he looked to both the Caribbean and the Far East for
American economic development. "It is a new and inviting field for
American enterprise and influence that opens Porto Rico, Cuba, the
Isthmian Canal, Hawaii, the Carolines and the Philippine Islands
to fair trade and good government," he wrote in 1898, and declared
a month later that the nation should "improve the opportunities
that the war with Spain have [*sic*] placed within our reach, by
acquiring military outposts and harbors of refuge for the protection
of our commerce . . . ."[20]

After the Spanish-American War, the Alabama Senator began
to seek political as well as economic benefits for the South through
expansion. He was particularly eager to annex Cuba and to admit
it to statehood in the American union, on the theory that it would

join the Southern bloc in Congress and increase the region's political power. This proposal revived an old dream of pre-Civil War expansionists, who had hoped to add Cuba to the roster of slave states during the 1850s. "As a Southern man, I claim an increase of Southern power in the Senate . . . , " Morgan wrote William Jennings Bryan in 1900, claiming that the Congressional opposition to future statehood for Puerto Rico and the Philippines was "a clear indication that the north and west intend to keep the South in this state of impotence in the Senate." In Hawaii, however, statehood was a future possibility, and in Cuba it could be achieved at once, Morgan thought. Seeing the South's numerical inferiority in the Senate as "a frightful forecast of dangers that threaten our future," he came to view the new territorial acquisitions as a source of additional states whose agrarian interests and climatic similarities would lead them to vote with the South when regional interests were involved.[21]

Most of the time, however, the Senator's chief concern was the economic rehabilitation of his region. He hoped for the rise of Southern industry, and saw cotton textiles as a good beginning, since it would use one of the leading local raw materials. The drive for needed foreign markets, to be sought in Latin America and the Far East, could be significantly aided by the construction of an isthmian canal and by the acquisition of strategic overseas bases, all to be protected by a powerful navy. Morgan had completed the main elements of this synthesis in the 1880s, and thereafter merely modified and elaborated it, the acquisitions of 1898 in particular requiring a considerable reworking of details.[22]

A younger generation of expansionists went even further in marrying economics to foreign policy. With typical exuberance, Albert J. Beveridge paraphrased the French imperialist Jules Ferry in the spring of 1898: "American factories are making more than the American people can consume. Fate has written our policy for us; the trade of the world must and shall be ours. And we will get it as our mother has told us how. We will establish trading posts throughout the world as distributing-points for American products.

We will build a navy to the measure of our greatness. Great colonies governing themselves, flying our flag and trading with us, will grow about our posts of trade. Our institutions will follow our flag on the wings of our commerce."[23]

In the following year, ex-Senator W. A. Peffer of Kansas echoed the same theme. "Providentially," he wrote, "the war with Spain affords us opportunities . . . to relieve the situation at home and improve conditions abroad." With the recent territorial acquisitions, "a new commercial tide" would set in, which could create employment and investment openings in the United States. The chance must be seized, for "with production vastly in excess of home requirements, with narrow profit margins . . . , with . . . idle money accumulating . . . , with much of our labor compulsorily idle all the time and demanding work," the nation had no choice.[24]

Overseas possessions were necessary for strategic purposes as well as for more directly economic uses. If economic salvation lay in increased overseas trade, and if that trade could be obtained only in the teeth of active international rivalry, then it must be protected from foreign threats. As exports grew, they should be carried increasingly in American merchant ships, and this shipping must be guarded by an effective naval force. The alternative, a rich but unprotected trade which was vulnerable to attack, would tempt less successful but better armed rivals to turn a commercial struggle into a physical one.

To Senator Morgan and his colleagues, these ideas had become commonplaces of debate by the late 1880s, and they were then codified and popularized by Alfred Thayer Mahan. But Mahan stressed the fact that naval power consisted, not merely of warships, but of bases from which they could operate far from their own coasts. The United States navy must have outlying bases if it were not to be wholly ineffective outside of its home waters. At the same time, such bases must be denied to rival fleets wherever they could be used to threaten the American shoreline. Once dug, an isthmian canal would be the most strategic point of all, and must be brought under the naval control of the United States, but other fleet bases would be required in the Caribbean and the Pacific, Mahan thought. All this meant sea power, the final link in the "chain of maritime power" which consisted of national productivity, overseas markets, a connecting carrying trade, and a protecting naval presence.[25]

Of the new possessions, the Philippines were most directly tied by market expansionists to the opening of new markets. Truxtun Beale, who had recently held diplomatic posts in the Balkans and Middle East, and who had travelled widely in Eastern Asia, believed that "if we guard it properly, nature will assure us almost a monopoly of trade with the greater part of the Continent of Asia." The ideal place from which to "guard" this prospective monopoly, he thought, was the Philippine Islands, and therefore "their importance cannot be overestimated." Assistant Secretary of the Treasury Frank Vanderlip called the Philippines "a vantage-point more valuable than the prizes for which the great nations of Europe have been striving." Properly developed, they would become "the gateway to all the trade of lower China and the countries south" of there, with Manila probably eclipsing Hong Kong as an entrepôt.[26]

In a similar vein, Albert J. Beveridge insisted that "China is our natural customer" and that the Philippines "give us a base at the door of all the East." Senator Lodge wrote in the spring of 1898 that: "All Europe is seizing on China and if we do not establish ourselves in the East that vast trade, from which we must draw our future prosperity . . . will be practically closed to us forever." A year later, John Foord was willing to "admit that had we no interests in China, the possession of the Philippines would be meaningless . . . ."[27]

As always, there were dissenters. To Henry Adams, this Philippine-based approach to Asian markets came to seem "a false start in a wrong direction." Why ape the English, and compete with them in South China where they were strongest? "The North Pacific is my line, not the South; our own race, and not the niggers, my instruments," Adams declared, denouncing a policy which "leads us into a *cul de sac* in the tropics."[28]

Whatever their disagreements, however, most commercial expansionists felt that some overseas outposts were essential to gaining the necessary increase in American markets. Senator Orville H. Platt of Connecticut had said in 1894 that "while I have no disposition to acquire territory for the sake of territory . . . I firmly believe that when any territory outside the present limits of the United States becomes necessary for our defense or essential for our commercial development, we ought to lose no time in acquiring it . . . , " if it could honorably be done.[29] Few expansionists would have dissented from this simple guideline, even if they were not always certain how to apply it.

Anti-imperialists, it was true, hoped for commercial expansion with a minimum of accompanying territorial gains. Senator John C. Spooner of Wisconsin, a member of the Senate's inner circle, exemplified this view. Chairman of the influential Rules Committee, member of the Senate's Finance Committee and the Republican Steering Committee, and intimate of Senators Orville Platt, William B. Allison, and Nelson Aldrich, who with himself constituted the Senate's "big four" of the period, Spooner came near an open break with his friends on the expansion issue. He refused to support Hawaiian annexation, opposed the acquisition of Cuba, and was only slowly reconciled to keeping the Philippines, which he called "one of the bitterest fruits of the war."[30]

Describing himself as a "commercial expansionist," the Wisconsin Senator favored a revived merchant marine, a large navy, an isthmian canal, and even the acquisition, if necessary, of small naval bases. He drew the line, however, at annexing large, distant territories "inhabited by peoples alien to us . . . . Every argument which has been made in support of this doctrine of territorial expansion . . . seems to me to be superficial, some of them sentimental, and some of them fantastic." Yet Spooner's opposition was largely immobilized, not only by his position in the power structure, but by his own logic. Hostile though he was to acquiring colonies *per se,* his desire for foreign markets and his belief in sea power made it impossible for him to deny that some minimum of overseas bases and government activity were necessary. A grudging and minimal expansionist, he was forced to become an expansionist all the same.[31]

While Senator Spooner was a commercial expansionist who regarded the non-commercial aspects of expansion as necessary evils, some of those who used the rhetoric of the market place seemed more expansionist than commercial. The language of these enthusiasts contrasted sharply with Senator Spooner's cautious and relucant posture. According to Whitelaw Reid:

> The Pacific Ocean . . . is in our hands now. Practically we own more than half the coast on this side, dominate the rest, and have midway stations in the Sandwich [Hawaiian] and Aleutian Islands. To extend now the authority of the United States over the great Philippine Archipelago is to fence in the China Sea and secure an almost equally commanding position on the other side of the Pacific—doubling our control of it and of the fabulous trade the Twentieth Century will see it bear. Rightly used, it enables the United States to convert the Pacific Ocean almost into an American lake.

Albert J. Beveridge, now a United States Senator, asserted in his maiden speech that "the power that rules the Pacific is the power that rules the world," and, with the acquisition of the Philippines, "that power is and will forever be the American Republic."[32]

Such men spoke of "the race for commercial supremacy" in terms that sounded more military than commercial. Indeed, it was a commonplace of the period to put commercial rivalry into a framework of Darwinian struggle. "It is not unusual to hear trade spoken of as peaceful," noted the *Bankers' Magazine* in 1898. "All trade, however, implies a contest," especially when foreign markets were involved; the nation had better continue to enlarge its navy, the article warned. Nor were such expressions confined to the United States. Late in 1897, Count Agenor von Goluchowski, Austro-Hungarian Minister of Foreign Affairs, made a speech to his countrymen which shocked the western world. Alarmed by the "destructive competition" of American exports in the markets of Europe, Goluchowski called upon all Europeans to unite and "fight shoulder to shoulder against the common danger" with all the means at their disposal. "Just as the sixteenth and seventeenth centuries were absorbed by religious wars, as the eighteenth century was distinguished by the triumph of liberal ideals, and our own century by the appearance of nationality questions," the Count said, so the twentieth century would be "a period marked by a struggle for existence in the politico-commercial sphere."[33]

Statements of this sort often reflected a belief that economic power was basic to other forms of national power, and that the emerging struggle for supremacy between the great powers of the world would be decided as much by commercial as by military conquests. Even Senator Lodge wrote solemnly that "in this age the economic tendencies are those which are finally dominant in the affairs of the world." By 1901, Lodge was worried about the dangers which he saw arising from his country's rapid economic growth. "We are putting a terrible pressure on Europe, and this situation may produce war at any time. The economic forces will not be the ostensible cause of the trouble, but they will be the real cause . . . ."[34] Clearly, talk of commercial competition in these terms had a larger than economic significance. If some men were concerned with the profits of specific business interests, and others with the prosperity of various regions or social groups, still others saw in international trade a principal mechanism of international rivalry, and merged economic factors into essentially nationalistic formulations.

An example of this broader view of commerce could be found in a much quoted magazine article written in 1897 by John R. Proctor, a Kentuckian who had been Theodore Roosevelt's colleague on the National Civil Service Commission. Proctor believed that the most successful expansionist nations in the nineteenth century had been Great Britain, Russia, and the United States. While the English-speaking peoples controlled the seas and were first in wealth, Russia had a very large population and an enormous land area. She was now tying herself to the Far East by means of the

Trans-Siberian Railroad, Proctor said, and threatening to extend her control over China. If achieved, such control would in time give her a dangerous degree of wealth and power. At the same time, the European powers, having finished off Africa, now nibbled at China's edges from the south and west, while the rise of Japan and the unification of Canada had created additional Pacific powers. The Pacific, in fact, had become the center of world rivalry, and the United States, too, must become a Pacific power, annexing Hawaii and moving to bolster her market position in the Far East.

Harking back to traditional concepts, Proctor announced that "the application of the Monroe Doctrine to the North Pacific is of more importance today than it was in 1823." As the United States and Great Britain had cooperated to produce the original doctrine, they must now bring it up to date by declaring their opposition in the Far East "to any Power forcing its system, to our exclusion and detriment, on countries with which we have commercial treaties." Japan, too, might adhere to this declaration, which would protect American markets and influence in Asia by blocking its further partition. Proctor repeated the plan a year later, with modifications reflecting the events of 1898.[35]

Proctor's formulations were repeated in more elaborate form by Brooks Adams. Adams, too, saw commercial rivalry primarily as a form of international struggle, writing that "war is only an extreme phase of economic competition." Conversely, economic competition, if carried far enough, must end in war. The Spanish-American War was, to Adams, merely an incident in the great continuing struggle for the control of the world's trade routes, possession of which had always led to wealth and power. "The United States thus stands face to face with the greatest conjuncture that can confront a people. She must protect the outlets of her trade, or run the risk of suffocation." Specifically, "those who are excluded from the Eastern trade have always lagged behind in the race for life."[36]

The United States, therefore, must make common cause with her natural ally, Great Britain, in the Pacific basin, and the two nations must dominate the region in their joint interests. This might require

war, but Adams felt that unless the Anglo-Saxon "race" had declined in martial qualities, it had "little to fear in a trial of strength."
A successful Anglo-American partnership, he thought, would be
decisive in the world's affairs. "Probably human society would then
be absolutely dominated by a vast combination of peoples whose
right wing would rest upon the British Isles, whose left would over-
hang the middle provinces of China, whose center would approach
the Pacific . . . . " Later, in 1902, Adams foresaw a time when the
United States alone would "outweigh any single empire, if not all
empires combined. The whole world will pay her tribute. Commerce will flow to her both from east and west, and the order which
has existed from the dawn of time will be reversed."[37]

These grandiose visions characterized an age in which the language of economics was often appropriated to express the Darwinian struggle for survival of the fittest, resulting in a confusion of
words and thoughts which made unlike ideas seem much the same.
Deeply influenced by a concept of life as a form of competitive
struggle, many Americans tended, consciously or unconsciously, to
limit the process to the realm of economics. War, they thought, was
becoming archaic, at least between the major civilized powers, as
man's progress enabled him to move his field of combat from the
battleground to the market place. Just as business leaders were the
purest product of natural selection within a national society, the
"fitness" of the several nations could best be tested by their success
in economic competition. To others, like Adams, military and commercial struggle were merely the two extremes of a single continu-
um. Thus a tendency to equate national power with economic
power was paralleled by a tendency to equate national worth and
vitality with economic success. The effect was frequently to draw
into an economic matrix the expressions of men whose real interests
and purposes were primarily non-economic, as well as to enable
conventional profit-seekers to broaden their public appeals sufficiently to encompass national patriotism and even progress itself.

10 Charles Denby: The China market

THE CONNECTION between Philippine annexation and Chinese markets was apparent to many Americans in the late 1890s, but to none did it seem more obvious or more central than to Colonel Charles Denby, who left China in the summer of 1898 after thirteen years of duty as United States Minister to that country. Destined to enter personally into the making of Philippine policy, Denby was an arresting figure when he returned to his homeland to publicize the policies in which he believed. At sixty-eight he was still handsome; though white-haired and distinguished looking, as befitted his age, his face was still smooth, his nose straight, his chin firm. Amiable of manner and a gracious host, the Colonel's charm and enthusiasm had made him popular with those whose interests took them so far afield as China, while his long service there under Presidents of both parties made him a national rather than a partisan figure.[1]

Denby's entire life had been marked by a certain cosmopolitanism. His father, a Virginia ship owner, held the post of United States Naval Agent at Marseilles during the 1830s, and Denby thus spent a part of his boyhood in France, where he acquired a lasting command of the French language. From Marseilles the family returned at length to Virginia, where Denby grew to manhood. Newly graduated from Virginia Military Institute, he began the 1850s as an instructor of military tactics at a small Alabama college and ended them a lawyer, politician, and newspaper editor in Evansville, Indiana. By the time the Civil War began, he had served a term in the state legislature and married the daughter of a United States Senator. Like many others from southern Indiana, Denby was both a Democrat and a unionist. Singled out because of his military training, he helped to raise a regiment of volunteers in 1861, and by the end of the following year held the rank of colonel in the Union Army. He was badly wounded, however, at the Battle of Perryville, and discharged for medical reasons in 1863.

The next twenty years saw the Colonel back in Evansville, as a moderately successful railroad lawyer and director. At the same time he remained an active Democrat. Though never again a candidate for elective office, he regularly attended Democratic National Conventions as a delegate from Indiana, and campaigned for the ticket in election years. It was this double connection, with railroad interests and Democratic party circles, which procured for Denby the appointment as Minister to China in 1885.[2]

In the first place, Denby was a long-time supporter of Indiana's Thomas A. Hendricks, newly elected Vice President of the United States. The Cleveland administration followed a generation of Republican chief executives, and in the general redistribution of federal offices Hendricks was able to pay off old political debts. In addition, Denby was identified with the railroad business, and the new administration came into office in a year when every report from China contained references to ambitious plans on the part of the Chinese government to build a national railroad system. In response, the same New York interests which recruited James Harrison Wilson to go to China and to secure them a share of this bounty threw their support behind the appointment of Denby as Minister there.[3]

Thomas F. Bayard, the new Secretary of State, was eager to help in the quest for Chinese contracts. He wrote to General Wilson in cordial terms, commending his proposed enterprise and referring him to Denby. "Colonel Denby you know personally," Bayard recalled, while Wilson declared approvingly that Denby's appointment had "encouraged myself and associates to undergo the expense and take the risk of our venture." It was understood all around that one of Denby's first tasks in China should be to help American business concerns to secure railroad construction contracts there. From the beginning, the Colonel regarded himself as a representative of his nation's economic interests in the Far East.[4]

The Colonel's interest in Chinese railroads was closely related to his visions of potentially large Chinese markets for American exports. An early herald of the China market, in time Denby became a publicist for it. By 1898, he could write that American "merchants and manufacturers were beginning to seize the trade of *our own sea,* the Pacific—*our* sea that washes our coast and the coast of Asia . . . [Denby's italics]." He declared: "We cannot sell at home all that we manufacture," and spoke of China as "the greatest commercial sphere, which was ours by natural right . . . . " A little earlier, he had stated: "China is our natural market."[5] But experience soon taught Denby the difficulties that stood between the promise and the reality of Chinese development, difficulties which he thought could be overcome only by the building of railroads. While still intensely interested in railroad contracts and concessions for their own sake, he came to see them in a wider setting, as the key that could unlock China to the world.

These ambitious hopes and plans had crystallized in Denby's mind by the time he had finished his first year in Peking. An adequate railroad system would provide cheap access to China's interior, and to the teeming millions who lived there. It would enable the general introduction of western products, and expose the Chinese to modern ideas and attitudes. All this would weaken traditional prejudices, Denby believed, and "destroy anti-foreign feeling here," eliminating another obstacle to the full development of trade. But there was an important condition: "These railways should be constructed by Americans." In one of his early interviews with the Chinese authorities, the Colonel showed his hand: "I, as delicately as I could, suggested that in the event of the building of railroads, it would be very agreeable to me if American engineers could be employed, and railroad supplies purchased in the United

States."[6]

Colonel Denby began his tenure at Peking as a vigorous partici-
pant in the struggle of the syndicate represented by General Wilson
to secure railroad contracts. To Chinese officials, he emphasized
the argument that the United States had no territorial designs on
China, while other powers had; it would be safer, therefore, to
encourage American influence than that of Europeans. On these
and other grounds he urged the Wilson syndicate on the Chinese,
supported strongly by his superiors in Washington. Secretary Bayard wrote that the State Department was making an all-out effort
on the group's behalf, and that General Wilson himself was ready
to "rattle all the China in the National cupboard" if the situation
demanded it.[7]

The Wilson group, however, found itself incapable of financing
its construction project within the terms imposed by the Chinese
government. It was at this juncture that Denby made his suggestion
to Wilson that the scheme might be reorganized as a private Chinese corporation, thus evading the rigid limitations of Chinese
government financing. Meeting the discouraged Wilson in Shang-
hai in the summer of 1886, Denby quickly revived the moribund
venture. "I said to him 'General, you and I have been soldiers. We
have failed in a direct attack, let us try a flank movement.' . . . He
replied 'You can try your flank movement.' "[8]

Drawing on his own railroad experience, Denby immediately
drew up a charter modelled on the railroad incorporation laws of
Indiana, with modifications to fit Chinese conditions. He and Wilson then added provisions enlarging the rights of the corporation
in several particulars, and Wilson began a new campaign to persuade the Chinese authorities to recast their plans along the lines
of this charter. In the end, the Chinese did so. They reorganized
the Kaiping Railway Company, and, following the lines of the
Denby-Wilson charter, transformed it into the China Railway
Company. In the process, however, they decided to freeze out all
foreign participation, including that of the Wilson syndicate.[9]

It was a hard blow. Denby had never lost faith until the end, making his disappointment the more bitter. As if the Wilson defeat were not enough, a syndicate from Philadelphia appeared hard on its heels, hoping to secure concessions to operate telephones, to build railroads, and to engage in banking and financial activities. The failure of this group to achieve any of its objects was also discouraging, although it had not worked so closely with Denby as had Wilson. Taking stock of his position in 1887, Denby wrote: "It was my fondest dream in coming to China to accomplish some notable service to our commercial and manufacturing interests. I have had success in my grasp but, without fault or negligence of my own, it has slipped away . . . . "[10]

After the passage of several relatively uneventful years, China's defeat in the Sino-Japanese War of 1894–95 revived Denby's hopes for American business opportunities. The United States government had offered its good offices to end the war, and although the Japanese rejected American mediation, the offer led to clarification of the terms upon which direct Sino-Japanese peace talks could begin. Denby himself acted as a presumably neutral intermediary in connection with the peace negotiations which followed. The resulting situation seemed to Denby highly favorable to American interests. As a part of the peace terms, Japan imposed a large indemnity upon the Chinese, forcing them to renew their endless search for money. "The most practical mode [for China to raise money] is to dispose of her valuable franchises which are still untouched . . . . " Denby wrote. "My present purpose is simply to suggest to American capitalists, railroad men, ship-builders, bankers, and merchants to consider the desirability of securing for themselves the great franchises to which I have alluded."

Nor should this be left to chance. The United States had helped China extricate herself from a disastrous war; why should she not demand return favors? "It is suggested that the influence secured by diplomatic work would assist our countrymen in securing commercial privileges . . . . " the Colonel wrote candidly, and forwarded the suggestion to Washington. The reaction of Secretary of State Walter Q. Gresham was not, however, what Denby had hoped.

Officially, Gresham was cool to the idea; unofficially, he warned his subordinate to be more discreet: "Everybody does not know you as I do, and in your honest efforts to aid others you may compromise yourself in the minds of strangers."[11]

Undismayed, the American Minister continued to plan and to hope. It was Denby who first suggested the scheme for a Russian-American combine to develop a North China-Manchuria railroad system, which was so energetically taken up by General Wilson and John J. McCook. During the latters' efforts to implement the plan, Denby was in direct correspondence with them, advising them at every point; one of the group's member firms offered Denby's son, who served as legation secretary, a salary for such services as he could render. When the second Wilson effort fell through in 1897, the Colonel busied himself in aiding the China Development Company, which represented another American railroad group. This last company actually got a contract in 1898, in the closing months of Denby's long ministry, but later backed out of it after failing to gain more favorable terms.[12]

Though encouraged by this one small victory, the Colonel frankly recognized that his overall record in aiding American enterprise was not what he had pictured when he began his mission. Several years later, he offered a partial explanation: "If one were asked why the most adventurous nation in the world—as Americans are—becomes the least so in its dealings with other nations, the answer would probably be that our system of protection provides our manufacturers with a highly paid home market, and they do not feel the necessity of cultivating foreign markets." It was an attitude, the Colonel insisted, which must be abandoned.[13]

Denby also felt that, during much of his tenure, his government had given him insufficient backing. Standing instructions issued in 1887 forbade him to apply pressure in favor of individual American capitalists without the specific approval of the State Department on each separate occasion. Not only did this inhibit quick action, Denby complained, but all too often the Department refused to approve any really significant action at all. Time after time Denby's efforts were greeted with indifference or disapproval, while Gresham's rebuke in 1895 was accompanied by a formal reaffirmation of the 1887 policy. Only a year later, however, in a significant change of direction, Secretary of State Richard Olney reversed this stand and gave Denby the freedom of action which he had so long desired. Olney now instructed him to "use your personal and official influence and lend all proper assistance to secure for reputable representatives of [American] concerns the [same] facilities for . . . contracts as are enjoyed by any other foreign commercial enterprises in the country." In the short time left to him in China, Denby took what advantage he could of this new liberty.[14]

There had been another difference with the State Department: the energetic Minister believed in a greater use of force than did his government. He conceded readily that the Chinese "would hail with joy the departure *en masse* of the foreigners in China," and that "they hate us almost universally . . . . They prefer their own ways, habits, and customs to ours. They look down upon us vastly more than we look down upon them." Since Westerners were unwelcome in China, they must protect their position there with force, or be ousted. Quoting the adage that "when two men ride a horse one must ride behind," Denby insisted that Western domination must be made good. "It may seem brutal to adopt this theory which rests on force . . . nevertheless, its existence rests on the supreme necessity of self-defense."[15]

It also rested on western superiority. While granting to Chinese civilization some genuine achievements, Denby considered it, on the whole, unworthy of survival. Perhaps too much coercion was wrong, but "if by means of gentle persuasion we can introduce Western modes and methods into China, we are simply doing for her what has been done, in one way or another, for every nation on the globe." In addition, the Colonel cited what he called "well-recognized" principles of international law which held "that no nation had the right to exclude itself against intercourse with other nations, that the ports which nature provided could not be closed to the world, and that international law authorized and sanctioned that every country should be open to foreign trade."[16]

THE ESCAPED COW (with apologies to Dupre).
— The Denver *Times*.
Reprinted in the *Literary Digest*, Jan. 13, 1900.

Without qualms or apologies, therefore, Denby called for a firm hand in China, and strict enforcement of Western treaty rights: "The first head demanded by a foreign power after a riot should be, not that of an obscure rioter, but of the highest official in the locality." The United States, he wrote in 1889, should send a fleet of small, fast gunboats to operate on Chinese rivers and use its guns to protect missionaries and businessmen in the interior. Upset by continuing anti-missionary violence, Denby urged a similar solution in 1895: "If a town had been recently the scene of a serious riot . . . it should be battered down by ships of the injured nationality . . . it is quite likely that in the neighborhood there would be no more riots." In case the disturbance occurred at a point inaccessible to ships, then "the nearest seaport would be bombarded." If, as a former colleague wrote, Denby possessed "one of the kindest hearts that ever beat," then these statements tell much about the outlook of "old China hands" in the late nineteenth century.[17]

Denby's concern for the safety of the missionaries rested, presumably, upon both humanitarianism and the general principle of foreign inviolability in China, but it was also intimately connected with his interest in future economic development. The Colonel, like his colleagues, found many of his knottiest problems arising from the scrapes into which the missionaries seemed continually embroiled, and he was not above grumbling at times over their propensity for mischief. Nevertheless, he viewed them as the pioneers of westernization in China, and westernization as the first step toward his own goals. In Denby's day, the American missionaries in China were virtually all Protestants, and the Colonel thought the "Protestant system" much superior to that of the Roman Catholics. Under Catholic tutelage, he complained, "the convert remains as devoted a Chinaman as he was before conversion." In the Protestant practice, however, "the convert learns to reason, to argue, to think . . . . His mind is enlarged . . . . In many cases he learns English, and the acquisition of the language makes him a new man." He began, in fact, to become "civilized," and when a "semi-civilized people become completely civilized, new wants arise which commerce supplies."[18]

Now the chain of reasoning was complete. "The missionary . . . is the forerunner of commerce. Inspired by holy zeal, he goes into the interior where the white man's foot has never trod . . . . He effects a lodgement in the heart of the country. The drummer follows behind, and foreign commerce begins." It only remained to spell out the possibilities: "Fancy what would happen to the cotton trade if every Chinese wore a shirt! Well, the missionaries are teaching them to wear shirts. How the hat trade would boom, if every Chinese wore a hat! The Japanese have taken to wearing hats—why not the Chinese?" The missionaries would plant the seeds and prepare the harvest for "the great, able, untiring body of that justly honored class— the commercial travellers—familiarly known as 'drummers.' "[19]

So the Colonel's thinking ran when, yielding to Congressional pressure for patronage, President McKinley replaced him with a Republican in the summer of 1898. When Denby returned to the United States in September, he was just in time to add his voice and visions to the great debate over expansion which reached its peak during the following winter. Furthermore, he was to remain in close contact with the government; although McKinley had been forced to relieve him as Minister to China, he had no intention of foregoing Denby's services entirely. The ex-Minister's views favored the President's purposes, while his Democratic background gave a bipartisan flavor to the bodies of which he became a member. In the first year after he left China, Denby served on two important presidential commissions, while becoming well known to the public through his writing and speaking on Far Eastern affairs.

The Colonel had barely had time to unpack his steamer trunks when he found himself one of the nine members of the so-called Dodge Commission, which was appointed by the President to investigate the conduct of the War Department during the war just ended. There was bitter public criticism of the Department's wartime performance, and particularly of the Secretary of War, Russell A. Alger. Unmoved by the unbroken successes of the armed forces, the critics asserted that the Army's victories had come only in spite of the inadequacy of its Washington headquarters. To satisfy public demands, and to forestall a possible Congressional investigation, McKinley called together his own group, composed of prominent Civil War veterans and headed by General Grenville M. Dodge, to look into the charges.

The Dodge Commission began public hearings in September, 1898, and reported its findings in February, 1899. Much of the testimony which it heard did more to raise new controversies than to settle the old ones. Its deliberations were accompanied by noisy newspaper sensations, and a large part of the public regarded its final report as a whitewash, although it contained a thoughtful critique of the War Department's administrative system. Membership in such a group was not highly desirable, and Denby must have been glad to see its work ended.[20] He had, in fact, been appointed to more congenial duties in January, 1899, even before the Dodge Commission had submitted its report.

The First Philippine Commission was more commonly known as the Schurman Commission, after its chairman, President Jacob G. Schurman of Cornell University. Its original mission was to investigate the situation in the Philippines and to report back to the President on conditions there, formulating recommendations for his future action. In addition to Schurman, the group contained four other members. The military and naval commanders in the islands, General Elwell S. Otis and Admiral George Dewey, were appointed ex-officio. Dean C. Worcester was a professor of zoology at the University of Michigan who had done research in the islands before the war, and was presumed to be an authority on the area. Denby, the last to be named, was included for his knowledge of Far Eastern affairs.

By the time the commissioners left the United States, their mission had been complicated by the outbreak of fighting between American troops and the insurgent forces of the embryonic Philippine Republic, which embodied a vigorous Filipino independence movement. When the little group arrived in Luzon in March, 1899, it found the island torn by full-scale warfare, and Otis and Dewey preoccupied with the conduct of a military campaign. To their fact-finding duties, the three civilians promptly added an adventure in peace-making which made their position a trifle anomalous. "It looks like a contradiction in fact," Denby wrote afterward, "that, while the army was engaged in active hostile operations, a respectable body of gentlemen accredited by the President was endeavoring to induce the enemy to quit fighting, but that was the actual situation."[21]

Shortly after its arrival in Manila, the Commission issued a proclamation promising the Filipinos all of the basic civil rights if they would accept American rule. While this was being printed in English, Spanish, and Tagalog, and circulated in enormous quantities, the group attempted to begin direct negotiations with the insurgent authorities. The President of the Philippine Republic and commander of its armed forces was an energetic and determined young man named Emilio Aguinaldo. Aguinaldo was unwilling to settle for anything less than recognition of his own organization as the rightful government of the Philippines, although he might have considered an unobtrusive American protectorate which left him in immediate control. Since the commissioners could not grant him recognition, there was probably never much chance of success in their attempts to restore peace. Nevertheless, Aguinaldo soon found his army outmatched by the Americans, and proved willing at least to explore the situation. The Philippine Republic would send a two-man delegation to confer with the Schurman Commission.

The commissioners hastily wired Washington to ascertain what they could tell Aguinaldo's representatives about the future government of the islands. The reply left them little room to maneuver. The administration to be established would be headed by a governor chosen by the President of the United States. This governor would possess a strong veto power, and would himself appoint the insular cabinet, composed of the heads of executive departments. An independent judiciary would be selected directly by the President. How were the Filipinos to share in this government? They would elect a "general Advisory Council" with unspecified powers.[22]

What is surprising is not that Aguinaldo refused to accept this unabashedly colonial scheme, but that, in time, he sent a new delegation to talk further with the commissioners. This group listened, asked questions, said little, and promised an answer in three weeks. The reply never came, nor could Aguinaldo ever be persuaded to come in person to discuss terms with the Americans, either on their territory or his own. By mid-summer, it was clear that the Commission's diplomatic efforts had failed. The dispirited Schurman now advocated concessions to Aguinaldo's demands in order to stop the fighting, but Denby and Worcester joined the service heads in arguing that the war must be fought through to victory.[23]

Between peace feelers, Denby and his colleagues spent the summer gathering testimony about various aspects of Philippine life, travelling about trying to win over the people in the hinterland to acceptance of American rule, and assisting in erecting new local governments on several outlying islands to replace the vanished power of Spain. According to Worcester, Colonel Denby was particularly popular with the Filipinos, and did effective work in gaining their confidence. In the autumn the civilian commissioners returned to the United States, submitting their report to the President in November, 1899. It proved to be a complete justification of the McKinley policies.[24]

The Philippine Islands, the report indicated, were pearls of great price, and the richness of the archipelago's resources was only a part of its value. A greater consideration was that it "should soon become one of the great trade centers of the East." Prospective hub of a network of steamship lines, the city of Manila had an especially glittering future, as "a distributing center for China, Siam, the Straits Settlements, Tonquin, Annam, and Australia."

Since no nation in its senses would reject such a windfall, the real question was simply how it should be governed. The Commission firmly rejected the idea of self-government by the Filipinos: "Their lack of education and political experience, combined with their racial and linguistic diversities, disqualify them . . . to undertake the task of governing the archipelago at the present time." The current political capacity of the inhabitants, the report said, would be sufficient only to enable them to cooperate with their rulers, perhaps holding offices but always "subject to American control or guidance." Were American power withdrawn, the islands would lapse into anarchy, and other nations would intervene to control or partition them. "Only through American occupation, therefore, is the idea of a free, self-governing, and united Philippine commonwealth at all conceivable."

It was conceivable, but it would take time. With education and experience, the "natives" could gradually be entrusted with a larger share of their own government. The ultimate goal, of course, was complete self-government, but by the time the people were prepared for it, they would have "become more American than the Americans themselves" under the guidance and influence of their protectors.

In the meantime, the insurrection, which represented only the delusions of some Filipinos, must be crushed. It was not even a true national movement, the commissioners declared, but a mere tribal power-play by the Tagalogs of Luzon. Aguinaldo's rule was actually misrule, replete with extortion, terrorism, and plundering. The Filipinos themselves were becoming disillusioned with it, or soon would be, if the United States remained steadfast and the Army kept up its systematic hammering at insurgent power. Nor could the struggle have been evaded. "Deplorable as war is, the one in which we are now engaged was unavoidable by us . . . . No alternative was left to us, except ignominious retreat." The nation must keep up the fight "until the insurgents are reduced to submission."[25]

Though it was the work of a committee, the Schurman report closely reflected Denby's own views. He had publicly argued for the retention of the Philippines before McKinley put him on the Schurman Commission, and he continued to do so after it had disbanded. He was interested in the islands less for their own sake than for their relation to the situation on the Asiatic mainland. Beginning in 1897, the accelerated international race for the acquisition of ports and "concessions" on the coast of China seriously alarmed the Colonel, for he thought it likely to end in the partition of China between the powers. On the one hand, he had urged that the State Department announce to the world that the United States would not tolerate discrimination against American goods in any "spheres of influence" which the European powers might succeed in establishing in China, a recommendation which foreshadowed the Open Door policy. On the other hand, Denby was eager to see the position of the United States grow so strong in the Far East that it could hope to prevent partition entirely. Possession of the Philippines seemed to him to offer a shortcut to that kind of position.[26]

Colonel Denby afterward wrote that ". . . I advocated the acquisition of these islands chiefly on the ground that their possession would enable us to prevent the partition of China. Holding enormous territories in the Far East, we have the right to intervene in any matter which points to the destruction of our interests, and there is little doubt that such intervention would be heeded . . . . " Once this were assured, the China market would remain safely available, and having served to keep it so, the Philippine base would also offer an entry point from which to exploit it. At this stage the chief value of the Philippines became "the advantage that their location gives us to increase our trade with China."[27]

To support his main objectives, Denby used the standard imperialist justifications. American rule, he said, would bring to the Philippines "liberty and hope and happiness . . . . The dusky East rises at our coming; and the Filipino springs to his feet and becomes a free man." In defense of the white man's burden, he told his readers that "you will respect your race more than ever, because you will contemplate it engaged in building up among people, whose complexions are darker than yours, institutions pointing toward the elevation of all races and conditions of men." And rather airily he declared that some day, "if we find that the Filipinos will always prove unfit to become American citizens, we will grant them their independence."[28]

But in other, blunter statements, the Colonel seemed to ignore the civilizing mission, or to put it distinctly second to more mundane matters. "We are after markets, the greatest markets now existing in the world," he stated, but added: "Along with these markets will go our beneficent institutions; and humanity will bless us." At times he was more direct: "With all proper respect for humanitarians, I must insist that the main object of government is to increase the material well-being of its people." And baldest of all: "Will the possession of these islands benefit us as a nation? If it will not, set them free tomorrow, and let their people, if they please, cut each others' throats, or play what pranks they please."[29]

The contrast between these statements and those couched in the metaphor of idealism has led critics, from his day to ours, to accuse Denby of hypocrisy, or at least of muddled thinking.[30] And it is true that the economic system for which the Colonel labored was set in no such ideological framework as was, for example, that of General Wilson. Charles Denby was simply an economic expansionist who had no objection to an adventure in imperialism if it promised to serve his ends. To him, the important question was whether it all had worked. Shortly before his death in 1904, Denby confessed that the China market had not met his expectations. Perhaps it would never be the fabulous bonanza which so many had described: "Some writers and lecturers on this subject portray a future in which this trade will reach billions, but I am not inclined to indulge in their roseate dreams . . . ."[31]

Nevertheless, he still had faith in China's future, though cast now on a more modest scale. With the increased Western penetration, and railroads at last under construction on a large scale, progress was inevitable. China might even "emulate or surpass Japan, which, in less than fifty years, has gotten rid of her old customs, and has leaped fully equipped into the arena of modern nations." Already American exports to China were having their effect on some branches of production: "Oregon sends lumber and railroad ties; Denver sends mining plants; South Carolina and Alabama send cotton." There were also "piece goods and kerosene oil . . . iron, flour, drugs . . . " and even Baldwin locomotives, and this was a mere beginning. At any rate, the nation had no choice but to continue the drive for foreign markets, to struggle unceasingly for whatever successes could be obtained. For in the end, Denby could only repeat the familiar litany: "Our condition at home is forcing us to commercial expansion . . . . Day by day production is exceding home consumption."[32]

11 Charles A. Conant: The Implications of Commercial Struggle

WHILE COLONEL Denby yearned for massive sales of American goods in China, his younger contemporary, Charles A. Conant, evolved a more complex and sophisticated approach to economic foreign policy. Both a popularizer and in some respects a pioneer thinker, Conant helped introduce the concept of oversaving to the American public, and attempted to shift the attention of the business world from foreign markets to overseas investment opportunities. His efforts to keep up with the latest European thinking on economic subjects made him a transmitter of current continental, and particularly French, ideas to readers in the United States. Conversely, Conant's own synthesis of international relations and economic expansion anticipated much of the thinking of the Englishman John A. Hobson, and of the even better known V. I. Lenin. The difference was that, unlike the famous Europeans, Conant approved of what he described.

He was a self-educated intellectual. Born in Winchester, Massachusetts, in 1861, he began adult life as a newspaper reporter for the Boston *Post,* and soon became interested in both politics and economics. In part, these interests grew out of a long stint as Washington correspondent of the New York *Journal of Commerce,* a leading business paper. The currency issue dominated both economic and political discussions in the 1890s, and Conant made himself an authority on it. A Democrat, he stood for the gold standard and against the inflationist silver wing of the party, unsuccessfully running for Congress in 1894 at the age of thirty-three. In 1896 he was a Massachusetts delegate to the National Gold Democratic Convention, a body which rejected the silvery banner of William Jennings Bryan and eventually bolted to the Republicans.

Conant's political aspirations ended with the bitter party struggles of 1896, but in the same year he published his first book, a *History of Modern Banks of Issue.* His conservative views on the currency question and his growing erudition about financial matters gained Conant the respect of bankers and Treasury officials while still a relatively young man, and by 1898 he was becoming a recognized expert in the field. His paper, the *Journal of Commerce,* was one of the most enthusiastic boosters of the China market, and as a leading contributor, Conant had also become closely identified with that cause by 1897.[1] It was in 1898, however, that he began to see new dimensions in the problem of solving the nation's domestic ills through overseas economic activity. Beginning in that year, he published a number of magazine articles which summarized his rapidly coalescing thoughts. Seven of these were brought together in 1900 as *The United States in the Orient,* forming a truly remarkable book about American foreign relations.[2]

The book's first article, originally printed in September, 1898, was entitled "The Economic Basis of 'Imperialism'," and contained the essential analysis upon which his conclusions rested. According to the author, saving for investment—that is, saving for the sake of an income without impairment of the capital—was a purely modern phenomenon, and one of central importance to the economy. It had made possible the enormous fixed investment required by industrialization, and the modern business corporation had developed as a mechanism for absorbing such savings on a vast scale in order to apply them to productive uses. By the late nineteenth century, however, the rich, advanced nations found that they possessed an excess supply of accumulated capital. These surplus savings, applied to unnecessary duplication of plant capacity, had led directly to that overproduction so widely deplored by contemporary observers. Thus the glut theory of production, Conant

argued, was superficial, because it considered the problems of overproduction without considering its causes. As a substitute, Conant
offered a glut theory of capital.

About 1870, this theory held, "the great civilized nations first
appear to have become fully capitalized to meet all demands for
consumable goods . . . . " Since then, periodic overproduction and
a recurrent boom-bust cycle had plagued every advanced country,
regardless of individual differences in their tariff or monetary policies. The competition of investors for profitable investments was
reflected in Europe by a steady fall in the rate of return, accompanied by a drop in interest rates. All this Conant illustrated by elaborate documentation, freely borrowing both data and ideas from
Paul Leroy-Beaulieu, an influential French writer on the economics
of empire. The problem fully identified, it only remained to point
out "how necessary to the salvation of these countries is an outlet
for their surplus savings, if the entire fabric of the present economic
order is not to be shaken by a social revolution."[3]

There were, at least in theory, three possible solutions for the
problem of oversaving, Conant declared. The first of these was
socialism, in which the state applied accumulated savings to current
consumption by improving the lot of the poor and the aged. But
the author quickly dismissed socialism as irrelevant for the present:
"It will be long before this solution will be accepted in a compre-
hensive form in any modern civilized state." A second possibility
was to continue to increase domestic consumer demands by introducing new wants. While this approach had promise as long as
human nature remained unchanged, Conant held that it had become impossible to expand domestic consumption as rapidly as
accumulating capital could expand production. National consumption could be greatly increased, of course, by the massive wastage
of war, but this was hardly desirable for its own sake. Thus it was
necessary to turn to the third solution: "There remains . . . as the
final resource, the equipment of new countries with the means of
production and exchange."

The surplus capital of the advanced western countries should be applied, not to an endless expansion of domestic production, with its concomitant struggle to market all that was produced, but to the task of developing the economies of areas which had remained at a low level of productivity. Asia and Africa were the most promising areas, Conant believed, and since Africa had fallen to European partition, the United States must turn its attention to the Orient. Although Americans were still large users of European capital, they were already moving toward a capital surplus similar to that of the Europeans, as their own overproduction and falling interest rates proved. Like the Europeans, they must find ways to invest their money abroad.[4]

As to the crucial question of how the nation was to seek these capital outlets, Conant was at first curiously indifferent: "In pointing out the necessity that the United States shall enter upon a broad national policy, it need not be determined in just what manner that policy shall be worked out. Whether the United States shall actually acquire territorial possessions, shall set up captain-generalships and garrisons, whether they shall adopt the middle ground of protecting sovereignties nominally independent, or whether they shall content themselves with naval stations and diplomatic representatives as the basis for asserting their rights to the free commerce of the East, is a matter of detail." Colonies, protectorates, or mere diplomatic influence—it mattered little, so long as the results were adequate, "but upon the economic side of the question there is but one choice . . . to enter by some means upon the competition for the employment of American capital and enterprise in these countries . . . ."[5]

It was not long, however, before Conant developed more specific views on methodology. If all the great powers were to abandon tariff protection and adopt non-restrictive economic policies—policies of "commercial freedom"—then, he granted, nations would not need to apply political or military power in order to create outlets for their goods and capital. But of all the powers, only Great Britain followed such policies. The prevailing trend was rather for each power to secure territory or spheres of influence of its own, to be guarded against the competition of rivals. The control of the civilized nations was "being rapidly extended over the decadent and undeveloped nations" in the race for economic supremacy.[6]

"Our turn has come to participate in the struggle for foreign markets," Conant wrote in 1899, "and apparently as the result of an accident in Havana Harbor, the path of destiny has been suddenly opened for us in the East. Accidents are only the ripening of opportunity. It has been by no series of accidents . . . that the great civilized states have been expanding their spheres of influence in all quarters of the world. It was an economic necessity which precipitated the British occupation of Egypt; and it was the pressure of surplus capital which led to the opening of 'the Dark Continent' . . . . The threatened partition of China . . . is another phase of the same great movement . . . . [T]he inexorable progress of economic tendencies has made expansion the inevitable policy of states which would survive in the future."[7]

By 1900, Conant had arrived at a formulation of international relations which bore a startling resemblance to that soon to be publicized by the Marxists: "It is when the 'trust' has swallowed up its rivals for the control of the local market, and reaches out for the control of foreign markets, that it seeks to bring political power to the aid of economic efficiency or inefficiency," thereby projecting market rivalries into the realm of international relations. "It is this struggle between the great political powers of the world for bolstering up national economic power which constitutes the cardinal fact of modern diplomacy."[8]

Like many other turn-of-the-century Americans, Conant regarded Russia as the most formidable rival of the Anglo-American bloc in the contest for "the commercial and military supremacy of the world." Autocratic and single-minded, advancing steadily toward control of North China, vast in population and resources, Russia, he said, was undergoing economic development at a rate which in thirty years would "make her almost irresistible." Much depended, therefore, upon the events of the next generation, and Conant did not exclude the possibility of war. Any nation which meant to succeed in the economic contest must be prepared for the final test of force, and it was conceivable that many appeals to arms lay in the future. Economic and military struggles were, in fact, closely related, and the real basis of national power was "capacity for competitive production."[9]

It was this world of harsh conflict, bounded by implacable economic imperatives, into which Conant saw his country emerging. There was not even a choice of whether or not to enter the fray, for "those states which timidly withdraw from competition with powerful rivals . . . will sentence themselves to the fate of the decadent countries"—countries like Persia, Turkey, or Spain, which had once been powerful but were now at the mercy of the more energetic northern races. The United States must win out, and to do so she must acquire colonies, and remain active overseas. In this regard the Philippine Islands were particularly important, not merely for their own sake, but "as a lever for keeping open the door of China." The latter country offered a huge potential for economic development, and Conant, like Denby, saw possession of the Philippines as assuring that the United States would participate in Asian opportunities. While the United States might also have a "mission . . . in portions of Latin America," the Far East came first in significance.[10]

Conant expressed impatience with the common assumption that the economic benefit of colonies lay mainly in their function as markets for the products of the mother country. While this was, of course, a serious consideration, it was distinctly secondary to the role of colonial areas in providing investment opportunities. "Whether trade follows the flag or not, the real question" was to find fields for the profitable investment of capital, and colonies would provide such fields. They would, in turn, be greatly benefited, for colonialism meant using the surplus capital of the developed countries to bring forward the undeveloped ones. Conant foresaw nothing less than "the equipment of the whole world with a producing plant, and with means of communication and exchange, which will raise the undeveloped portions . . . to the level of comfort, producing power, and civilization of the more advanced

portions." Only this would enable the advanced societies to maintain their own social systems intact, yet the advantage would be
mutual, and civilization would be advanced. The task, in fact, was
"the mission of the great civilized states today."[11]

It was, above all, the mission of the English-speaking peoples.
"To the Anglo-Saxon race, by the historical evolution of events, has
been committed this cause of modern social progress." Civilization
must either advance or decay, and while its advance was closely
related to economic considerations, it was also "a mission of the
highest altruism" which could not be avoided, "unless the world is
to sink backward into another long night like that of the Dark
Ages." Nor would Americans try to evade their fate; their own
natures forbade it. "The instinctive tendency of a race or civilization
often outruns the wisdom of its leaders. Whether for good or ill,
the inborn tendencies of the race . . . prevail by a sort of instinct."
It was for this reason as much as any other that the people of the
United States were entering on "a path marked out for them as the
children of the Anglo-Saxon race."[12]

To this Anglo-Saxonism, Conant added a dash of manifest destiny.
Like the other great expansive peoples, Americans had already
come far along on their appointed path. Settling and absorbing the
Northwest Territory, the Louisiana Purchase, Florida, Texas, and
California had been a fitting prelude to new feats like the recent
expulsion of Spain from Cuba and Puerto Rico, or future achievements in the Far East. "While Russia advances with giant strides
in Central Asia, the great republic of the West is pursuing the same
inevitable destiny, and tending to put herself upon an equal plane
for the contest . . . ."[13]

There could be no turning back; the nation had acquired colonies, and the problem now was to govern and develop them. In this
connection, debates about colonial self-government, particularly in
the Philippines, merely confused the issue, but fortunately "the
English-speaking races are preeminently practical rather than se-
verely logical. They do not permit themselves to be carried away
by a syllogism to extreme conclusions." The argument that a gov-

ernment's just power rested upon the consent of the governed must not be misapplied. The founding fathers had meant by this only that self-government should not be denied to those competent to exercise it. To extend it uncritically to anyone and everyone would be "to carry an abstract theory to a merciless conclusion." Anglo-Saxon liberty was a plant of slow growth, which could not simply be "torn up by the roots and transplanted in its entirety to foreign soil."

The wisest policy in the Philippines, the author declared, was to make no rash promises for the future, but simply to establish orderly government and begin a slow tutelage. Little more could yet be attempted in a society "where the sanctions of order and justice which promote industrial development are scarcely understood." And what was true in the Philippines was true elsewhere: "Only by the firm hand of the responsible governing races . . . can the assurance of uninterrupted progress be conveyed to the tropical and undeveloped countries."[14]

Conant also considered the longer-term questions which his program posed. If the only salvation of the advanced countries now lay in industrializing the backward ones, what would happen once this had been achieved? Would not the human race arrive at a "jumping-off place" when Africa and Asia were "capitalized"? And had not the process of "capitalization" proved extraordinarily rapid of late in places like the American West, Germany, and Russia? Where could salvation be found when the entire world suffered from oversaving and overproduction? Admitting that he could not answer these questions, Conant argued that the future would bring changes which could not be predicted, and that each generation must meet the challenges of its own time. Another era might see inventions and discoveries yet undreamed of, which would revolutionize production. A growing world population might overcome prospective food shortages through the intensive development of chemical farming, for example; whole new industries could arise, absorbing vast amounts of capital.[15]

Conant was more deeply concerned with the implications of his theory in his own day. To him much of the contemporary discussion about domestic social and economic problems seemed irrelevant or obsolete. A protective tariff, for instance, was useful in stimulating infant industries, but it became "a relic of medievalism" when applied to a state of national overproduction and rivalry for foreign markets. Similarly, many other traditional issues were "shriveling up—settled and sent to the lumber-room of the political theatre, or tinged with strange, new light by the flash of Dewey's guns in the Bay of Manila." It was necessary for political parties to realign along the new issues associated with keeping open the world's markets and business opportunities. He who offered effective policies for that purpose would gain the support, not only of the business community, but of "all far-seeing men who desire the perpetuation of the ideals of Anglo-Saxon civilization."[16]

More rigorously than most of his fellows, Conant spelled out the consequences of his logic. From his original economic analysis he deduced not only a foreign policy, but bold conclusions about domestic affairs as well. Indeed, perhaps his most arresting statements were those which described how domestic society must be reshaped in order to compete successfully in the international contest. From every facet, they reflected the conviction that the nation must be made as efficient as possible. While social efficiency had many aspects, the most obvious place to seek it was in the national political structure. "Concentration of power, in order to permit prompt and efficient action, will be an almost essential factor in the struggle for world empire . . . . The people of the United States may have something to learn in this respect." They could learn it, in particular, from Russia, which Conant regarded as the prime example of centralization of power and singleness of purpose, and, to a much lesser extent, from the British, who at least honored the principle of continuity in foreign policy.

The government of the United States would require "a degree of harmony and symmetry which will permit the direction of the whole power of the state toward definite and intelligent policies." If the Constitution, which was framed in another era to meet other needs, was no longer adequate to the national purposes, then it must be amended. Ideally, "an absolute government, like that of Russia" enjoyed advantages in its ability to make and execute quick decisions, independent of parliamentary maneuver or public opinion. While it was too much to expect Americans to accept a tsarist absolutism, they must at least see the need to extend far broader powers to the executive branch of the government, especially in the field of foreign affairs. A strengthened presidency should be accompanied by a professionalized, career foreign service which had been lifted out of politics. "In this direction, as in all others, the highest efficiency will turn the scale between nations . . . ."[17]

As the role of the executive branch was increasing in importance, that of the legislative was decreasing. "Public opinon," said the journalist-expert, "is no longer formed by debates in Congress, but by the expression of the best opinion of experts through the press." With the executive to take action, and an informed public opinion to guide him, the policy-making function of Congress had become redundant. There must, of course, be a separate legislative power, but its duties were no longer such as to require superior ability, or to justify a central role. And under the circumstances, a greater concentration of power in the hands of the President "need not be inconsistent with industrial liberty and the freedom of political discussion at home."[18]

At least as important as political centralization was the problem of making an optimum use of the nation's brain power. Since the crucial field of activity was the economic, it followed that the highest intelligence must be channelled into managerial functions; it was clearly "desirable that the supreme productive power of the best minds should be applied to industry." To insure this, it was essential that the rewards of business leadership should be great, and its public prestige high. While American reformers might complain because the ablest people failed to go into politics and to accept governmental office, Conant considered the tendency a positive advantage. A higher level of personnel would naturally improve the performance of legislative bodies, for example, but "the diversion of the best minds to such a service might involve an economic waste which would react disastrously upon the real interests of the country in its competition with foreign rivals." It was simply uneconomical to waste an undue share of the nation's human resources upon the machinery of government.

Another American advantage was the absence of an entrenched militarism, the glamor and prestige of which might divert too many men of superior ability into the barren service of arms. The greatest cost of militarism to Europe was not the vast financial burden which it entailed, but the perversion of values which shut up "the keenest and most ambitious minds in the narrow treadmill of official routine or military ostentation...." It was, of course essential that the nation have effective armed forces and be prepared, if necessary, to fight for its interests, but this must be achieved with the smallest possible subtraction of brain power from the main currents of industrial development.[19]

There were admittedly other considerations besides that of efficiency in the utilization of society's talents. Literature, art, and the world of ideas had their own claims, which must be honored, but there was no real conflict, Conant insisted, between commercialism and "the higher ideals." There would always be those to whom the gratifications of intellectual and artistic pursuits were more compelling than tangible rewards or material success. The process of natural selection could be trusted to provide an ample supply of such people, provided that society had sufficient surplus wealth to support them adequately. Historically, the wealthier societies had nurtured the highest cultural achievements, indicating that, "rather than being antithetical, commercial and cultural growth *go together*, for a wealthy society can best support the arts" [Conant's italics]. Let the nation look to its economy, then, and the rest would follow.[20]

The maintenance of a high degree of social mobility was also vital. "Only when new blood is constantly poured into the so-called 'upper' grades of society from beneath, or into the city from the country, does their vitality remain unimpaired; and only under such conditions can a people go forward in the field of industry, of art, and of world empire from victory unto victory." Any tendency to stratify society, or lessen the equality of opportunity, was dangerous, while a hereditary aristocracy would be disastrous to national efficiency. A nation which had no self-made men, no Horatio Alger tradition, would eventually find itself in peril.[21]

Conant denied, however, that he was interested solely in the men at the top, since the problems he discussed were of vital interest to working men as well as capitalists, to farmers as well as executives. Business interests were centrally at stake, it was true, but so were the jobs and the prosperity which would flow to all levels of society from the success of American economic expansion. Even the welfare of the increasing number of working-class small investors must be considered; a good return on his investment was more important to the thrifty laborer than to the rich speculator. And, most important of all, a failure to solve underlying economic questions risked the collapse of the entire society. While the world struggle brought great dangers, it made possible correspondingly great gains, not the least of which was the alleviation of domestic social problems. "Those who do not welcome the responsibilities and the opportunity which this situation creates," Conant warned, "are fostering the discontent within the old civilized countries which breeds social and political revolution."[22]

Although unquestionably innovative as a synthesis, *The United States in the Orient* shared some of the more obvious inconsistencies of other formulations of the period which pleaded the cause of economic imperialism. Rigidly economic in purpose and logic, Conant nevertheless found it necessary to make appeals to Anglo-Saxonism, destiny, altruistic mission, and other elements superfluous to a purely economic argument. It is easy to dismiss these as manifestations of hypocrisy, mere sugar-coating, yet it is equally possible that the author found that his bleak world view became more livable when softened by an infusion of non-material values. Indeed, the blending of economics, politics, and idealism which marked Conant's discussions of the development of undeveloped economies is no more characteristic of his own era than of similar discussions about foreign aid programs in the years of the Cold War.

It is possible, in fact, to exaggerate the book's originality. As we have seen, Conant's contemporaries also viewed the world through the perspective of an international struggle for economic supremacy. Conant did help to integrate this viewpoint into the general theory of imperialism, particularly through his diagnosis of the economic problem as stemming from oversaving. He is even credited by one authority as being the first writer to propound a fully developed system of economic imperialism.[23] Such a claim, however, seems to overlook the extent to which Conant borrowed from continental writers, and especially from Paul Leroy-Beaulieu, who as early as 1874 published a famous work which linked colonies with the disposal of the surplus capital of the mother country.[24]

Even Conant's approach to domestic policy falls within a recognizable contemporary trend toward efficiency in every aspect of American life. The mugwumps, with their distrust of legislators and their enthusiasm for civil service reform and administrative efficiency, foreshadowed Conant's political ideas, while the emerging progressive movement was to make a fetish of "social efficiency" in general.[25] In short, like most synthesizers, Conant worked with ideas that were readily available to him rather than spontaneously creating wholly new elements. Nevertheless, it was he who early made a coherent and consistent system out of these varied elements, and put them into a form which was to become universally known under the attacks of later and better-remembered writers.

Having theorized so boldly about colonies, Conant soon had an opportunity to face colonial problems at first hand. By the time *The United States in the Orient* was published in 1900, his reputation as an authority on money and finance was firmly established, and in the following year it led to the beginning of a long career as a government consultant on monetary problems. In July, 1901, Secretary of War Elihu Root invited Conant to go to the Philippines, study financial conditions there, and prepare plans for a new

Philippine currency system. In addition, he was to suggest banking reforms which would broaden and strengthen local credit. According to Root, it was Secretary of the Treasury Lyman Gage, whom Conant knew well, who had originally consulted Conant about the Philippine currency and who suggested him to the Secretary of War.[26]

Conant promptly went out to Manila, arriving late in the summer and staying in the Far East for about three months. In November, back in the United States, he submitted to Root a "Special Report on Coinage and Banking in the Philippine Islands," which embodied his recommendations. Their adoption, he said in the report, would "hold out the inducement to the large investment of American capital" in the islands, by solving problems of credit and exchange. The chief problem was that the Philippines, like most of the Far East, depended upon Mexican silver dollars for their principal medium of exchange. Conant believed it unwise to leave the islands' exchange system subject to the fluctuations of a foreign currency, but he feared that the introduction of United States currency would be too drastic a change, especially in an area accustomed to a silver medium. As an advocate of the gold standard, he suggested a compromise. The Philippines should have their own separate coinage, but the new silver peso would be tightly pegged to the United States' gold dollar, making it in reality an extension of the American currency. In addition, Conant's report urged the authorization of private banks empowered to issue bank notes, thereby adding another element to the money supply. An important feature of his plan was its provision for branch banking in the Philippines by national banks in the United States, which would introduce American financial institutions directly into the economic life of the islands.[27]

The next step was to get Congress to pass the laws needed to implement these changes. The campaign began at once, and, at Root's request, Conant became one of the chief lobbyists for his own programs. William Howard Taft, the civil governor of the Philippines, had reported to the Secretary of War that Conant had been "exceedingly useful to us" and was "a remarkably clear-headed writer"; he would undoubtedly be an effective witness before Congressional committees, Taft added. But "how much influence he has with the prominent members of the House and Senate, I do not know," the governor wrote doubtfully. Nevertheless, Conant went manfully to work, calling on legislators, mobilizing support from his colleagues of the financial press, and personally writing several magazine articles in support of his proposals. He also attempted to interest New York banking houses in Philippine possibilities, and thus get them behind his proposed banking law.[28]

In spite of all of their efforts, however, Root and Conant found progress slow. Money and banking were politically sensitive subjects in the United States, and it proved difficult to get both Houses of Congress to unite on any single plan. Conant's banking recommendations were never implemented, and his currency bill was adopted only after a long, hard fight. Blocked all through 1902 because the Senate stood out for a silver standard in the Philippines, the bill finally became law in March, 1903. Its adoption made Conant "the father of the Philippine coinage." When the new pesos were put into circulation, the Filipinos promptly dubbed them "conants" to distinguish them from the old silver pieces, henceforth known as "mex." After his death, Conant's picture actually appeared on the paper one-peso notes.[29]

The transition to "conants" proved to be almost as difficult as their creation. The sudden need for over seven million dollars worth of silver for the new coinage forced up American silver prices sharply, and brought windfall profits to western silver-mining interests. In the Philippines, the lack of provision for taking the old Mexican dollars out of circulation resulted in confusion, dualism, and the hoarding of the more valuable "conants" until their use was eventually required by government action. Some critics charged Conant with failing to foresee the problems of changing money systems, and consequently blamed him in part for the difficulties which developed.[30]

Nevertheless, these high-level connections with the government provided the final element necessary for the success of Conant's career. He remained a leading monetary consultant until his death, keeping a permanently close relation with the War Department's Bureau of Insular Affairs. Between 1903 and 1912 he represented the United States government on three separate international commissions dealing with problems of money and exchange, building a trans-Atlantic reputation in the process. He also remained close to colonial problems; he advised the United States government on currency reforms in Panama and Nicaragua, and was on a similar mission in Cuba when he died in Havana of stomach cancer in 1915. In addition, Conant pursued an active private career. From 1902 to 1906, he was Treasurer of the Morton Trust Company of New York, then one of the largest institutions of its kind in the country, and he became a director of several corporations. He also continued to write about banking and finance, publishing a two-volume work on the *Principles of Money and Banking* in 1905, and producing eight books in all.[31]

Among his varied activities, Conant continued to take an interest in the Philippines. As late as 1907, he wrote a detailed defense of the retention of the islands,[32] but his attention was increasingly focused on the technics of money and exchange. A life-long bachelor, Conant lived quietly, devoting himself to his work. Self-assured but modest, he concealed both charm and wit behind his serious, and rather humorless, public expressions. Yet essentially he was a scholar, an "expert," a man of books and figures, and most of all, a theorist, with the theorist's passion for finding a single key to the multiform riddles of society.

PART III
The Issues

12 The Anti-Imperialist Movement

THE ARGUMENT against overseas expansion, like the argument in favor of it, developed in the United States well in advance of the events and issues of 1898. As several observers have pointed out, the anti-imperialist case in the 1890s incorporated most of the arguments used against President Grant's schemes of Caribbean expansion a generation before.[1] In addition, the controversy over Hawaiian annexation in 1893, the Venezuelan crisis of 1895–96, and the rising tide of jingoism which preceded the Spanish War, all evoked a stiffening resistance from those who distrusted the new directions discernible in American foreign policy.

The continuity of this resistance is best illustrated by the career of Carl Schurz, who enunciated the anti-expansion position upon every new occasion from the presidency of Grant to that of Theodore Roosevelt. An immigrant who had achieved celebrity by his heroics during the unsuccessful German revolutionary movement of 1848, Schurz entered American politics within a few years of his arrival in the new country in 1852. His staunch opposition to slavery led him into the Republican party, where he made himself so useful in rallying German-Americans behind the Union cause that Abraham Lincoln made him in turn a diplomat and a general. After the war Schurz became a United States Senator from Missouri, and Secretary of the Interior under President Rutherford Hayes. After Hayes left office in 1881, Schurz's increasingly independent and reformist tendencies undermined his position in the Republican

213

party, and he spent his later years as a controversial journalist, lecturer, and champion of causes. He became a leading figure among the "mugwumps," a like-minded group of political independents who deserted the Republican party to help achieve the defeat of James G. Blaine in the presidential campaign of 1884. Arrogant and tactless, Schurz ended as a perennial gadfly of the national scene.[2]

When Ulysses Grant attempted to secure the annexation of Santo Domingo to the United States in 1870, Carl Schurz joined Massachusetts Senator Charles Sumner in leading the fight in Congress against the scheme, and in January, 1871, he made his major Senate speech on the issue. To Schurz, the question involved far more than the fate of one small nearby country, for he believed that the adoption of Grant's Dominican plan would inevitably draw the United States into the chaotic power vacuum of the American tropics. Once involved in that troubled region, the nation would find it necessary to subdue it all, from the neighboring waters of the Caribbean to the Isthmus of Darien. This, in turn, would raise the problem of what to do with the millions of inhabitants who would be brought under United States control. Alien, turbulent, and backward, they were in Schurz's eyes spectacularly unfit to be citizens of the United States, yet any other relationship would violate American principles of government, raising the specter of tyranny abroad and militarism and corruption at home. Whether incorporated as citizens or ruled arbitrarily as subjects, these tropical populations would create a deadly danger to American democratic institutions.[3]

From the beginning, Schurz's anti-imperialism partook both of geographic determinism and of Teutonic prejudices. In his Santo Domingo speech, he bewailed the new manifest destiny as another example of that "romantic longing for the south" so often displayed by Northern peoples, comparing it with the German urge toward Italy. Quite simply, people who lived in Southern climes degenerated; there were laws of nature which could not be repealed. When the white man, even the Teuton, moved to the tropics, he too degenerated. If he assimilated with the natives, he assimilated downward to their level, Schurz insisted in an argument which anticipated the thesis of Benjamin Kidd. Because warm climates induced laziness, the efficient mobilization of tropical labor required coercion of the workers; subtly but surely, the climate led toward slavery, and thence toward violence and degeneration. The United States had already spread dangerously far toward the tropics, and had reaped the fruits in its recent history of slavery, civil war, and the problems of reconstruction. Now the nation was asked to add to those disturbing influences others far worse. Vividly, Schurz pictured ten or twelve new tropical states arising in the future, their people ignorant and anarchic, yet fully represented in Congress and making common cause with the former Confederacy. " . . . Have we not enough with our own South?" he asked passionately. "Can we afford to buy another one?"[4]

The proper approach to expansion was two-fold, Schurz suggested in a little-noticed alternative to Grant's scheme. On the one hand, Germany's example showed the way to a purely commercial expansion which could serve the nation's economic needs without involving it in territorial annexations of the wrong kind. On the other hand, there lay to the north "a magnificent field left for our ambition of aggrandizement." The future held territorial expansion in plenty, but the territory to be acquired was Canada, where "Teutons" were in their own element and nature's rigors kept them fit. The Canadians could easily be assimilated: "if we annex them today they would be good Americans and republicans tomorrow." In time, and by voluntary agreement, North America would be unified from the arctic to the Rio Grande. For the rest, he warned, "beware of every addition in that quarter where the very sun hatches out the serpent's eggs of danger to our republican institutions . . . "; in short, "beware of the tropics."[5]

When the Harrison administration attempted the annexation of Hawaii in 1893, Schurz's reaction closely resembled his Dominican position of over twenty years earlier. Hawaii, too, was tropical, alien, and non-contiguous, and again Schurz viewed its annexation as only the first step in a broader program of tropical expansion. Thus his major utterances on the Hawaiian issue incorporated most of what he had said about the Dominican one, sometimes in virtually the same words. He insisted still that the United States could legitimately acquire large territories only with the intention of admitting them to full statehood within a reasonable time. Once more he dwelt upon the degeneracy of tropical peoples, this time envisioning "fifteen or twenty, or even more, States" added to the union from these dangerous materials, and polluting the nation's political life. Again he suggested the Canadian alternative as the proper form of American expansionism. But to these earlier arguments, he added a strategic one which he had touched upon only lightly in 1871.[6]

At the time, Schurz pointed out, the United States was the only one of the world's principal nations that was not threatened by powerful neighbors. Occupying a large but contiguous area, isolated by its flanking oceans, and bordered by states too weak to be a danger to its security, the nation had been spared the burden of armaments and the necessity of war. The militarily formidable powers all lay overseas, and while these might effectively attack the maritime commerce of the United States or raid its coasts, none of them could strike a really crippling blow at the New World Colossus without enormous and time-consuming preparations. By the time a European enemy could mount a full-scale invasion, Americans would be prepared for it, their numbers, spirit, and large territory insuring a long and bloody struggle. But no European power would dare to commit itself so fully in America, when its own territory was menaced by dangerous rivals close at hand. Thus the very conditions of invading the United States insured that the only powers capable of attempting it would never do so. "In other words," Schurz reasoned, "in our compact continental stronghold we are substantially unassailable." The American position was so strong that, as matters stood, "we can hardly get into a war unless it be of our own seeking."

The acquisition of major overseas possessions would negate many of these advantages at a blow. Such possessions would present vulnerable points to potential enemies, and require the maintenance of strong armed forces for their defense. Committed to defending them, the United States would have to do so at a disadvantage, its forces posted far from their impregnable continental stronghold, and brought to battle on terms and in places chosen by the enemy. Rather than adding to the national security, the new acquisitions would gravely lessen it, while requiring large peacetime armaments, raising the burden of taxes, and engendering the spirit of militarism. Their acquisition would furnish new causes for war with other nations, and embroil the United States in a general rivalry which it was to her advantage to avoid. So ran Schurz's analysis, which added a strategic dimension to the ideological and ethnic-geographic bases of his anti-imperialism.[7]

Occupying a strongly reasoned position which he had expounded and developed over more than a quarter of a century, Carl Schurz was fully prepared to combat the expansionist fever that accompanied the Spanish-American War. It was only necessary to refurbish his time-tested arguments and apply them to the current issues, while adding detail here and there. Thus, to answer the claim that colonies promoted foreign trade, he merely pointed out that Great Britain was rapidly being overhauled in the world's markets by two commercial rivals, the United States and Germany. "What? Great Britain, the greatest colonial Power in the world, losing in competition with two nations one of which had, so far, no colonies or dependencies at all, and the other none of any commercial importance?" The point was clear: colonies were not needed for trade expansion, nor was their possession any protection against the loss of existing overseas trade.[8]

To such reasoning, Schurz could put an impressive peroration:

> If this democracy, after all the intoxication of triumph in war, conscientiously remembers its professions and pledges, and soberly reflects on its duties to itself and others, and then deliberately resists the temptation of conquest, it will achieve the grandest triumph of the democratic idea that history knows

of . . . . It will put its detractors to shame, and its voice will be
heard in the council of nations with more sincere respect and
more deference than ever. The American people . . . will stand
infinitely mightier before the world than any number of subju-
gated vassals could make them . . . .

This, Schurz declared, would be genuine glory.[9]

To a remarkable degree, Carl Schurz and a little circle of collabo-
rators were the pioneers and architects of the anti-imperialist stand.
Through the years, his reasoning was echoed and supplemented by
allies like E. L. Godkin, the acidulous editor of *The Nation* and idol
of the mugwump breed of independents. Like Schurz, the Anglo-
Irish Godkin came to the United States in the 1850s, went into
journalism, and espoused such governmental reforms as a merit-
based, career civil service. Godkin was intensely upset by the
growth of that belligerent chauvinism which characterized so much
of the nation's public expressions in the 1890s, and the Venezuelan
crisis of 1895 evoked from him an analysis which has became classic:
"The situation to me seems this: An immense democracy,
mostly ignorant, and completely secluded from foreign influence,
and without any knowledge of other states of society, with great
contempt for history and experience, finds itself in possession of
enormous power and is eager to use it in brutal fashion against anyone who comes along, *without knowing how to do it,* and is therefore constantly on the brink of some frightful catastrophe like that
which overtook France in 1870."[10]

Schurz and Godkin were charter members of a tightly knit group
of moderate reformers who had long worked together on the American political scene. Many of them traced their intellectual roots
back to the anti-slavery movement, while their revulsion against
the scandals of "Grantism" and the grosser crudities of Republican
Reconstruction policies had alienated them from any fixed party
loyalty. Favoring civil service reform, honest government, and
sound money, suspicious of labor unions, the "New Immigration"
from Southern and Eastern Europe, and most varieties of radical-
ism, these men had learned from long practice how to unite quickly

into an organized lobbying group. Mostly educated, successful city-dwellers, the group contained editors like Godkin and Samuel Bowles of the Springfield, Massachusetts, *Republican,* businessmen like Edward Atkinson and Charles Francis Adams, Jr., prominent lawyers like Moorfield Storey, and college professors like Harvard's Charles Eliot Norton. Some of them espoused the heresy of free trade, and many of them, repelled alike by Republican corruption and Democratic rabble-rousing, had at last found a political instrument in that impeccably conservative Democrat, Grover Cleveland.[11]

Distributed thickly in and about Boston and New York, members of this group began late in 1898 to organize "Anti-Imperialist Leagues" in the major Eastern cities. In the course of 1899 the movement was carried westward across the nation, and the local bodies were consolidated into a single American Anti-Imperialist League, although a disproportionate influence continued to reside in the Boston chapter. Flooding the country with printed propaganda, holding numerous congresses and conferences on the subject of colonial policy, providing a seemingly endless supply of speakers, the new movement energetically took the issue to the people.[12] Given their crucial role in creating a platform, providing organizational forms, and lending the movement their highly literate respectability, it is natural that the Eastern-based mugwumps for whom Carl Schurz spoke should have attracted more notice, in their own time and since, than the other components of the anti-imperialist crusade. The movement was, nevertheless, possessed of an almost infinite variety of disciples, and valid generalizations about it are correspondingly difficult to formulate.

On the far left could be found the fiery Socialist, Morrison I. Swift, the vehemence of whose attacks on the administration shocked even some of the more orthodox anti-imperialists. Swift charged in 1899 that American foreign policy had been handed over to the plutocracy, and that the real goal of expansion was "the expansion of billionaires." He dismissed altruistic appeals to the white man's burden as the grossest kind of hypocrisy, and flayed "military hucksters" like Theodore Roosevelt for suggesting that the nation needed wars to keep it healthy. Swift saved his bitterest execrations, however, for President McKinley, whose position in regard to the coming of the war with Spain he characterized as follows: "Yes, I am morally certain that I can prevent war with its immediate horrors and terrible aftermath; but if I do it I antagonize my party chiefs, I disrupt my party harmony, I dash my hopes of reelection. Lord, it is too much, let this cup pass from me!" For his weak-kneed complicity in the scheme of conquest, Swift thundered, McKinley deserved the name of traitor to his country, and should be impeached and jailed. No citizen should obey the traitor president and his government. "I declare," Swift wrote boldly, "that it is treason to support the army," and he called upon the soldiers themselves to refuse to fight against the Filipinos: "You swore allegiance to your nation, not to a popinjay president, not to traitor Hanna, not to all-earth monopolists." It was strong stuff, and not every dissenter could stomach it.[13]

In contrast to the radical Swift stood Andrew Carnegie, the steel king, who put his immense wealth at the disposal of the movement. "You have brains and I have dollars," Carnegie wrote Carl Schurz, in an offer to print and distribute a Schurz speech against imperialism. "I can devote some of my dollars to spreading your brains." Since few other economic titans enlisted in the fight, Carnegie's dollars were to be exceedingly welcome, and he made good his promise by freely providing them.[14]

Between the agitator and the industrialist were farm and labor representatives who opposed imperialism in the name of their respective interest groups. Samuel Gompers, the long-time head of the American Federation of Labor, became one of the forty-nine vice-presidents of the Anti-Imperialist League. Gompers feared that Hawaiian annexation would lead to the legalization in the United States of the vicious contract-labor system which already prevailed on Hawaiian plantations, and he warned of the flooding of the American labor market by cheap oriental labor from both Hawaii and the Philippines. Furthermore, authoritarian rule in the colonies would undermine respect for the common people's rights

THE OLD FAIRY STORY.

McKINLEY: "Now, son, if you ever find the end
of that rainbow, you'll get a great bag of gold."
— The St. Louis *Republic*.
Reprinted in the *Literary Digest*, Aug. 4, 1900.

at home, while an enlarged and prestigious army could be put all
the more effectively to strike breaking, as it had been in the ill-fated
Pullman Strike of 1894. Similarly, the *American Agriculturalist*
proclaimed the danger that colonial sugar and tobacco, produced
as it was by native cheap labor, would be admitted to the United
States free of tariff, and speedily drive American growers out of
business.[15]

There were ethnic as well as economic factors. The German-
American press was solidly anti-imperialist, according to a *Literary
Digest* survey in 1898 which sought to find the common features of
this opposition. The *Digest* analysis found two. One was the anti-
militarism of a generation so many of whom came to America

precisely to escape conscription and militarism at home. The other was the fear that the new colonial policy meant an increasing German-American rivalry, and perhaps even war. The frictions already visible in the Philippines fed this apprehension, as did the rising anti-German feeling in the United States which they produced. This factor was accentuated by the effects of the new policy in bringing about an Anglo-American *rapprochement,* and in the explicit Anglo-Saxonism of so much of the expansionist propaganda. German-Americans thought that the new imperialism had the effect of making them unpopular in their adopted country, while their lot would be even worse if the "large policy" ended in a war between the old fatherland and the new.[16]

While the elements of anti-imperialist support were numerous and varied, politically the result was unsatisfactory. The central core of mugwump activists were self-consciously elitist, rather than mass oriented, and eschewed party alignment as a matter of principle. While Gompers managed to put the American Federation of Labor on record against colonialism, the labor movement as a whole was cool to the anti-imperialist appeal, and union men individually showed a distressing tendency to support McKinley. Some prominent Republicans, it was true, broke with the administration on the expansion issue, most notably Thomas Brackett Reed, the powerful Speaker of the House. In addition there were Senators George F. Hoar of Massachusetts, Eugene Hale of Maine, and Justin Morrill of Vermont, though Morrill died late in 1898, before the decisive battle had been joined. Elderly leaders from the past, these men were supported by such venerable relics as John Sherman, George S. Boutwell, and George F. Edmunds, all once notable Senators and all survivors of the great crusade of the 1860s. More surprisingly, they were joined by ex-President Benjamin Harrison, although Harrison muted his public criticism of the administration out of deference to party loyalty. Yet on the whole, the administration succeeded in maintaining substantial unity in the regular party ranks, and in securing full and consistent Republican party support for its programs. And the dissident Republicans found it hard to work with those very mugwumps whose defection from Republican ranks they had up to then so bitterly resented.[17]

On the Democratic side, the picture appeared brighter. Grover Cleveland had made a partisan issue of expansion when he rejected the annexation of Hawaii in 1893, after it had been negotiated by his Republican predecessor, Benjamin Harrison. Democratic rhetoric on that occasion had lingered long enough in the public's ear to identify the party as at least skeptical of the virtues of overseas acquisitions.[18] The campaign of 1896, which turned upon domestic social issues, had split the Democrats into two rival factions, a conservative minority centered about Cleveland, and a reform-oriented majority wing led by William Jennings Bryan, the young presidential candidate. The expansion issue, however, promised for a time to reunite the two camps, since both leaders were unequivocal in their anti-imperialism. Cleveland's opposition was prompt and unflagging, and he was able to count no less than eight of his own former cabinet members among his fellow protesters, as well as most of his remaining personal following.

The Cleveland Democrats, it was true, were the fading remnant of a defeated faction, and their leadership reflected that tendency toward old age and political obsolescence that characterized so much of the anti-imperialist movement. But these terms could hardly be applied to the young and vital William Jennings Bryan, titular head of the Democratic party and active idol of millions of voters. Among the numerous celebrities and chieftains of the anti-imperialist forces, Bryan alone had a current political following large enough to challenge the Republican leadership at the polls. By committing his party to the anti-imperialist position, Bryan did the movement a service which no other American could have done it, and insured a genuine political testing of the administration's strength.

Nor was it as easy as appearances might have indicated for the Nebraska orator to hold his party to his own position. The evidence suggests that, without Bryan, the Democratic stand on foreign policy would have differed considerably from that to which he led

it. Such expansionist Democrats as Senator John T. Morgan of
Alabama and the Louisville editor Henry Watterson had a considerable following and preferred another posture; indeed, Senator
Hoar taunted Bryan with the charge that: "A very large number of
your influential supporters are what are called Expansionists, and
the Democratic party seems to support them with as much cheerful-
ness as it supports you." Watterson urged Bryan to make a distinction between "expansion" and "imperialism," reserving his attacks
for the latter. In essence, he favored launching a partisan attack on
the administration's performance rather than its principles, empha-
sizing the frustrations of the Philippine War and the administrative
failures in Cuba and Puerto Rico. "We should deny the Republicans the cry of 'copperheadism' against us," Watterson explained,
"and should force them to defend their maladministration . . . ."[19]

A far-western Democrat cautiously suggested to Bryan that anti-
imperialism need not get in the way of economic advantage. Expansion could mean, not direct territorial government, but merely
"commercial interest from a territory to be governed friendly to
our own country . . . . I believe in the main, that we all agree to a
certain extent, but that we do not all understand the intention of
others who want the same result," this advice ran cryptically. A
blunter critic wrote Senator Morgan that the Democratic party had
the opportunity to put itself at the head of the new manifest destiny,
but that "fate allows it to be run by fools," chief among them "that
talking automaton in Nebraska."[20]

William Randolph Hearst revealed the thinking of a good many
such Democrats in an exchange with Bryan in the summer of 1899.
Bryan was particularly anxious to convert Hearst to anti-imperialism because the latter's New York *Journal*, which had hitherto
supported Bryan, was the principal Democratic newspaper in the
urban northeast. Hearst had championed the Cuban intervention
which began the Spanish-American War, but his pro-Cuban sym-
pathies prevented him from advocating the annexation of that
island. He did, however, approve of the other annexations, particularly that of the Philippines, and on this question he differed openly

with Bryan.

In a long personal letter, the editor argued his case to the politician, stoutly asserting that "I am much more anxious to convert
you than you are to convert me." The Filipinos, he said, would not
gain freedom if left to themselves, but would fall under a military
despotism; their best chance for individual liberty lay in becoming
citizens of the United States. From the American point of view, the
islands would be of immense advantage in developing increased
trade with Asia, and the nation's leaders, Hearst insisted, could not
"afford altogether to overlook material advantage, as the wealth of
the country means largely the wellfare [sic] of its citizens." Besides,
expansion was good Democratic doctrine, and had been accomplished under Democratic presidents in the past. Finally, the
Democratic party was seriously injuring its chances of electoral
success by opposing expansion, running "the risk of returning to its
hopelessly unsuccessful policy of obstruction and opposition . . . . "
Like Watterson, Hearst preferred to attack the "favoritism, mis-
management and corruption" of the Republican regime, and to
denounce its "unnecessary war" in the Philippines, while advocating the retention of the islands, but promising them more liberal
treatment in the future.[21]

There was considerable appeal in the Hearst-Watterson blend of
political opportunism and economic aspiration, but Bryan consistently rejected such trimming and evasion. He had, it was true,
been hampered in developing his stand on foreign policy by the
fact that he was on active duty as a volunteer army colonel during
the latter half of 1898. Although he had not been among those
Democrats who urged Cuban intervention to embarrass the McKinley administration, Bryan came in the end to approve of such intervention in order to end the chaos and suffering in Cuba. He may
also have hoped that participation in the war would enhance his
political appeal, but he made it clear that he endorsed that war
only so far as it freed the Cubans, not to conquer someone else.
In June, 1898, just before embarking on his army service, the prospective colonel asked an Omaha audience: "Our guns destroyed a

Spanish fleet [at Manila Bay], but can they destroy that self-evident
truth that governments derive their just powers—not from force—
but from the consent of governed?"[22]

Silenced by his military position during the rest of 1898, Bryan
escaped to civilian life early in the following year, and promptly
took up the cudgels against imperialism. His first major speech at
this juncture proved that the orator had not lost his eloquence.
"Imperialism might expand the nation's territory," he declared,
"but it would contract the nation's purpose. It is not a step forward
toward a broader destiny; it is a step backward, toward the narrow
views of kings and emperors." And a little later, in a scathing
response to McKinley's plea that events had passed beyond the
control of mere mortals, he said: "Whether a man steals much or
little may depend upon his opportunities, but whether he steals at
all depends upon his own volition." Bryan's position was essentially
a moral and ideological one, and at his best he achieved a ringing
sincerity that added weight to his arguments.[23]

Yet the addition of this notable champion to their cause, while
giving the anti-imperialists their principal chance for electoral
victory, also presented them with their greatest obstacle to unity.
Besides their devotion to anti-imperialism, a common bond for the
mugwump elite, Regular Republicans, and Gold Democrats in the
movement was the disapproval, and even revulsion, with which
they all regarded William Jennings Bryan. The difficulty in making
common cause with him was reflected in the cautious overture of
Rollo Ogden, an editor of E. L. Godkin's New York *Evening Post*.
"You may be surprised, sir, to learn that an editor of the *Evening
Post* has any sympathy with your cause," Ogden wrote Bryan in
evident embarrassment. Desperate for a standard bearer, the inescapable fact that it had to be Bryan, whom they viewed as a
demagogue and a radical, drove the non-Bryanites to the brink of
a new desperation. Thus, as leader of the political phase of the anti-
imperialist movement, it fell to Bryan to attempt to unite two con-
stituencies as alien as oil and water. The "original Bryan men" were
men of few issues, partisans of a social struggle typified for them

by the questions of the currency, the tariff, and the trusts. While their loyalty to their hero insured that they would follow his leadership on foreign policy, it was a field in which they were not primarily interested. The hard core of zealous anti-imperialists, on the other hand, showed a clear preference for orthodoxy in domestic affairs, and regarded the Bryanite platform with something akin to loathing.[24]

All this was bad enough, but the very first occasion upon which Bryan joined the struggle ended amid circumstances which confirmed the worst suspicions of the anti-Bryan faction. The Nebraska leader got out of the army just as the fight over the confirmation of the peace treaty with Spain was at its peak. The terms of the treaty included the cession of Puerto Rico and the Philippines to the United States, and the anti-imperialist strategy was to defeat its ratification in the Senate, thus forcing the administration to negotiate a new peace which omitted the annexations. Since ratification required the approval of two-thirds of the Senators, the defeat of the treaty appeared distinctly feasible, and in their furious campaign toward that end the anti-imperialists seemed at last to have achieved a genuinely effective unity.

To their utter horror, however, Bryan announced publicly that the treaty should be ratified, throwing Senate Democrats into confusion. While most held fast to their opposition, a few ultimately changed sides, a change for which Bryan was widely held responsible. The treaty was ratified by the narrowest of margins, after what Senator Lodge described as "the closest, hardest fight I have ever known." Bitter in their defeat, which proved to be a crucial one, the anti-treaty leaders saw in Bryan's action proof of his essential levity and lack of scruples. To them it was clear that he wished the annexations approved so that he could preserve the issue for use in the presidential campaign of 1900. Some of Bryan's later explanations seemed to add weight to this theory, such as his statement that "we are now in a better position to wage a successful contest against imperialism than we would have been had the treaty been rejected."[25]

In fact, Bryan's motives for his position included some perfectly proper ones, and he publicly explained his reasoning on several occasions. To defeat the peace treaty would have left the nation still at war with Spain, postponing the demobilization of the army and the disposition of many vital questions. But why wait upon the slow and uncertain processes of diplomacy? If the treaty were ratified, the United States government would be left with complete discretion as to the future of the Spanish colonies. Surely such matters could be better settled in Washington than in Paris, Bryan insisted. Furthermore, Bryan shared the administration's concern about the possibility of an international clash over the Philippines, if the fate of the islands were left too long undecided. To approve the treaty would formally put the area under American control, insulating it against foreign meddling and providing time to work out a just solution. "If the treaty had been rejected the opponents of imperialism would have been held responsible for any international complications which might have arisen before the ratification of another treaty," he pointed out.

The more correct course was first to ratify the peace treaty, and then to secure congressional action to give self-government to the Filipinos, Bryan thought. "I was among the number of those who believed it better to ratify the treaty and end the war, release the volunteers, remove the excuse for war expenditures and then give the Filipinos the independence which might be forced from Spain by a new treaty," he declared in 1900, explaining that he "thought it safer to trust the American people to give independence to the Filipinos than to trust the accomplishment of that purpose to diplomacy with an unfriendly nation." In all of this, the question of the volunteer soldiers represented an important underlying factor. When Bryan took his stand on the peace treaty, his own regiment was still fretting in camp amid the Florida sands, eagerly awaiting the same discharge that their colonel had already obtained for himself. To advocate a course which would leave them there indefinitely must have seemed to him like disloyalty to his men, and he chose instead to work for a plan which would do justice to the soldiers and to the alien islanders at the same time.[26]

Unfortunately, the Peerless Leader's calculations proved faulty. As anticipated, Senator Augustus O. Bacon of Georgia introduced a resolution in the Senate which declared that it was not the purpose of the United States to retain the Philippine Islands permanently, but rather "to give the people thereof their liberty" when order was restored. Offered as a substitute for a much more vague resolution, the Bacon Amendment came to a Senate vote in the same month in which the peace treaty had been ratified, and the struggle which it precipitated proved even closer matched than that on the treaty. After an incredible tie vote, the impasse was broken by the vote of Vice President Garrett A. Hobart. The fact that thirty-two Senators did not vote at all provided additional evidence of the Senate's lack of enthusiasm for the Philippine venture, but the defeat of Bacon's proposal left the Bryan strategy utterly discredited.[27]

The damage to the unity of the cause was fatal. Andrew Carnegie later recalled that he felt so strongly about Bryan's actions that, he said, "I could not be cordial to him for years afterwards." Senator Hoar told Bryan that the ratification of the peace treaty was the greatest single disappointment of his public life, and that he held Bryan personally responsible for it. When Bryan gained a second nomination for the presidency in 1900, it was still impossible for many anti-imperialists to support him, even though he campaigned vigorously against McKinley's expansionist record. Moorfield Storey reflected the common dilemma when he wrote Hoar that he wanted to vote against imperialism, but not for Bryan. To Storey, it indicated "a certain amount of decay that in a crisis like this the country should not have strength enough to present some other candidate than Bryan."[28]

Charles Francis Adams, Jr., who had once called Bryan "a pinchbeck Christ," found it impossible to vote for either Bryan or McKinley, as did Grover Cleveland and Thomas Brackett Reed. Schurz and Carnegie led an effort to organize a third party which would run solely on an anti-imperialist platform, but the attempt collapsed for lack of support. Carnegie eventually joined Senator Hoar in reluctantly supporting McKinley as the lesser of two evils, while Schurz's endorsements of Bryan were so lukewarm and so qualified as to seem almost like repudiation. While Bryan held the support of his own Democratic followers, he lost that of many of the mugwumps, and found so little enthusiasm for anti-imperialism among the voters at large that he shifted the emphasis of the campaign to the traditional currency, tariff, and trust issues. The result was a decisive defeat at the polls, and the final disintegration of the anti-imperialist movement. After the election, Carl Schurz wrote the verdict of the mugwumps: "Whatever good qualities Bryan may possess, I have always considered him the evil genius of the anti-imperialist cause. To vote for him was the most distasteful thing I ever did . . . . "[29]

In the wake of the disaster, Charles Francis Adams, Jr., drew an unkind picture of his fellows in the movement: "We are the most impracticable set of cranks probably to be found on the face of the earth. By 'we' I refer to our [anti] imperialist crowd. We cannot agree on anything: and the standards we set up are so exalted and all embracing, and any infringements upon them are so objectionable, that to reach an agreement is impossible, and our influence is, therefore, wasted."[30] While there was truth in Adams' evaluation, it did the anti-imperialists less than justice. Deeply divided upon domestic policy, unable to agree upon the strategy of their common cause, and saddled by fate with a presidential candidate almost uniquely unacceptable to many of their most effective members, they could hardly be blamed for falling prey to the dissidence of dissent. The more surprising feature of their crusade was that it almost succeeded anyway; on two occasions in February, 1899, the expansionist program stood in jeopardy, to be saved in the Senate only by the slightest of margins.

The problem of the anti-expansionists was further compounded by the fact that the administration secured its annexations just at the moment when war broke out in the Philippines. As the struggle to subdue the Filipinos dragged along, enthusiasm for overseas commitments cooled perceptibly in the United States, and opponents found ready to hand the most effective ammunition that they were ever likely to possess in their attack upon imperialism. To civilize an area through the bloody conquest of its inhabitants was to put the proposition in its crudest terms, and there was no question but that public opinion was sharply affected. Yet the moment of decision had passed, and could not be recalled. Intense as was the long debate on the Philippine war, it began too late to affect the first crucial decisions. It never resulted in the reversal of existing policy, nor were its effects sufficient to tilt the balance against the administration in the election of 1900.

The anti-imperialists fought three major fights: against the annexation of Hawaii in 1897 and 1898; against ratification of the peace treaty in 1899; and against the re-election of McKinley in 1900. They lost them all. Politically, the anti-imperialist crusade had failed. By 1904, Charles Francis Adams, Jr., could write: "The whole question of the Philippines is now a dead issue. The discussion attracts no sort of attention; and, when it is brought to the fore, people turn away from it with a sense of weariness."[31]

13 Conflict and Consensus

THE GREAT national debate on foreign policy which marked the closing years of the nineteenth century threw the light of inquiry on every aspect of America's relation to the rest of the world. As the domestic politics of the 1890s reflected an intense interest in the relations between sections and classes within the United States, so the issue of imperialism led to fresh attempts to define the nature of American institutions and of the American mission, and to find where the national interest most truly lay. These attempts touched upon many facets of the nation's life, and contributed to that mood of energetic self-examination which gave birth to the Progressive movement.

A central belief of the anti-imperialists was that the acquisition of a colonial empire violated the letter, or at least the spirit, of the constitution, and was a negation of the American belief in self-government. It had long been a habit in American politics to discuss public issues as constitutional questions, and Senate anti-imperialists quickly took constitutional grounds in their opposition to the proposed annexations. In December of 1898, Senator George G. Vest of Missouri introduced his joint resolution stating that "under the Constitution of the United States no power is given to the Federal Government to acquire territory to be held and governed permanently as colonies." Except for small areas needed for coaling stations and the like, Vest's resolution declared, any lands which the nation acquired must ultimately be organized into territories suitable for admission into the union as states.[1]

Vest argued his case in the traditional manner, citing legal precedents and Supreme Court decisions, and setting off a full-scale constitutional debate in which the numerous lawyers in the Senate enthusiastically joined. For the next two weeks, the Senate chamber periodically rang with legal and historical arguments about the powers of the federal government which recalled the days of Webster and Calhoun. Ultimately, however, the anti-imperialists found themselves baffled by the very simplicity of their opponents' position. Selected by the astute Senator Orville H. Platt of Connecticut, who made the first major speech against the Vest Resolution, it was that the federal government possessed "every sovereign power not reserved in its Constitution to the states or the people," including the power to acquire territory as it pleased. As Senator Joseph B. Foraker of Ohio pointed out, Vest had raised a question about power, and Vest's answer to that question would leave the government of the United States inferior in power to those of all other sovereign nations. Even Senator John C. Spooner of Wisconsin, who did not wish the annexation of the Philippines, vigorously defended the legal right of the government to take colonies if it wanted to, although he expressed grave doubts about the expediency of doing so.[2]

One purpose of the Vest Resolution was to provide an opportunity for public debate in Congress on the issues presented by the peace treaty. Treaties were debated in executive session, from which the public was barred and of which no public record was kept. It was therefore a part of Vest's strategy to raise the issues of the peace settlement in an openly debatable form, and to make Senate members take a public stand on them. Thus the wrangling over the Vest Resolution, which never came to a vote, was an integral part of the debate on the peace settlement, and everyone knew it. Senator Edward O. Wolcott of Colorado, who gave his votes to the administration but often argued on the side of its opponents, called the resolution an improper device for forcing an open discussion of matters that ought to be discussed privately.[3] Yet, by putting the question on essentially legalistic grounds, Vest probably did the anti-imperialist cause a disservice. The effect was to drain off much of the argument into the old, clogged channels of constitutional theory, rather than fighting the battle on straightforward grounds of morality and expediency. The better question was not whether the government had the theoretical right to acquire colonies, but whether it was wise and proper to do so.

Nevertheless, the debate on the Vest Resolution did touch frequently upon the spirit as well as the letter of the constitution. Vest himself appealed to Jefferson's principle that "all governments derive their just powers from the consent of the governed," and this proposition figured prominently in the debate. Senator George F. Hoar of Massachusetts interrupted Platt's speech to demand the Connecticut Senator's stand on the principle. Facing the issue squarely, Platt answered, "From the consent of *some* of the governed," evoking a gasp of dismay from Hoar. After all, Platt pointed out, women and illiterates were generally denied the vote; furthermore, there were a quarter of a million Americans living in the District of Columbia who were governed without their consent, and no one seemed concerned about them. Senator Henry M. Teller of Colorado returned to the issue the next day during a discussion of the future of Cuba. Although his own Teller Resolution had promised the Cubans self-government, the Senator explained that it was not necessary to "invite every man in Cuba to participate in the government that we there establish. We have the right to see that they exclude from participation . . . such elements as we know would render the government unstable and unsafe, or else do it ourselves." In short, these Senators took the ground that the consent required to legitimize a government need come only from certain essential segments of a society, not from the society as a whole. From thence they could argue that, whatever the level of opposition to American rule in a given colony, the "best" elements consented to it and that they outweighed the rest.[4]

The Senate debate on these matters was echoed in the nation at large, where partisans hotly argued the correct application of the principles of self-government to the new acquisitions. Most expansionists clung to traditional liberal values, claiming that colonial expansion would actually spread self-government by preparing for it peoples who were currently incapable of its exercise. But a minority, hard pressed by their opponents' attacks, impatiently questioned the egalitarian tradition itself. One writer thought that the constitution needed modernizing. If the American form of government was incompatible with colonial empire, then it should be changed. "Is it not possible that our interpretation of government, even of the popular type, has been provincial, or at least western-continental, and not applicable to a world-policy?" he asked.[5]

A contributor to the venerable *North American Review* posed an even more fundamental challenge to democratic assumptions. Charging that the framers of the Declaration of Independence had "consecrated to perpetuity some of the most obvious fallacies that were ever promulgated to mislead men," he insisted that all men were clearly *not* created equal. Nor did their creator endow them with any rights; rights were acquired slowly as society advanced, and were not inalienable, but subject to modification, extension, or withdrawal as conditions changed. As for governments deriving their just powers from the consent of the governed, the entire proposition was too fuzzy and theoretical even to debate in that form. Rejecting the whole concept of universal rights of man, the author made those rights relative, evolutionary, and dependent upon circumstances. Such questions as the government of the Philippines, he said, must be decided on the basis of their specific realities, not by "delusive fallacies solemnly promulgated a century and a quarter ago."[6]

While representing an extreme position, statements like these lent weight to William Graham Sumner's famous accusation that "we have beaten Spain in a military conflict, but we are submitting to be conquered by her on the field of ideas and policies." A distinguished Yale professor of political and social science, Sumner was well known for his controversial expressions on current national issues. The war with Spain, he thought, had produced a state of

excitement and "nervous intoxication" in the United States which
threatened to carry the country far from its original principles. The
United States was built on the premise that men were individually
equal, just as its federal union was workable only as a group of
equal partners. Heterogeneous or unequal elements introduced into
the national fabric would act as a solvent upon it, warping or
destroying the underlying pattern. While American ideals had
never been completely fulfilled in practice, Sumner said, the unique
conception behind them had made the nation stand for "something
unique and grand in the history of mankind." To compromise those
ideals for the tinsel glory of empire seemed to him a poor bargain
indeed.[7]

Sumner shared much of the mugwump political position, favoring
sound money, free trade, and civil service reform, and opposing
imperialist expansion as both inexpedient and incompatible with
American principles. Always an independent thinker, he viewed
the advance of the civilized peoples upon the uncivilized as inevitable, however. Those who could not adapt to civilization were
doomed, he concluded; philanthropy could delay their fate, but
not avert it. Futhermore, he made an important distinction between
settlement colonies, in which the ruling race actually went themselves to populate their conquests and build new societies there,
and conquest colonies, in which they merely seized control of an
existing, alien society. He thought the former much more worthy
of respect than the latter, and approved of past American expansion because it fell in the settlement category.

Sumner also distinguished between "economic earth hunger" and
"political earth hunger," finding it rational to seek economic advantage in undeveloped regions but irrational to assume unnecessarily
the burden of political control. The shrewdest American policy, he
held, would be to encourage the British to absorb as much as
possible of the uncivilized world into their empire, since their free
trade policy would make the economic benefits available to all
while they alone would bear the trouble and expense of governing.
Sumner granted that any civilized power, even the United States,

might find it necessary at some point to assume jurisdiction over an uncivilized area, but "if the industrial use could be got without taking the political jurisdiction, it would be far better." A mixture of ideological and practical considerations, therefore, had led Sumner into the anti-imperialist camp.[8]

It was William Jennings Bryan, however, who hit most squarely the ideological issue involved: "Once admit that some people are capable of self-government and that others are not and that the capable people have a right to seize upon and govern the incapable, and you make force—brute force—the only foundation of government and invite the reign of a despot." To E. L. Godkin, imperialism meant the death of republican government in the United States: "Forms may be kept up as at Rome, but the spirit will be gone." The anti-imperialists believed that the denial of liberty and self-government by Americans anywhere weakened them at home, and that the rationalizations required to justify undemocratic practice abroad would inevitably pervert American political principles. However much they might sympathize with Filipinos or others, their gravest fears were for their own society.[9]

As to the white man's burden, the anti-imperialist position was much less clear-cut. Anti-imperialists were not only deeply divided about the nature of the duty which the civilized societies owed to the uncivilized, but individually they often showed great ambiguity on the subject. Some, like Sumner, simply dismissed the notion of tutelage to backward peoples as a hypocritical excuse for conquest. Others found the imperialist argument preposterous on its own terms. Senator Edward M. Carmack of Tennessee seized upon the imperialists' penchant for talking in terms of centuries when they spoke of the uplift of the "lower races." Theodore Roosevelt, he told the Senate, had explained that it had taken the Anglo-Saxon race a thousand years to master the art of self-government, and Roosevelt believed the Filipinos to be less apt pupils than his own race. Thus, Carmack declared, "We are not to hold them [the Philippines] permanently. We want to experiment with them for only a thousand years or so." This seemed a long time to wait, he told his laughing colleagues, to anyone who lacked the "serene and composed and restful temper" of the ebullient Rough Rider. Sumner put the case more brutally. "We talk of civilizing lower races, but we have never done it yet," he wrote; "we have exterminated them."[10]

Others challenged the assumption that one people could teach self-government to another. Moorfield Storey believed that "no people in the history of the world has ever learned how to govern itself without trying." The art could be mastered by practice alone; an alien tutelage, therefore, merely postponed the day when a people could successfully manage its own affairs. Charles Francis Adams, Jr., recalled that the United States withdrew its occupation of Mexico in 1848 even though that country was then in complete chaos. Furthermore, the United States had opposed the French attempt to impose order upon that troubled region in the 1860s. The result of giving the Mexicans ample time and freedom to work out their own problems was the eventual creation of an orderly and stable government, which represented a purely Mexican achievement. Rather than getting involved in endless quarrels and entanglements by trying to uplift the Mexicans, Adams asserted, the United States had found a wiser and more practical course, and one which harmonized with American principles as well. Senator Hoar took a similar position toward the Philippines, arguing that the regime of Emilio Aguinaldo promised, if let alone, to evolve into as good a republic as most of those south of the Rio Grande. "For years and for generations, and perhaps for centuries, there would have been turbulence, disorder, and revolution," Hoar conceded. "But in her own way Destiny would have evolved for them a form of civic rule best adapted to their need."[11]

If some anti-imperialists rejected the whole idea of tutelage, however, others accepted the need for this function, but denied that the United States could exercise it. Americans commonly regarded the British empire as the best example of enlightened imperialism, and tended to a surprising degree to approve of its achievements in ruling subject peoples. Imperialists in the United

States frequently pointed to the British empire as a model to be emulated. Rather than questioning this favorable view, their opponents often accepted it, agreeing to the validity of the civilizing mission in principle, but denying that the United States was capable of fulfilling it properly. Such men held that the white man's burden should be left to the British, who were especially suited to bear it. "No other agency of civilization has been so potent as England's enlightened selfishness," admitted the anti-imperialist president of Stanford University, David Starr Jordan, but Jordan thought that America's national development must follow other lines. Carl Schurz argued that "monarchies or aristocracies can do certain things which democracies cannot do as well," and Senator Hoar, while praising British rule in India, felt that its successes could only have been achieved under an aristocratic political system like that of England.[12]

A recent scholar has charged that the anti-imperialists as a group occupied a weak moral position. Since they shared the general belief in the backwardness of the colonial peoples and in their unreadiness for self-government, the opponents of expansion showed themselves callous to the fate of others when they refused to take up the white man's burden, according to this critic. Even granting that a majority of anti-imperialists actually did believe in racial inequality and in the civilizing mission, however, they also advocated a kind of division of labor among the civilized powers, each doing that for which it was best suited. "The question is not whether Great Britain or the United States has the better form of government or the nobler civic mission," David Starr Jordan insisted. "There is room in the world for two types of Anglo-Saxon nations, and nothing has yet happened to show that civilization would gain if either were to take up the function of the other."[13]

The function of England, Jordan thought, was to carry good government about the world, and it was a valuable and worthy service. But the object of democracy was not good government: "better government than any republic has yet enjoyed could be had in simpler and cheaper ways." Democracy's object was self-government, and its purpose was to build men, not states. Individual Americans could properly go to the lesser regions to advance their development, but the government's duty was at home. Let England police far-off islands for populations unready for self-rule, while the United States showed all the world what democratic self-government meant among those who were prepared for it. Each task played a role in advancing the level of civilization, while expressing the unique qualities of the society which performed it.[14]

Besides sharing the conviction that an egalitarian tradition was a poor basis for authoritarian rule, anti-imperialists believed that American politics were too steeped in patronage and corruption to promise well for the treatment of helpless subjects, while the past national record in dealing with non-white races was so dismal as to offer little encouragement for further ventures. Denying that Americans were paragons of good government, Carl Schurz predicted sarcastically that Havana and Ponce "may get municipal administration almost as good as New York has under Tammany rule; and Manila may have a city council not much less virtuous than that of Chicago." "So far as yet appears," agreed Sumner, "Americans cannot govern a city of one hundred thousand inhabitants so as to get comfort and convenience in it at a low cost and without jobbery." Such being the case, it was presumption indeed to offer to govern someone else![15] As a result of this kind of argument, the American domestic record came in for sharp scrutiny. Critics particularly charged that the people of the United States had systematically discriminated against Indians, Negroes, and Chinese, denying them opportunity and justice. Although *The Outlook* undertook editorially to defend its countrymen against these accusations, it visibly found the task difficult. The present condition of some domestic minorities might indeed discourage those, one editorial granted, "who fail to recognize the fact that character is a plant of slow growth," but presumably all would come right in the end. More striking was the skepticism of Booker T. Washington, who asked "whether this Government can do for the millions of dark-skinned races to be found in Cuba, Porto Rico, Hawaii, and the Philippine

Islands that which it has not been able to do for the now nearly 10,000,000 negroes and Indians" within the United States.[16]

To one group in particular, the question of domestic race relations dominated that of foreign imperialism. With the exception of some genuine expansionists like John T. Morgan, Southern Democrats tended to concentrate on seizing the arguments by which Northern Republicans justified colonialism, and using them to disarm their former critics. Led by the fearsome Senator Benjamin R. ("Pitchfork Ben") Tillman of South Carolina, they insisted upon the essential hypocrisy of the expansionist position. Many of the same men who for years had preached that all men were equal, and had assailed the South for her treatment of the Negro, now announced that the white race must take other peoples under tutelage and that not everyone was fit for self-government. If this were true, why was not the South's racial policy right? Tillman's triumphant claim that Republican leaders would no longer dare to question the disfranchisement of Southern Negroes convinced Senator Hoar that any doctrine of inequality applied to colonial peoples would further undermine the position of the Negro at home.[17]

Southerners also used the opportunity to renew their old grudge about Radical Reconstruction policies after the Civil War. From the debate over the war resolutions in the spring of 1898 to that on the Philippine Organic Act in 1902, Congress heard continual comparisons of military rule in the new colonies and in the old Reconstruction South. Even before the declaration of war with Spain, Senator Tillman thundered that his state had lived through a military occupation, and that he would not vote to fix such a burden upon the Cubans. Four years later, Senator Carmack was still asking how anyone could expect gentle or compassionate treatment of the Filipinos at the hands of an American army of occupation, when a similar army had perpetrated such horrors upon its own countrymen during Reconstruction. To Southerners, the issues of imperialism seemed intimately related to the familiar sources of sectional conflict within the United States. It was thus to their own situation, past and present, that they reacted, more than to that in Cuba or the Philippines, and their main animus was less against imperialism than against their old Republican enemies.[18]

There were at least two aspects to the discussion of imperialism, one concerned with principles and duty, the other with benefits and the national advantage. Anti-imperialists not only charged that the acquisition of colonies was wrong for the United States, but denied that they would bring the nation any important benefits. David Starr Jordan found the proposition that war and colonial rule would improve the tone of American society simply "detestable." War had a degrading influence, not an ennobling one, Jordan held. It gave occasion for corruption and profiteering, turned men's attention away from sober civic affairs, and brought appalling suffering and carnage. "To waste good blood is pure murder . . . ," he cried indignantly. Senator Wolcott ridiculed the notion that entrusting the government of the Philippines to American politicians, perhaps including "the precinct committeemen of Indiana and other states," would produce such spotless rule in the islands that "a reflected glory and purity would shine across to our land, which would make at once our civic institutions pure and stainless."[19]

The alleged economic advantage of empire also received a critical examination. Carl Schurz stressed the simple fact that the United States, lacking colonies, had been rapidly expanding its overseas markets at the expense of Great Britain, which had so many of them. Effective as this was, it was soon supplemented by equally strong arguments. In a remarkable analysis of America's foreign trade, Edward Atkinson came to conclusions which should have deflated the myth of the China market. Noting that Europeans bought almost 80 per cent of United States exports, Atkinson established a correlation between productivity and purchasing power. Advanced regions like the United States and Europe had a far higher level of productivity than the rest of the world, owing to their scientific and technological superiority. This in turn made them wealthier than other societies, and thus able to buy more. Great markets were not to be found in areas of great population, like China, Atkinson said, but in areas of great buying power, like Europe. Thus the advanced, industrialized states were not merely commercial rivals, but each others' best customers as well, and would necessarily continue to be. The imperialist assumption that markets should be sought primarily in undeveloped economies which lacked competing industry was wrong. They must be secured, Atkinson showed, by finding ways to increase commercial intercourse with Europe.[20]

If colonies would not help the population as a whole, who would they help? William Jennings Bryan undertook to answer that question: "Imperialism would be profitable to the army contractors; it would be profitable to the ship owners, who would carry live soldiers to the Philippines and bring dead soldiers back; it would be profitable to those who would seize upon the franchises, and it would be profitable to the officials whose salaries would be fixt [sic] here and paid over there; but to the farmer, to the laboring man and to the vast majority of those engaged in other occupations it would bring expenditure without return and risk without reward."[21]

Claims that the Spanish War and the new territories which it brought had made the United States a world power and enhanced her international status evoked an angry response from the sardonic Sumner. "My patriotism is of the kind which is outraged by the notion that the United States never was a great nation until in a petty three months campaign it knocked to pieces a poor, decrepit, bankrupt old state like Spain." And in the end, it was their disparate views of national greatness which most fundamentally separated the imperialists and their opponents. "The danger," declared Senator Hoar, "is that we are to be transformed from a republic founded on the Declaration of Independence . . . into a vulgar, commonplace empire founded upon physical force . . . ."[22]

The differences between imperialists and anti-imperialists were obvious and significant; their areas of agreement were less obvious, but hardly less significant, for the outlook of a society is defined as much by the assumptions which it shares as by those about which it quarrels. From this point of view, the two groups shared a common frame of reference, from which they usually reasoned their way to opposing conclusions. While the enormous diversity of positions among both groups makes generalizations risky, a majority on both sides seems to have held a number of beliefs in common.

As we have already seen, there was a very wide consensus about the desirability of the United States acquiring additional territory; there was little objection in any quarter to the voluntary annexation of Canada, should it seem feasible, and most anti-imperialists were interested in acquiring at the least a few naval bases in the western hemisphere, if not more ambitious additions. What the political status of new territory should be, or whether it should be sought beyond the limits of the hemisphere, were matters of dispute. Even here, however, there was a good deal of common ground: most partisans on either side were strongly opposed to granting statehood to non-contiguous areas with alien populations. Whether the colonial peoples were seen as innately inferior, or merely as too different to assimilate to American institutions, made little practical difference. In either case, they must not be permitted to join in the central councils of the nation. The expansionists concluded from this that the new peoples must be governed as colonial subjects, while their opponents believed that no large alien populations must be allowed to come within the jurisdiction of the American political system at all.

A different but closely related phenomenon was the disinclination of both groups to share the benefits of the American system in any direct way. Even annexationists were reluctant to grant United States citizenship to the inhabitants of the newly acquired areas, fearing that it might be a step toward statehood. The most obviously appropriate concessions, such as removing American tariff barriers for colonies like Puerto Rico, or lowering them for protectorates like Cuba, were made only grudgingly and after great presidential prodding. There was absolute hostility to the possibility that the new subjects might emigrate to the United States. It was not only political participation which was to be denied the colonies, but any real membership in the American system. Colonies were something to be kept apart, and to be civilized at arm's length. There were, of course, honorable exceptions to all of these things. The expansionist Senator John T. Morgan fought hard to secure American citizenship for the colonial peoples, as well as a larger share of self-government and, in the case of Hawaii, statehood itself. On the other side, Moorfield Storey admitted "the dangers and difficulties of giving a people of this sort citizenship," but declared that if they were held permanently, he would struggle as long as he lived to secure the islanders "every right that a citizen of Massachusetts enjoys, including a right to be represented in Congress."[23] Theodore Roosevelt and Elihu Root labored mightily to gain the tariff concessions which seemed to them demanded by justice. Yet the fact remains that the attitude of Americans toward their colonies was essentially niggardly, to an extent that gave a hollow sound to much of the rhetoric about uplift.

It is also true that the prevalent racism of the time influenced anti-imperialists as well as their opponents. Carl Schurz was one of many who thought tropical peoples degenerate. He called the Cubans "a sorry lot" of Spanish creoles and Negroes, and the Filipinos a "mass of more or less barbarous Asiatics" leavened by Spaniards and their half-breed offspring. David Starr Jordan thought Cuban society characterized by "vice, superstition and revenge," and the Cubans brutal and indolent. In describing the population of the Philippines he included "a substratus of Malays, lazy and revengeful," "a surface scum of the wanderers of all the world," and, in the interior, tribes of "untamed black imps." Senator Vest saw the same people as "half-civilized, piratical, muck-running" semi-savages. To Thomas Reed they were "yellow-bellies." "I s'posed we had niggers enough in this country without buyin' any more of 'em," he was alleged to have said.[24]

After the anti-imperialists made the Philippine War a central rallying point for their cause, their tone regarding the Filipinos changed visibly. In place of the previous denigration, the new line expressed a greatly increased confidence in the readiness of Fili-

pinos for self-government, and a more favorable view of their level
of civilization. It was a position to which they were forced by the
exigencies of debate, however, and which never wholly replaced
the earlier and more genuine feelings with which the anti-imperialists regarded tropical islanders.[25] And if people like Moorfield Storey, Senator Hoar, or Bryan exhibited less prejudiced attitudes
throughout, they were the exceptions which proved the rule.

The concept of a superior western civilization, which must in
time be imposed upon the greater or lesser barbarism of everyone
else, was similarly popular. It was a universal truism that civilization must inevitably prevail, and "civilization," upon examination,
turned out to be the norms and achievements of western European
society. The highest manifestation of this western culture was to be
found in the United States, whose institutions were superior to all
others. It was a lively question, of course, as to whether those institutions were suitable for export, or whether they must be nurtured
at home; whether they could serve as a universal model, or whether
only Americans were capable of life in such a rarified political
atmosphere. But surely non-western cultures must in time adopt
western religion and values, western products and customs, western styles of thought and ways of doing things. They must become
civilized, and that was what civilization entailed, according to a
popular definition with which few would have argued.

In all the debate over American foreign policy, virtually no one
seriously questioned the need for American trade expansion overseas. Even William Jennings Bryan acknowledged the duty of his
party to work for this goal, and arguments about it centered solely
on the means by which it could best be achieved. Would overseas
empire facilitate the expansion of trade, was it simply irrelevant to
that purpose, or would the resulting military and naval costs and
the heightened risk of international conflict prove an actual burden
to economic expansion abroad? Should the new markets be sought
in backward or advanced regions, within the hemisphere or without, in Europe or in Asia? All these quarrels only emphasized the
eagerness with which everyone pursued the common goal.

The differences about specific policies failed to obscure a broad, underlying consensus in the American world view. However troubled by the hard decisions of their time, however fearful of taking a wrong course in foreign or domestic policy, the fundamental note was one of enormous confidence in at least the *potential* of the American future. Men believed that their country did have something unique to teach the rest of the world, and that their institutions were indeed superior, their civilization higher, than was true of other societies. They believed that the United States was already great and strong, that it was not only the richest of nations but that it must grow richer. They saw that it stood alone as the only great power in the western hemisphere, and they took for granted the resulting hegemony in the area, which they symbolized by the name "Monroe Doctrine." The most important fact about their goals for the nation, however they differed in detail, was the universal certainty that those goals were achievable and near at hand. It was fear of jeopardizing a magnificent future which made man quarrel so bitterly, and the prize they envisioned seemed worth a struggle. For both imperialists and anti-imperialists foresaw for the United States nothing less than the moral and material leadership of the world.

Conclusion

ALTHOUGH THE events of 1898 insured an American presence in Cuba and the Philippines, Puerto Rico, and Hawaii, they left the exact status of those areas still to be decided. Not even the treaty of peace with Spain dealt with these questions in any clear-cut way, supposedly leaving them to be settled at leisure. While the McKinley administration knew in general where it was going, the steps by which it moved were deceptively gradual, so much so that Carl Schurz charged that the President had worked a "confidence game" upon his own people. First, said Schurz, McKinley sent an army to the Philippines, presumably to follow up Dewey's victory against Spain, and labelled as unpatriotic those who dared question his intentions while the fighting raged. Then he procured a peace treaty which annexed the Philippines to the United States, but told opponents of the treaty that they must not endanger the successful conclusion of the war, assuring them that the actual disposition of the islands was yet to be determined by Congress. Once the treaty was ratified, however, a new pronouncement claimed that the entire matter was settled, by the final and solemn action of the government. "Oh no, gentlemen, this will not do," cried Schurz. "This artful dodge has been played long enough, and too long."[1]

In contrast, the future status of Cuba was supposedly settled at the outset by the Teller Resolution, which pledged the United States to withdraw after pacifying the island, leaving all further matters to the sole discretion of the inhabitants. Having fought a war over Cuba, however, the McKinley administration showed little disposition merely to walk away afterward. If Cuba was important enough to fight about, then the United States must retain some influence over events there. Thus the American military occupation of Cuba stretched on and on, and the Teller Resolution came to pose more questions than it answered. Two years after the fighting ended, it was still unclear what the administration intended for Cuba, and a Yankee general still ruled in Havana.

In the meantime, Congress showed no eagerness to act. Having spent so much time and energy debating general principles, its members found it irritating to face the mass of detailed work that remained after the more dramatic decisions were made. Repeatedly, bills dealing with the governmental machinery of the new dependencies were postponed, and immediate decisions were largely delegated to the executive branch. Eventually, however, the new forms emerged. Hawaii became a self-governing territory, virtually under its pre-annexation government, and was treated in the traditional territorial way. Puerto Rico received an Organic Act in 1900, and the Philippines in 1902, each granting an elective legislative body but holding the reins of executive power in Washington. Cuba, though in theory a sovereign state, became a formal protectorate of the United States by the terms of the Platt Amendment in 1901. Hawaiians had the status of United States citizens, but all the others were mere "nationals" for many years. Citizenship went to the people of Puerto Rico in 1917, and of Guam in 1950. The Filipinos were never citizens of the United States, but were the first of the new "nationals" to receive a bill of rights, in 1902. Puerto Rico's did not come until 1917, while Hawaii, being an "incorporated" territory, needed none. And so it went, a gradual patchwork of legislation growing up to define the nature of the new empire in the years between 1900 and 1917.[2]

A more immediate concern was the establishment of a system of colonial administration. This could not wait upon the ponderous workings of Congress, but must begin at once. The first impulse was

to seek vicarious experience. Most Americans thought of Great
Britain as preeminent in the art of colonial rule. By far the most
experienced nation, its achievements in the field were regarded as
most worthy of emulation, and it quickly became a commonplace
that the United States must learn from the British example. "I only
hope that our people will take advantage in her Colonizing plans
of England's four hundred years experience," the United States
consul at Hong Kong wrote John Hay. "It would be too bad if we
commenced back, and went through the very costly school out of
which her present almost perfect colonial system graduated." One
of the President's closest friends, Russell Hastings, gave similar
advice to McKinley, offering to send him a book by the Governor
General of Gibraltar which described "the whole colonial system
of the British Empire." Elihu Root, on becoming Secretary of War
in 1899 and finding himself in charge of military governments in
Cuba, Puerto Rico, and the Philippines, read not one book, but
many, toiling through a whole list of standard works on the history
and government of the British Empire.[3]

Nor were Englishmen backward about proffering the desired
advice. From Alleyne Ireland's *Tropical Colonization* in 1899 to
Archibald Colquhoun's *Greater America* in 1904, British writers
directed a steady stream of information and guidance at the American public. Even the respected James Bryce, who personally disapproved of American imperialism, felt impelled to add his bit,
though it proved more cautious in tone and less sweeping in gen-
eralization than most such offerings. While numerous and diverse,
these expressions tended to reiterate a few basic principles of colonial rule as the fruit of the British experience. First of all, liberties
taken for granted in temperate countries must be restricted when
dealing with tropical peoples; Bryce joined the others in endorsing
this point. At home, overall authority should be concentrated in
a single colonial office, isolated from politics and allowed broad
autonomy and continuity of policy. In the colonies, power should
be exercised by a select, career civil service, competitively chosen,
well paid, and serving for life. The Indian Civil Service was the

favorite example of this ideal administrative body, and it was usually made clear that an American service, like the Indian model, should contain no members from the colonial population. The latter could participate in government through an advisory council or some similar device, but must be kept out of administration proper.[4]

All of this became the common knowledge of the well read in the United States. At the annual meeting of the American Academy of Political and Social Science in the spring of 1899, a panel on the government of dependencies heard speaker after speaker discuss these same basic principles and make references to British methods. A Yale history professor described in the *North American Review* a proposed training-school for future colonial administrators, where they would learn "Geography and Ethnology, History, Economics and Law, Languages, Religions, and Folk Psychology." In the meantime, with this special service yet to be created, many observers thought that the needed administrators could be supplied from the officer corps of the armed forces, a suggestion which reflected the actual practice by which military governments initiated American rule in all of the new dependencies except Hawaii.[5]

There was deep concern, particularly among reformers, that a political "spoils system" might reduce colonial offices to the level of the machine patronage in American cities or post offices. One informant wrote Elihu Root that, having travelled widely in the United States, he found that the chief objection to the expansion policy arose from the fear that "our colonial management will have too much politics, and savour too much of our municipal government." The public could be most readily won over, he said, by convincing it that only competent men would hold colonial offices. James B. Reynolds, a prominent New York social worker, added further qualifications, writing Root that these officials must not only be educated and intelligent, but must possess "an understanding of the social forces which make the life of the people." The habits and feelings of the alien peoples involved could not be understood in Anglo-Saxon terms, Reynolds explained; " . . . I have seen intelligent people make as bad mistakes as ignorant people in trying to do for our foreign population simply because they did not understand the real forces which make their lives comfortable or uncomfortable and do not understand or appreciate the real root of their prejudices and desires." To Reynolds, the colonial problem seemed "essentially a sociological problem, and in many respects similar to the problem which social reformers are seeking to solve in our large cities."[6]

This ideal of rule by a trained and select elite was to fail in practice, however, like most of the other sacred tenets of British colonialism. The United States never established a career colonial service, and never attempted to train its colonial officials for government, social work, or anything else. It never even created a colonial office. Although the War Department developed a Bureau of Insular Affairs which was in some ways comparable to such an office, it possessed only limited powers, and did not have jurisdiction over all of the new dependencies: Guam and American Samoa were under the Navy Department, while Hawaii went at once to the Department of the Interior. On the other hand, American practice soon allowed the colonials a larger share in their own government than most British theorists advocated for tropical peoples.[7]

In general, the United States evolved its own methods for governing dependencies, rather than slavishly copying the British example. The original discussion of principles was significant, not in providing a blueprint for the future, but in demonstrating the positivist bent of contemporary thinking about colonies, whose people were envisioned as being ruled in their own interest by cooler and wiser heads from the mother country. This longing for government by an expert elite was further demonstrated by the fact that, while upper class, educated Americans regarded most "natives" as unfit for high office, they were almost equally skeptical of the fitness of the bulk of their own fellow citizens. The art of government, they thought, required a special competence which was substantially lacking in tropical peoples, and appeared in only a minority of members of even the "highest" races.

As the United States never really created a colonial system, so it showed little further interest in creating an empire, at least in the formal sense. The novelty of possessing colonies quickly lost its charm, and public interest in the acquisitions of 1898 plummeted after 1900. Yet neither expansionism nor imperialism disappeared. In the years from the Spanish-American War to the First World War, the United States created a network of Caribbean protectorates that formally included Cuba, Panama, Nicaragua, Haiti, and the Dominican Republic, and informally touched the other Caribbean countries as well. This process, which the events of 1898 did much to precipitate, cannot be explained solely as a result of the Spanish War, however, since it had roots in the programs of expansionists from 1895 on, if not earlier. Furthermore, traditional United States interest in Cuba, Central America, and the Caribbean had given a measure of continuity to the nation's activities in the western hemisphere since the 1840s.

The most crucial effect of the expansionism of the 1890s was neither the creation of an empire, nor the acceleration of the growth of American influence within the hemisphere, although these things occurred. Rather, it was to begin the demolition of a basic guideline of American foreign policy, the "theory of the two hemispheres," which gripped the minds of policy makers and the public from the birth of the nation. This view held that the United States must stand aloof from the Old World while dominating the New. In spite of cultural and historical ties to Europe, in spite of the most intimate and vital economic relationships, in spite of the actual physical transfer of tens of millions of Europeans to the United States, it was an article of faith that the nation must have no formal transatlantic political commitments: "European entanglements" were tabu. Imperialists still subscribed to this traditional doctrine in 1900, at least as stated in its traditional form. To proclaim a national interest in the Far East seemed no contradiction of the theory of the two hemispheres; the Orient was seen as a neutral ground where Europeans and Americans might compete or cooperate as they pleased. Americans had been active there since the 1840s, securing trade treaties and safeguards for their citizens on

the coattails of European aggressions. They had even toyed with
force themselves, as in Perry's opening of Japan via an implied
threat of naval attack.

Never, however, had the United States been prepared to wage
serious large-scale warfare for Far Eastern goals, nor were trade
treaties in themselves necessarily an evidence of expansionism.
While exhibiting a fairly continuous interest in the Far East for
half a century before the Spanish-American War, the United States
had, until the 1890s, consistently refused to commit its power in
that region. The establishment of a power commitment that lay
outside the North American orbit, outside even the hemisphere,
was a fateful step. The nation was visibly approaching the day
when the Jeffersonian dream should be realized, when it would be
supreme in one hemisphere and able to defy challenges from the
other. Led on by events, the expansionists of 1898 decided, irrevocably, that this was not enough. By abandoning the historic limits
of American policy, they opened the way for the nation's transformation from a regional power to a world colossus.

A second heritage of 1898 was the insistence that the national
mission must be fulfilled, not only by example, but by actual tutelage, not solely at home, but abroad as well. While the issue continued to be argued through the decades of the twentieth century,
the new view steadily gained ground, and Americans found themselves increasingly engaged in offering guidance to peoples they
hardly knew. Self-confident, rich, and powerful, they came at last
to laugh at the quaintness and the crudities of the effusions of 1898,
while moving in practice toward the new directions in which those
half-forgotten expressions pointed. A revolution in rhetoric disguised the extent to which many of the old assumptions survived,
their aged features half-hidden by their modern dress.

Obviously, the questions raised in the 1890s have yet to find a
final answer. Where can security be found in a threatening world?
How important are overseas business activities to the health of the
economy, and how and to what extent should the government
support them? What is the true mission of America, and what duty

do Americans owe to the rest of mankind? Put in these terms, the issues of expansion are still with us.

Finally, there is an even broader relevance attaching to these matters, which transcends the limits of time and place. In considering how the United States became first a regional power and then a global one, it is inadequate to view the American case in isolation. In modern history, those nations which were capable of extending their power or influence beyond their own borders have normally sought a way to do so. In the twentieth century it is hard to find an exception to the pattern. Germany, Italy, China, Japan, Egypt, Indonesia, the defunct Austro-Hungarian Empire, and Argentina are examples of actual or would-be regional powers, while the United States, Great Britain, Russia, and to a lesser extent, France, have played power roles that extended beyond the bounds of any one geographical region. Thus to ask why the United States chose to become a world power when it did is to confront a problem in general behavior. Those who control power also harbor goals and aspirations, and it is not strange that they should use the one to serve the other. There were, of course, serious questions in the 1890s—as in the 1960s—as to the proper objects, permissible techniques, and practical limits of the application of power. Yet to possess great potential power without eventually seeking to apply it toward desired ends would be a queer condition indeed.

REFERENCE MATTER

Notes

Chapter 1: *A World of Empires*

1 Stephen Gwynn, *The Letters and Friendships of Sir Cecil Spring-Rice,* 2 vols. (Boston and New York, 1929), 1:115–16.
2 *New York Tribune,* 1897: June 23, 27.
3 Ibid., June 22, 1897.
4 Ibid., June 20, 1897; *Public Opinion,* 23 (July 1, 1897):9–10.
5 For the diplomatic history of European expansion in the late nineteenth century, see William L. Langer, *The Diplomacy of Imperialism* (New York, 1935).
6 Quoted in Walter E. Houghton, *The Victorian Frame of Mind, 1830–1870* (New Haven and London, 1957), p. 41; see also pp. 27–33, 41–42.
7 For a provocative study of the development of these ideas, see Philip D. Curtin, *The Image of Africa: British Ideas and Action, 1780–1850* (Madison, Wis., 1964).
8 Walter Bagehot, *Physics and Politics* (New York, 1904), pp. 8, 44; see also Houghton, *Victorian Frame of Mind,* p. 145.
9 Quoted in J. W. Burrows, *Evolution and Society* (Cambridge, England, 1966), p. 275.
10 These ideas are lucidly discussed ibid., esp. pp. 98–99, and in Curtin, *Image of Africa,* esp. Chap. 10.
11 John W. Burgess, *Sovereignty and Liberty,* Vol. 1 in *Political Science and Comparative Constitutional Law* (Boston and London, 1893), pp. 45–46.
12 J. A. Cramb, *The Origins and Destiny of Imperial Britain and Nineteenth Century Europe* (New York, 1915), p. 11; Sir Frederick Lugard, *The Dual Mandate in British Tropical Africa* (London, 1929), p. 61. For the Dual Mandate see also C. E.

Carrington, *The British Overseas* (Cambridge, England, 1950), p. 829.

13 Thomas F. Power, *Jules Ferry and the Renaissance of French Imperialism* (New York, 1944), p. 193.

14 Langer, *Diplomacy of Imperialism*, p. 77; Joseph Chamberlain, *Foreign and Colonial Speeches* (London, 1897), pp. 131–33. See also J. L. Garvin, *The Life of Joseph Chamberlain*, 3 vols. (London, 1932–34), 3:19–20.

15 Sir J. R. Seeley, *The Expansion of England* (Boston, 1920), pp. 88–89; see also C. A. Bodelson, *Studies in Mid-Victorian Imperialism* (Copenhagen, 1924), pp. 81–82.

16 Charles H. Pearson, *National Life and Character: A Forecast* (London and New York, 1894) pp. 14, 89–90.

17 Garvin, *Life of Joseph Chamberlain*, 3:249.

18 Elihu Root to Samuel L. Parrish, Dec. 1, 1899, Elihu Root Papers, Library of Congress. Ernest R. May stresses the European influence on the American elite in *American Imperialism: A Speculative Essay* (New York, 1968); see esp. pp. 86–94.

19 See Dexter Perkins, *A History of the Monroe Doctrine* (Boston, 1941), Chap. IV, for a fuller discussion of these events.

20 Ibid., pp. 161-64; James D. Richardson, *A Compilation of the Messages and Papers of the Presidents, 1789–1897*, 10 vols. (Washington, D.C., 1898), 7:585–86.

21 See John A. S. Grenville and George B. Young, *Politics, Strategy, and American Diplomacy* (New Haven and London, 1966), pp. 76–83; and Nelson M. Blake, "Background of Cleveland's Venezuelan Policy," *American Historical Review*, 47 (1942):259–77.

22 Cushman K. Davis, *A Treatise on International Law Including American Diplomacy* (St. Paul, Minn., 1901), pp. 273–86.

23 *Congressional Record*, 53 Cong., 3 sess. (1895), 27:3082–84.

24 Ibid., pp. 3077, 3089; Henry Cabot Lodge, "England, Venezuela, and the Monroe Doctrine," *North American Review*, 160 (June, 1895):651–58.

25 Richard Olney to Thomas F. Bayard, July 20, 1895, U.S. State Department, *Papers Relating to the Foreign Relations of the United States, 1895*, Part I (Washington, D.C., 1896), 557–60.

26 Quoted in Geoffrey Seed, "British Views of American Policy in the Philippines Reflected in Journals of Opinion, 1898–1907," *Journal of American Studies*, 2 (April, 1968):49–50.

27 Sir Walter Besant, "The Future of the Anglo-Saxon Race," *North American Review*, 163 (Aug., 1896):133.

28 Editorial, *Review of Reviews*, 1 (Jan., 1890):3; William T. Stead, *The Americanization of the World* (London, 1902), quotations from pp. 5, 10, 13.

29 John Fiske, *American Political Ideas Viewed from the Standpoint of Universal History* (New York, 1885), pp. 125, 109, 145–49.

30 See Geoffrey Seed, "British Reactions to American Imperialism Reflected in Journals of Opinion, 1898–1900," *Political Science Quarterly*, 73 (June, 1958):254–72; Richard Koebner, "The Concept of Economic Imperialism," *Economic History Review*, 2nd s., 2 (1949):19–21; and Peter Henry King, "The White Man's Burden" (Ph.D. dissertation, University of California at Los Angeles, 1958), pp. 85–100.

31 Quoted in Garvin, *Life of Joseph Chamberlain*, 3:302–4.

32 Richard Olney, "International Isolation of the United States," *Atlantic Monthly*, 81 (May, 1898):588; Tyler Dennet, *John Hay from Poetry to Politics* (New York, 1934), p. 189; Roosevelt to Frederick Courteney Selous, February 7, 1900, in E. E. Morison, ed., *The Letters of Theodore Roosevelt*, 8 vols. (Cambridge, Mass., 1951–54), 2:1176–77.

Chapter 2: *Destiny and Dollars*

1 Benjamin Harrison, *Views of an Ex-President* (Indianapolis, 1901), p. 185.

2 Theodore Roosevelt, *The Works of Theodore Roosevelt*, ed. Hermann Hagedorn, 24 vols. (New York, 1923–26), 15:337.

3 Quoted in Claude G. Bowers, *Beveridge and the Progressive Era* (Cambridge, Mass., 1932), pp. 74–75.

4 For a standard study, see Albert K. Weinberg, *Manifest Destiny* (Baltimore, 1935).

5 See Samuel Eliot Morison, *"Old Bruin": Commodore Matthew C. Perry, 1794–1858* (Boston, 1967), pp. 312–14, 425, 428–29; Basil Rauch, *American Interest in Cuba: 1848–1855* (New York, 1948); and C. Stanley Urban, "The Ideology of Southern Imperialism: New Orleans and the Caribbean, 1845–1860," *Louisiana Historical Quarterly*, 39 (Jan., 1956):48–73, for various aspects of pre-Civil War expansionism.

6 Glyndon Van Deusen, *William Henry Seward* (New York, 1967), pp. 488–548.

7 Frederic Bancroft, ed., *Speeches, Correspondence and Political*

Papers of Carl Schurz, 6 vols. (New York and London, 1913), 5:191.

8 Quoted in Russell B. Nye, *This Almost Chosen People* (East Lansing, Michigan, 1966), p. 24; see also pp. 1–42.

9 See Harold U. Faulkner, *Politics, Reform and Expansion, 1890–1900* (New York, 1959), pp. 72–73, 84–85; H. J. Habakkuk and M. Postan, eds., *The Cambridge Economic History of Europe,* Vol. 6 (Cambridge, Eng., 1965), 31, 53, 496, 673; and Heinrich E. Friedlander and Jacob Oser, *Economic History of Modern Europe* (New York, 1953), pp. 205, 220–22.

10 Nye, *This Almost Chosen People,* pp. 164–77; and Edward McNall Burns, *The American Idea of Mission* (New Brunswick, N.J., 1957), pp. 3–34.

11 John Fiske, *American Political Ideas Viewed from the Standpoint of Universal History* (New York, 1885), pp. 7–8.

12 Josiah Strong, *Our Country: Its Possible Future and Its Present Crisis,* ed. Jurgen Herbst (Cambridge, Mass., 1963), pp. 206–217.

13 Richard Olney, "International Isolation of the United States," *Atlantic Monthly,* 81 (May, 1898):587. This is the published version of an address delivered by Olney at Harvard College on March 2, 1898.

14 Hay to McKinley, Feb. 20, 1898, William McKinley Papers, Library of Congress.

15 John Higham, *Strangers in the Land,* 2nd. ed. (New York, 1963), pp. 68–105; the poem quoted is Thomas Bailey Aldrich, "Unguarded Gates," in *The Writings of Thomas Bailey Aldrich,* 9 vols. (Boston and New York, 1907), 2:71–72.

16 C. Vann Woodward, *The Strange Career of Jim Crow,* 2nd. rev. ed. (New York, 1966), pp. 69–71; William Graham Sumner, *The Conquest of the United States by Spain and Other Essays,* ed. Murray Polner (Chicago, n.d.), p. 168. See also John G. Sproat, *"The Best Man": Liberal Reformers in the Gilded Age* (New York, 1968), pp. 29–44.

17 *Cong. Record,* 48 Cong., 1 sess. (1884), 15:1454; *U.S. Senate Reports,* 49 Cong., 1 sess. (1886), 6:3; David M. Pletcher, *The Awkward Years* (Columbia, Mo., 1962), pp. 340–42.

18 James G. Blaine, *Political Discussions, Legislative, Diplomatic, and Popular, 1856–1886* (Norwich, Conn., 1887), pp. 186–93, 300–36, 411–19.

19 See Alice Felt Tyler, *The Foreign Policy of James G. Blaine*

(Minneapolis, Minn., 1927), pp. 165–90; and J. Lloyd Mecham, *The United States and Inter-American Security, 1889–1960* (Austin, Texas, 1961), pp. 48–58.

20 Harrison to Blaine, Oct. 1, 1891, in Albert T. Volwiler, ed., *The Correspondence Between Benjamin Harrison and James G. Blaine, 1882–1893* (Philadelphia, 1940), p. 202. See also Tyler, *The Foreign Policy of James G. Blaine,* pp. 128–64, 302–346; Frederick B. Pike, *Chile and the United States, 1880–1962* (Notre Dame, Ind., 1963), pp. 66–83; and William A. Russ, Jr., *The Hawaiian Revolution, 1893–94* (Gettysburg, Penn., 1959).

21 Harold and Margaret Sprout, *The Rise of American Naval Power, 1776–1918* (Princeton, N.J., 1939), pp. 188–89, 213–21.

22 Robert Seager II, "Ten Years Before Mahan: the Unofficial Case for the New Navy, 1880–1890," *Mississippi Valley Historical Review,* 40 (Dec., 1953):491–512; see esp. pp. 503–5.

23 Reprinted in Walter Millis, *American Military Thought* (New York, 1966), pp. 236–37. See also H. and M. Sprout, *Rise of American Naval Power,* pp. 210–11.

24 Adams to Charles M. Gaskell, April 28, 1894, in Worthington C. Ford, ed., *Letters of Henry Adams,* 2 vols. (Boston and New York, 1938), 2:47.

25 Eugene V. Smalley, "What Are Normal Times?" *Forum,* 23 (March, 1897):96–100.

26 See Richard Hofstadter, "Manifest Destiny and the Philippines," in *America in Crisis,* ed. Daniel Aaron (New York, 1952), pp. 173–200.

27 Arthur Krock, ed., *The Editorials of Henry Watterson* (New York, 1923), p. 269; Murat Halstead, "American Annexation and Armament," *Forum,* 24 (Sept., 1897):56–66; editor's introduction to Thomas B. Reed, "Empire Can Wait," *Illustrated American,* 22 (Dec. 4, 1897): 713.

Chapter 3: *Evolution of the New Imperialism*

1 Alfred Thayer Mahan, *The Problem of Asia* (Boston, 1900), p. 4.

2 W. J. Bryan, *Speeches of William Jennings Bryan,* 2 vols. (New York and London, 1913), 2:26.

3 Donald F. Warner, *The Idea of Continental Union; Agitation for the Annexation of Canada to the United States, 1849–1893* (Lexington, Ky., 1960), pp. 175–77, 234–35.

4 Ibid., pp. 96–97, 216.

5 Ibid., pp. 234–35; Robert Craig Brown, *Canada's National Policy, 1883–1900: A Study in Canadian-American Relations* (Princeton, N.J., 1964), p. 253; Charles M. Harvey, *The Republican National Convention, St. Louis, 1896* (St. Louis, 1896), p. 124.

6 New York *Tribune,* June 29, 1897.

7 Albert K. Weinberg, *Manifest Destiny* (Baltimore, 1935), pp. 65–68; *Cong. Record,* 53 Cong., 3 sess. (1895), 27:3084; George Frisbie Hoar, *Autobiography of Seventy Years,* 2 vols. (New York, 1903), 2:305–7, 310–11.

8 Charles Callan Tansill, *The Foreign Policy of Thomas Francis Bayard* (New York, 1940), pp. 455–56; George H. Bates, "Some Aspects of the Samoan Question," *Century,* 37 (April, 1889): 945–49.

9 John A. Garraty, *Henry Cabot Lodge, A Biography* (New York, 1953), p. 194; Oscar D. Lambert, *Stephen Benton Elkins* (Pittsburgh, 1955), pp. 239–40; August Carl Radke, "John Tyler Morgan, an Expansionist Senator, 1877–1907" (Ph.D. dissertation, University of Washington, 1953), pp. 241, 281–84; Morgan to William McKinley, March 23, 1898, William McKinley Papers, Library of Congress.

10 Whitelaw Reid, *Problems of Expansion, as Considered in Papers and Addresses* (New York, 1900), pp. 13–14; Reid to Sen. William E. Chandler, Jan. 22, 1900, printed in Royal Cortissoz, *The Life of Whitelaw Reid,* 2 vols. (London, 1921), 2:266; Andrew D. White, *Autobiography of Andrew Dickson White,* 2 vols. (New York, 1905), 2:162.

11 Garraty, *Henry Cabot Lodge,* p. 195; *Cong. Record,* 55 Cong., 3 sess. (1898), 32:20 (for Vest's resolution); Sen. William E. Chandler to Elihu Root, July 29, 1899, Elihu Root Papers, Library of Congress.

12 Bryan to W. J. Stone, June 30, 1900, William Jennings Bryan Papers, Library of Congress; Paolo E. Coletta, *William Jennings Bryan,* 3 vols. (Lincoln, Neb., 1964), 1:233; Chilton to Bryan, Dec. 31, 1898, Bryan Papers; Richard Olney, "Growth of Our Foreign Policy," *Atlantic Monthly,* 85 (March, 1900):289–301.

13 Andrew Carnegie, "Distant Possessions — the Parting of the Ways," *North American Review,* 167 (Aug., 1898):242–43; quotation from *Literary Digest,* 17 (Oct. 12, 1898):566; Hoar, *Autobiography,* 2:305–7; *Cong. Record,* 56 Cong., 2 sess. (1901), 34:3145; Thomas B. Reed, "Empire Can Wait," *Illustrated*

American, 22 (Dec. 4, 1897):713–14.

14 Frederic Bancroft, ed., *Speeches, Correspondence and Political Papers of Carl Schurz,* 6 vols. (New York and London, 1913), 5:196–97, 472–73.

15 "Who Will Get the Philippines?" reprinted in *Public Opinion,* 21 (Dec. 24, 1896):825.

16 Henry Cabot Lodge, "Our Blundering Foreign Policy," *Forum,* 19 (March, 1895):8–17; Garraty, *Henry Cabot Lodge,* pp. 184–85.

17 Cortissoz, *Life of Whitelaw Reid,* 2:214; Radke, "John Tyler Morgan," pp. 210–11, 319–29; John T. Morgan, "The Duty of Annexing Hawaii," *Forum,* 25 (March, 1898):11–16; Roosevelt to William Astor Chanler, Dec. 23, 1897, in E. E. Morison, ed., *The Letters of Theodore Roosevelt,* 8 vols. (Cambridge, Mass., 1951–54), 1:746; Henry Adams to Elizabeth Cameron, Dec. 4, 1898, in W. C. Ford, ed., *Letters of Henry Adams, 1892–1918,* 2 vols. (Boston and New York, 1938), 2:195.

18 Mahan, *Problem of Asia,* pp. 7–8.

19 John A. S. Grenville and George B. Young, *Politics, Strategy, and American Diplomacy* (New Haven, Conn., and London, 1966), pp. 272–78.

20 John A. S. Grenville, "American Naval Preparations for War with Spain, 1896–1898," *Journal of American Studies,* 2 (April, 1968):33–47. The quotation is from p. 43.

21 *Cong. Record,* 55 Cong., 2 sess. (1898), 31:3979–80; Claude G. Bowers, *Beveridge and the Progressive Era* (Cambridge, Mass., 1932), pp. 69–70; *Outlook,* 59 (May 7, 1898):2.

22 Quoted in *Public Opinion,* 24 (May 12, 1898):583–85; and *Literary Digest,* 16 (May 14, 1898):571–73.

23 Quoted ibid., 17 (July 2, 1898):2–4.

24 Thomas J. McCormick, *China Market: America's Quest for Informal Empire, 1893–1901* (Chicago, 1967), p. 211.

25 Garraty, *Henry Cabot Lodge,* pp. 197–98; Mahan to Lodge, July 27, 1898, printed in William E. Livezy, *Mahan on Sea Power* (Norman, Okla., 1947), pp. 182–83. See also Grenville and Young, *Politics, Strategy, and American Diplomacy,* pp. 292–94.

26 John T. Morgan, "What Shall We Do With the Conquered Islands?" *North American Review,* 166 (June, 1898):641–49; Morgan, "The Territorial Expansion of the United States," *Independent,* 50 (July 7, 1898):10–12.

27 *Cong. Record,* 57 Cong., 1 sess. (1902), 35:6089; Radke, "John Tyler Morgan," pp. 99, 307–10.

28 *Outlook,* 59 (May 14, 1898):112–13; (July 2, 1898):511–12; (August 6, 1898):813–15; 60 (Oct. 22, 1898):464–66; 61 (Jan. 7, 1899):10–12.

29 Margaret Leech, *In the Days of McKinley* (New York, 1959), pp. 209–12; U.S. War Department, *Correspondence Relating to the War with Spain,* 2 vols. (Washington, D.C., 1902), 2:635–49; Paolo E. Coletta, "McKinley, the Peace Negotiations and the Acquisition of the Philippines," *Pacific Historical Review,* 30 (Nov., 1961):343.

30 Lodge to Roosevelt, May 24, 1898, in Henry Cabot Lodge, ed., *Selections from the Correspondence of Theodore Roosevelt and Henry Cabot Lodge,* 2 vols. (New York and London, 1925), 1:299–300; William R. Day to John Hay, June 3, 1898, and June 14, 1898, both printed in Tyler Dennet, *John Hay* (New York, 1934), pp. 190–91.

31 William M. Laffan to Henry Cabot Lodge, July 14, 1898, quoted in Grenville and Young, *Politics, Strategy, and American Diplomacy,* pp. 285–86; H. Wayne Morgan, ed., *Making Peace With Spain: the Diary of Whitelaw Reid (September–December, 1898)* (Austin, Texas, 1965), pp. 30–31.

32 McKinley to Day, Oct. 25, 1898, in William McKinley Papers.

33 *Literary Digest,* 17 (Sept. 10, 1898):307–8.

34 See speech by Sen. John C. Spooner, *Cong. Record,* 55 Cong., 3 sess. (1899), 32:1376–88; Seth Low to William McKinley, Aug. 6, 1898, William McKinley Papers; Thomas J. Yount to John Hay, Dec. 5, 1898, in John Hay Papers, Library of Congress; John D. Long to unnamed correspondent, Nov. 1, 1898, printed in Lawrence Shaw Mayo, *America of Yesterday As Reflected in the Diary of John D. Long* (Boston, 1923). pp. 213–15; Theodore S. Woolsey, *America's Foreign Policy: Essays and Addresses* (New York, 1898), p. vi; Bancroft, *Speeches ... of Carl Schurz,* 6:80–87.

35 McKinley to William R. Day, Oct. 25, 1898, in William McKinley Papers; William McKinley, *Speeches and Addresses of William McKinley* (New York, 1900), p. 187.

36 Lionel M. Gelber, *The Rise of Anglo-American Friendship* (London, New York and Toronto, 1938), pp. 24, 27–30; McCormick, *China Market,* pp. 110–11; Thomas A. Bailey, "Dewey and the Germans at Manila Bay," *American Historical Review,*

45 (Oct., 1939):59–81.
37 McCormick, *China Market*, p. 111; Alfred L. P. Dennis, *Adventures in American Diplomacy, 1896–1906* (New York, 1928), pp. 94–98; Cecil Spring-Rice to John Hay, May 27, 1898, in John Hay Papers, Library of Congress; John Hay to William R. Day, July 28, 1898, in William McKinley Papers; Irving M. Scott to Charles A. Moore, Aug. 4, 1898, ibid.
38 See Reid, *Problems of Expansion*, pp. 11–12; Dean C. Worcester, "Knotty Problems of the Philippines," *Century*, n.s. 34 (Oct., 1898):873–79; Theodore Roosevelt, *The Works of Theodore Roosevelt*, ed. Hermann Hagedorn, 24 vols. (New York, 1923–26), 18:360–61.
39 *Literary Digest*, 17 (Aug. 27, 1898):241–42.
40 Mahan, *Problem of Asia*, pp. 8–9.

Chapter 4: *James Harrison Wilson*

1 For Wilson's own account of his Civil War career see James Harrison Wilson, *Under the Old Flag*, 2 vols. (New York, 1912). See also Fletcher Pratt, *Eleven Generals: Studies in American Command* (New York, 1949), pp. 217–32; William T. Sherman, *Memoirs*, 2 vols. (New York, 1875), 2:159–60; and Richard Taylor, *Destruction and Reconstruction* (New York, 1879), p. 220.
2 Wilson, *Under the Old Flag*, 2:389–400; E. H. Talbot and H. R. Hobart, *Biographical Directory of Railway Officials of America* (Chicago and New York, 1885), p. 267; George P. Baker, *The Formation of the New England Railroad System* (Cambridge, Mass., 1949), pp. 55–58; Alvin F. Harlow, *Steelways of New England* (New York, 1946), pp. 205–6; George W. Cullum, *Biographical Register of the Officers and Graduates of the United States Military Academy*, 4 vols. (Boston and New York, 1891), 2:740–42, and 4:117.
3 Ibid., 2:742 and 4:117; James Harrison Wilson, *China, Travels and Investigations in the Middle Kingdom*, 3rd ed. (New York, 1901), pp. xx–xxii; New York *Tribune*, April 27, 1884; J. H. Wilson obituary, Wilmington *Evening Journal*, Feb. 23, 1925.
4 This description is based upon the author's cumulative impressions, old photographs, and an article in the Wilmington *Every Evening*, May 24, 1929. The quotation is from Margaret Long, ed., *The Journal of John D. Long* (Rindge, N.H., 1956), p. 260.
5 Wilson, *Under the Old Flag*, 2:378–79.

6 Gary Pennanen, "American Interest in Commercial Union with Canada, 1854–1898," *Mid-America*, 47 (Jan., 1965):24–39; Robert C. Brown, *Canada's National Policy, 1883–1900* (Princeton, N.J., 1964), pp. 137–39.

7 "Remarks of General James H. Wilson in Joint Debate with Erastus Wiman, Esq., Before the Board of Trade and the Citizens of Wilmington, Delaware, on Our Relations with the Dominion of Canada, December 13, 1889" (Pamphlet, Wilmington, Del., 1890).

8 William J. Wilgus, *The Railway Interrelations of the United States and Canada* (New Haven, Conn., 1937), pp. 42, 156–57; James Morton Callahan, *American Foreign Policy in Canadian Relations* (New York, 1937), pp. 395–96; Chicago *Times*, 1888: April 23, and supplement, April 21.

9 New York *Tribune*, Feb. 11, 1888; New York *Sun*, 1888: Feb. 11, March 17.

10 See "Interesting to Shippers, Receivers, etc., etc., A Merchant's Reply and other matter in reference to General James H. Wilson's statement concerning Transportation in Bond over the Railways of the Dominion of Canada" (Pamphlet, Chicago, n.d.); and "The Canadian Railroad Question, Arguments and Facts submitted to a Committee of the United States Senate by E. W. Meddaugh and A. C. Raymond at a hearing in Detroit, Michigan, May 1, 1891" (Pamphlet, Detroit, 1891).

11 Wilson, *Under the Old Flag*, 2:466–67; Charles M. Harvey, *The Republican National Convention, St. Louis, 1896* (St. Louis, 1896), pp. 124, 140, 178; Joseph Benson Foraker, *Notes of a Busy Life*, 2 vols. (Cincinnati, 1916), 2:60.

12 Percy H. Kent, *Railway Enterprise in China* (London, 1907), pp. 22–27; Charles C. Tansill, *The Foreign Policy of Thomas F. Bayard* (New York, 1940), pp. 422–23; Charles Denby to Thomas F. Bayard, July 13, 1886, Diplomatic Despatches, Vol. 78, Division of State Dept. Archives, National Archives.

13 Wilson, *China*, pp. xx–xxiii, 91–100.

14 Ssu-yu Teng and John K. Fairbank, *China's Response to the West* (Cambridge, Mass., 1954), pp. 87, 110–11, 116; U.S. State Department, *Papers Relating to the Foreign Relations of the United States, 1885* (Washington, D.C., 1886), pp. 180–81; Tyler Dennett, *Americans in Eastern Asia* (New York, 1922), pp. 597–98; Tansill, *Foreign Policy of Bayard*, p. 431.

15 Wilson, *China*, pp. 140–41; Tansill, *Foreign Policy of Bayard*, pp. 424–25.

16 Denby to Bayard, July 13, 1886, and June 3, 1887, Diplomatic Despatches, Vol. 78, National Archives; Denby to Bayard, April 5, 1887, U.S. State Department, *Papers Relating to the Foreign Relations of the United States, 1888* (Washington, D.C., 1889), p. 208; Wilson, *China*, pp. 276–77.

17 McCook obituary, New York *Times*, Sept. 18, 1911. See also *Who Was Who In America*, Vol. I,*1897–1942* (Chicago, 1966): 803.

18 A. W. Bash to J. H. Wilson, Oct. 4, 1895, in James Harrison Wilson Papers, Library of Congress; a draft charter for "The American Syndicate," dated Oct., 1896, is ibid., which contains correspondence about the project. A good account of this venture can be found in Thomas J. McCormick, *China Market* (Chicago, 1967), pp. 78–83.

19 McCook to Wilson, Nov. 11 and Nov. 17, 1896, McCook to Secretary of State John Sherman, March 20, 1897, McCook to W. W. Rockhill, May 28, 1897, all in James H. Wilson Papers; McCormick, *China Market*, pp. 80–82.

20 McCook to Wilson, Feb. 26, 1897, and W. W. Rockhill to Wilson, May 12, 1897, James H. Wilson Papers; McCormick, *China Market*, pp. 82–83; Harold Bell Hancock, "The Political Career of John Edward Addicks in Delaware" (Typescript, Federal Writers' Project, 1939, in the possession of the Library of the University of Delaware), pp. 44, 47, 81–86.

21 McCormick, *China Market*, pp. 82–83.

22 James H. Wilson, "America's Interest in China," *North American Review*, 116 (Feb., 1898):129–41.

23 Wilson, *Under the Old Flag*, 2:416–59.

24 Ibid., pp. 470–73; Hermann Hagedorn, *Leonard Wood*, 2 vols. (New York, 1931), 1:144; Henry Cabot Lodge to James H. Wilson, May 4, May 6, June 2, and Dec. 1, 1898, James H. Wilson Papers.

25 Emeterio S. Santovenia and Joaquín Llaverías, eds., *Actas de las Asambleas de Representantes y del Consejo de Gobierno Durante la Guerra de Independencia*, 5 vols. (Havana, 1932), 3:68–70, 76–77, 115–16.

26 Ibid., 4:61–65; New York *Tribune*, Aug. 20, 1904; Herbert G. Squiers to Secretary of State John Hay, Sept. 9, 1904 (and attached memorandum), Despatches from U.S. Ministers to Cuba, 1902–1906, National Archives.

27 Wilson, *Under the Old Flag*, 2:482–89; David F. Healy, *The*

United States in Cuba, 1898–1902 (Madison, Wis., 1963), pp. 81–91.

28 Wilson to Joseph B. Foraker, May 12, 1899, James H. Wilson Papers; Hagedorn, *Leonard Wood*, 1:421; Wilson to Theodore Roosevelt, July 5, 1899, Theodore Roosevelt Papers, Library of Congress; Philip C. Jessup, *Elihu Root*, 2 vols. (New York, 1938), 1:310–11.

29 Joseph B. Foraker to Wilson, March 5, 1899, and William E. Frye to Wilson, March 20, 1899, James H. Wilson Papers; Theodore Roosevelt to Leonard Wood, March 8, 1899; and Roosevelt to Wilson, July 25 and Aug. 5, 1899, Theodore Roosevelt Papers.

30 Roosevelt to Lodge, July 21, 1899, and Wilson to Roosevelt, Sept. 8, 1899, ibid.; Wilson to Lodge, Nov. 1, 1899, and Wilson to Root, Nov. 3, 1899, James H. Wilson Papers. See also "Special Report of Brigadier General James H. Wilson, U.S.V.," in U.S. War Department, *Civil Report of Major General John R. Brooke, U.S. Army, Military Governor, Island of Cuba* (Washington, D.C., 1900), pp. 329–42.

31 See Healy, *The United States in Cuba*, pp. 164, 193–94.

32 McCook to McKinley, May 26, 1898, William McKinley Papers, Library of Congress.

33 McCook to McKinley, Nov. 26, 1898, ibid.

34 Roosevelt to Wilson, July 12, 1899, in E. E. Morison, ed., *The Letters of Theodore Roosevelt*, 8 vols. (Cambridge, Mass., 1951–54), 2:1032; New York *Times*, Dec. 20, 1898; Wilson, *Under the Old Flag*, 2:467–70.

35 New York *Times*, Dec. 21, 1898; Roosevelt to Wilson, July 12, 1899, in Morison, ed., *Letters*, 2:1032.

36 New York *Tribune*, April 29, 1900; Wilson, *Under the Old Flag*, 2:518–36.

37 "Remarks of General James H. Wilson in Joint Debate with Erastus Wiman," p. 13; Wilson, *China*, pp. 403–4.

38 "Remarks of General James H. Wilson in Joint Debate with Erastus Wiman," p. 13; "An Address on Our Trade Relations with the Tropics delivered by General James H. Wilson at Boston, Massachusetts, November 9, 1901" (Pamphlet, Boston, 1901), p. 18.

39 "Remarks of General James H. Wilson in Joint Debate with Erastus Wiman," p. 27.

40 Carl A. Bodelson, *Studies in Mid-Victorian Imperialism* (Copenhagen, 1924), pp. 52–57; *Dictionary of National Biography*,

Supplement, 1901–1911 (London, 1912), pp. 330–39. The Manchester school was an influential group of Englishmen who opposed government intervention in economic matters and looked to free trade for national prosperity and the easing of international tensions. They led the drive for free trade in England during the 1840's, but their following declined after 1860.

41 Goldwin Smith, *Canada and the Canadian Question* (London, New York and Toronto, 1891), pp. 1–3.

42 Ibid., pp. 261, 278–79.

43 Wilson, *Under the Old Flag,* 2:462–63.

44 See ibid., p. 501; New York *Tribune,* Jan. 14, 1900; Wilson to Goldwin Smith, March 3, 1899, James H. Wilson Papers; and "Special Report of General James H. Wilson," in U.S. War Dept., *Civil Report of Major General John R. Brooke,* p. 337.

45 "An Address on Our Trade Relations with the Tropics," p. 17.

46 "Our Relations with Cuba, An Address Delivered by General James H. Wilson at the request of the Commercial Club of Chicago at the Auditorium Hotel on the evening of October 25, 1902" (Pamphlet, Wilmington, Del., 1902), pp. 3–4.

47 Ibid., p. 4.

48 "An Address on Our Trade Relations with the Tropics," pp. 4–7.

49 J. Laurence Laughlin and H. Parker Willis, *Reciprocity* (New York, 1903), pp. 9–11, 133–38.

50 William L. Strauss, *Joseph Chamberlain and the Theory of Imperialism* (Washington, D.C., 1942), pp. 102–9. For a contemporary American discussion, see Michael G. Mulhall, "Thirty Years of American Trade," *North American Review,* 165 (Nov., 1897):572–81.

51 "An Address on Our Trade Relations with the Tropics," p. 21.

52 Ibid., pp. 6–7.

53 "Our Relations with Cuba," pp. 30–31.

Chapter 5: *The Tone of Society*

1 *Literary Digest,* 17 (Sept. 17, 1898):337.

2 Ibid., p. 336; ibid. (July 9, 1898):35–36; L. S. Rowe, "Influence of the War on Our Public Life," *Forum,* 27 (March, 1899):52–60; Howard H. Quint, "American Socialists and the Spanish-American War," *American Quarterly,* 10 (1958):131–41.

3 Philip C. Jessup, *Elihu Root,* 2 vols. (New York, 1938), 1:335.
4 Albert J. Beveridge, *The Meaning of the Times and Other Speeches* (Indianapolis, Ind., 1908), pp. 24–25. See also John G. Sproat, *"The Best Men": Liberal Reformers in the Gilded Age* (New York, 1968), pp. 148–53; and Richard Hofstadter, *The Age of Reform* (New York, 1955), pp. 631–40.
5 Brooks Adams, *The Law of Civilization and Decay* (New York and London, 1896). See especially pp. v–xi, and 362.
6 Stephen B. Luce, "The Benefits of War," *North American Review,* 153 (Dec., 1891):672–83.
7 Alfred Thayer Mahan, *The Interest of the United States in Sea Power* (Boston, 1897), pp. 120–22; Andrew D. White, *Autobiography of Andrew Dickson White,* 2 vols. (New York, 1905), 2:346–47. See also Peter Daggett Karsten, "The Naval Aristocracy: U.S. Naval Officers from the 1840's to the 1890's: Mahan's Messmates" (Ph.D. dissertation, University of Wisconsin, 1968), pp. 271–72, 333, 422, for naval officers' views of war.
8 Quoted in Daniel Levine, *Varieties of Reform Thought* (Madison, Wis., 1964), pp. 71–72.
9 William James, *Essays on Faith and Morals* (New York, London, and Toronto, 1947), pp. 316–28. "The Moral Equivalent of War" was originally published as a pamphlet by the Association of International Conciliation, and was also republished in 1910 by two different magazines, *McClure's* and *Popular Science Monthly.*
10 Sir Charles Dilke, *Greater Britain,* 2 vols. (London, 1869), 2:394–95; James Anthony Froude, *Oceana, or England and Her Colonies* (New York, 1886), pp. 355–56.
11 James Bryce, *The American Commonwealth,* 3rd ed., 2 vols. (New York and London, 1908), 2:69–71. See also pp. 521–34.
12 Geoffrey Seed, "British Views of American Policy in the Philippines Reflected in Journals of Opinion, 1898–1907," *Journal of American Studies,* 2 (April, 1968):58.
13 Alfred Thayer Mahan, *Lessons of the War With Spain, and Other Articles* (Boston, 1899), pp. 292–93; Mahan, *Retrospect and Prospect* (Boston, 1902), p. 17.
14 Julian Hawthorne, "A Side-Issue of Expansion," *Forum,* 27 June, 1899):441–44.
15 Edwin Lawrence Godkin, *Problems of Modern Democracy* (New York, 1896), pp. 180–98. See also Peter Henry King, "The White Man's Burden" (Ph.D. dissertation, University of Cali-

fornia at Los Angeles, 1958), pp. 126–31.

16 E. L. Godkin, "The Conditions of Good Colonial Government," *Forum*, 27 (April, 1899):190–203; Rollo Ogden, *Life and Letters of Edwin Lawrence Godkin*, 2 vols. (New York, 1907), 2:218.

17 Franklin Henry Giddings, *Democracy and Empire* (New York and London, 1900), pp. 273–75.

18 Quoted in John A. Garraty, *Henry Cabot Lodge* (New York, 1953), pp. 197, 206.

19 Brooks Adams, *America's Economic Supremacy* (New York, 1900), p. 99.

Chapter 6: *Theodore Roosevelt and the Sturdy Virtues*

1 For Dewey's attack at Manila see John A. S. Grenville and George B. Young, *Politics, Strategy, and American Diplomacy* (New Haven, Conn., and London, 1967), pp. 272–78; John A. S. Grenville, "American Naval Preparations for War With Spain, 1896–1898," *Journal of American Studies*, 2 (April 1968):33–47; and Roosevelt to Lodge, Sept. 26, 1898, in E. E. Morison, ed., *The Letters of Theodore Roosevelt*, 8 vols. (Cambridge, Mass., 1951–54), 2:880.

2 Roosevelt to Henry Cabot Lodge, Oct. 27, 1894, in Morison, ed., *Letters*, 1:318; Theodore Roosevelt, *The Works of Theodore Roosevelt*, ed. Hermann Hagedorn, 24 vols. (New York, 1923–26), 16:337–50.

3 Roosevelt to A. T. Mahan, May 3, 1897, in Morison, *Letters*, 1:607; Roosevelt to Lodge, Sept. 21, 1897, in Henry Cabot Lodge, *Selections from the Correspondence of Theodore Roosevelt and Henry Cabot Lodge, 1884–1918*, 2 vols. (New York and London, 1925), 1:278–79.

4 Roosevelt to Lodge, June 12, 1898, in Morison, ed., *Letters*, 2:842; to William Astor Chanler, Dec. 23, 1897, ibid., 1:746; Roosevelt, *Works*, 16:499–500, and 18:364–65.

5 Roosevelt to John D. Long, Sept. 30, 1897, in Morison, ed., *Letters*, 1:695; Roosevelt, *Works*, 15:252.

6 Grenville and Young, *Politics, Strategy, and American Diplomacy*, pp. 305–7. See also Roosevelt to Lodge, March 27, 1901, in Morison, ed., *Letters*, 3:31–32.

7 Roosevelt to Frederic Rene Coudert, July 3, 1901, ibid., 3:105; to Cecil Arthur Spring-Rice, Aug. 11, 1899, ibid., 2:1052; to same, Dec. 2, 1899, ibid., 2:1104.

8 Roosevelt, *Works,* 14:127–28.
9 Roosevelt to Anna Roosevelt Cowles, Dec. 17, 1899, in Morison, ed., *Letters,* 2:1112–13; to Spring-Rice, May 29, 1897, ibid., 1:620–21; to Granville Stanley Hall, Nov. 29, 1899, ibid., 2:1100.
10 Roosevelt, *Works,* 14:134–42.
11 Ibid., 15:10; Roosevelt to Spring-Rice, July 3, 1901, in Morison, ed., *Letters,* 3:107.
12 Roosevelt to George Otto Trevelyan, Oct. 1, 1911, ibid., 7:370.
13 Roosevelt to Edward Sanford Martin, Nov. 26, 1900, ibid., 2:1443; Roosevelt, *Works,* 14:482, 15:267.
14 Ibid., pp. 5–7.
15 Theodore Roosevelt and Henry Cabot Lodge, *Hero Tales from American History* (New York, 1895), p. ix; Walter E. Houghton, *The Victorian Frame of Mind, 1830–1870* (New Haven, Conn., and London, 1957), pp. 305, 313, 317–18.
16 Roosevelt, *Works,* 15:243, 257–58.
17 Roosevelt to Lodge, Aug. 10 and Aug. 20, 1886, in Morison, ed., *Letters,* 1:108–9; to Spring-Rice, April 14, 1889, ibid., p. 157; to Lodge, Dec. 27, 1895, ibid., pp. 503–4; to Anna Roosevelt Cowles, March 9, 1896, ibid., p. 521; Edward Sanford Martin, *The Life of Joseph Hodges Choate,* 2 vols. (New York, 1921), 2:34.
18 Roosevelt to Lodge, April 29, 1896, in Morison, ed., *Letters,* 1:535–36; to Robert Bacon, April 5, 1898, ibid., 2:811; to William Wert Kimball, Nov. 19, 1897, ibid., 1:717; Roosevelt, *Works,* 15:236.
19 Ibid., pp. 539–43.
20 Roosevelt to Lodge, July 19, 1898, in Lodge, *Selections,* 1:328; to Winthrop Chanler, March 23, 1899, in Morison, ed., *Letters,* 2:968–69; to Lodge, Dec. 6, 1898, ibid., p. 892.
21 Roosevelt to Maria Longworth Storer, Oct. 28, 1899, ibid., p. 1089; Roosevelt, *Works,* 15:240, 256, 563–64.
22 Roosevelt to Theodore E. Burton, Feb. 23, 1904, in Morison, ed., *Letters,* 4:737; to Edward Sanford Martin, Nov. 26, 1900, ibid., 2:1443.
23 Roosevelt to George F. Becker, Sept. 6, 1899, ibid., p. 1068.
24 Ibid.; Roosevelt, *Works,* 16:474.
25 Roosevelt to Mahan, Dec. 11, 1897, in Morison, ed., *Letters,* 1:741; Roosevelt, *Works,* 15:273, 16:499–500.
26 Roosevelt to Robert J. Thompson, April 30, 1900, in Morison, ed., *Letters,* 2:1274; to David B. Schneder, June 19, 1905, ibid., 4:1240; Roosevelt, *Works,* 14:195–203, 245, 15:291, 18:465.

27 Roosevelt to Winfred Thaxter Denison, Aug. 3, 1914, in Morison, ed., *Letters*, 7:792–93; Roosevelt, *Works*, 18:341, 346–47, 15:287.

28 Roosevelt to Arthur Hamilton Lee, Nov. 25, 1898, in Morison, ed., *Letters*, 2:890; to Spring-Rice, May 29 and Aug. 13, 1897, ibid., 1:620–21, 645; to Henry White, March 30, 1896, ibid., p. 523.

29 McCormick, *China Market*, n., p. 211; Theodore Roosevelt, "General Leonard Wood, A Model American Military Administrator," *Outlook*, 61 (Jan. 7, 1899):19, 22; Roosevelt, *Works*, 16:476.

30 Roosevelt to Adelbert Moot, Feb. 13, 1900, in Morison, ed., *Letters*, 2:1183; to Whitelaw Reid, Sept. 3, 1908, ibid., 6:1206; to Lyman Abbott, July 15, 1901, ibid., 3:119; to William Howard Taft, Aug. 21, 1907, copy in Elihu Root Papers, Library of Congress.

31 Roosevelt to Spring-Rice, Aug. 11, 1899, in Morison, ed., *Letters*, 2:1053.

32 Roosevelt to Edward Grey, Nov. 15, 1912, ibid., 7:648–49.

Chapter 7: *Civilization, Barbarism, and Christianity*

1 "Expansion; One Step At A Time," *Outlook*, 60 (Dec. 24, 1898): 996–97.

2 "Santiago," ibid., 59 (July 9, 1898):610.

3 David J. Hill, "The War and the Extension of Civilization," *Forum*, 26 (Feb., 1899):650–55; "Views of Prominent Men on the Policy of 'Imperialism'," *Literary Digest*, 17 (July 2, 1898):4; Cortlandt Parker to McKinley, Feb. 17, 1899, William McKinley Papers, Library of Congress; Albert Bushnell Hart, *Foundations of American Foreign Policy* (New York and London, 1901), p. 52.

4 William McKinley, *Speeches and Addresses of William McKinley* (New York, 1900), pp. 114, 134, 142, 153, 188.

5 Alfred T. Mahan, *The Interest of America in Sea Power* (Boston, 1897), pp. 118–19, 243–44, 267, 31–32. (This book is a collection of eight articles by Mahan which were originally published from 1890 through 1897.)

6 Alfred T. Mahan, *Lessons of the War With Spain* (Boston, 1899), p. 250; Mahan, *The Problem of Asia* (Boston, 1900), pp. 74, 87–88, 116. For a different view of Mahan see Peter Daggett

Karsten, "The Naval Aristocracy: U.S. Naval Officers from the 1840's to the 1890's: Mahan's Messmates" (Ph.D. dissertation, University of Wisconsin, 1968), pp. 405–447.

7 Josiah Strong, *Our Country,* ed. Jurgen Herbst (Cambridge, Mass., 1963), pp. 13–14, 17–18; Paul A. Varg, *Missionaries, Chinese, and Diplomats* (Princeton, N.J., 1958), p. 3.

8 Quoted in Louis A. Coolidge, *An Old-Fashioned Senator, Orville H. Platt* (New York, 1910), pp. 287, 291–93.

9 James Anthony Froude, *The English in the West Indies, or the Bow of Ulysses* (London, 1888), p. 182.

10 Benjamin Kidd, *The Control of the Tropics* (New York and London, 1898), pp. 3–5, 41, 50–54.

11 Ibid., pp. 57–60, 83–86; Benjamin Kidd, "The United States and the Control of the Tropics," *Atlantic Monthly,* 82 (Dec., 1898): 721–27.

12 See *Literary Digest,* 17 (Oct. 29, 1898):514–15; Abram S. Hewitt to McKinley, Sept. 12, 1898, in William McKinley Papers; Truxtun Beale, "The White Race and the Tropics," *Forum,* 27 (July, 1899):534–36; William Elliott Griffis, "The Anglo-Saxon in the Tropics," *Outlook,* 60 (Dec. 10, 1898):902–7; John R. Proctor, "Isolation or Imperialism?" *Forum,* 26 (Sept., 1898):22; *Literary Digest,* 17 (July 9, 1898):34.

13 "The Praise of Wrath," *Congregationalist,* 83 (July 21, 1898): 70; "Face to Face with Our Destiny," *Christian Herald,* 21 (May 25, 1898):448.

14 *Public Opinion,* 23 (Oct. 28, 1897):561; Varg, *Missionaries, Chinese, and Diplomats,* pp. 52, 58–62.

15 John R. Mott, *Strategic Points in the World's Conquest* (New York and Chicago, 1897), pp. 95, 104–6, 152–57, 166–68, 208–9, 212–13.

16 Varg, *Missionaries, Chinese, and Diplomats,* pp. 70–76; Robert E. Speer, *Missions and Modern History,* 2 vols. (New York and London, 1904), 2:667–69, 691–92.

17 The Reverend Francis E. Clark, D.D., "Do Foreign Missions Pay?" *North American Review,* 166 (March, 1898):268–80; Margherita Arlina Hamm, "The Secular Value of Foreign Missions," *Independent,* 52 (April 26, 1900):1000–3; Charles Denby, "The Influence of Mission Work on Commerce," *Independent,* 53 (Dec. 12, 1901):2960–62; Whitelaw Reid to John Hay, Sept. 18, 1900, in Whitelaw Reid Papers, Library of Congress.

18 See, for example, the remarks of the Reverend A. B. Leonard,

D.D., as reported in *Literary Digest*, 17 (Dec. 10, 1898):695; and the Reverend Judson Smith, "The Awakening of China," *North American Review*, 168 (Feb., 1899):229–39.

19 See Frank T. Reuter, *Catholic Influence on American Colonial Policies, 1898–1904* (Austin, Texas, and London, 1967), pp. 3–35.

20 John T. Farrell, "Archbishop Ireland and Manifest Destiny," *Catholic Historical Review*, 33 (Oct., 1947):269–301.

21 "Scenes in Our New Colonial Possessions in the Philippines," *Christian Herald*, 21 (May 18, 1898):431; *Literary Digest*, 17 (Sept. 3, 1898):290; the Reverend Randolph H. McKim, D.D., "Religious Reconstruction in Our New Possessions," *Outlook*, 63 (Oct. 28, 1899):504–6.

22 Reuter, *Catholic Influence on American Colonial Policies*, pp. 18–19; *Literary Digest*, 18 (June 17, 1899):706; Archbishop John Ireland, "The Religious Conditions in Our New Island Territory," *Outlook*, 62 (Aug. 26, 1899):933–34.

23 *Literary Digest*, 17 (Oct. 29, 1898):525–26.

24 Ibid., 20 (Feb. 10, 1900):188.

25 New York *Evening Post*, Aug. 19, 1898.

26 *Literary Digest*, 18 (April 22, 1899):447.

Chapter 8: *Elihu Root*

1 Robert Bacon and James Brown Scott, eds., *Addresses on Government and Citizenship by Elihu Root* (Cambridge, Mass., 1916), pp. 503–4.

2 Richard W. Leopold, *Elihu Root and the Conservative Tradition* (Boston, 1954), pp. 5–6, 12–19, 47; Philip C. Jessup, *Elihu Root*, 2 vols. (New York, 1938), 1:136–37, 164–65, 191–200; Margaret Leech, *In the Days of McKinley* (New York, 1959), pp. 379–80.

3 Jessup, *Elihu Root*, 1:196.

4 Root to Cornelius N. Bliss, April 2, 1898, copy in Elihu Root Papers, Library of Congress.

5 Jessup, *Elihu Root*, 1:329, 223.

6 See Leech, *In the Days of McKinley*, pp. 316–22, 366–69; and Jessup, *Elihu Root*, 1:329–71.

7 Robert Bacon and James Brown Scott, eds., *The Military and Colonial Policy of the United States; Addresses and Reports by Elihu Root* (Cambridge, Mass., 1916), pp. 9–10.

8 Ibid., pp. 42–43; Robert Bacon and James Brown Scott, eds., *Miscellaneous Addresses by Elihu Root* (Cambridge, Mass., 1917), p. 220.

9 Bacon and Scott, *Military and Colonial Policy*, pp. 164–65.

10 Root to Paul Dana, Jan. 16, 1900, copy in Elihu Root Papers; Bacon and Scott, *Military and Colonial Policy*, p. 11.

11 See Root to William C. Whitney, May 31, 1900; to William McKinley, Aug. 18, 1899; and to Leonard Wood, Jan. 19, 1901, and May 9, 1900; copies in Elihu Root Papers.

12 Bacon and Scott, *Military and Colonial Policy*, pp. 162–63.

13 Leopold, *Elihu Root and the Conservative Tradition*, pp. 26–28; Bacon and Scott, *Military and Colonial Policy*, p. 103; Jessup, *Elihu Root*, 1:378–79.

14 Bacon and Scott, *Military and Colonial Policy*, pp. 11–12.

15 See John R. Seeley, *The Expansion of England* (Boston, 1920), pp. 88–89.

16 Quoted in James L. Garvin, *The Life of Joseph Chamberlain*, 3 vols. (London, 1932–34), 3:281.

17 See Roland N. Stromberg, *Collective Security and American Foreign Policy* (New York, 1963), pp. 5–6

18 Theodore Roosevelt, *The Works of Theodore Roosevelt*, ed. Hermann Hagedorn, 24 vols. (New York, 1923–26), 15:285–86; John Fiske, *American Political Ideas* (New York, 1885), p. 146.

19 John Bassett Moore, "The Progress of International Law," in a special supplement to the New York *Evening Post*, Jan. 12, 1901.

20 From "Report of the [Cuban] Committee Appointed to Confer with the Government of the United States, Giving an Account of the Results of Its Labors," copy in Elihu Root Papers.

21 "Remarks of Elihu Root at Union League Club, Jan. 11, 1900," copy in Elihu Root Papers; "Report of the [Cuban] Committee . . . "; Bacon and Scott, *Military and Colonial Policy*, p. 100.

22 *Works of Theodore Roosevelt*, 17:299; Jessup, *Elihu Root*, 1:471.

23 See *Papers Relating to the Foreign Relations of the United States, 1907*, 2 vols. (Washington, D.C.,1910), 2:667–68, 673, 691–92, 697–700.

24 Robert Bacon and James Brown Scott, eds., *Men and Policies: Addresses, etc., by Elihu Root* (Cambridge, Mass., 1925), pp. 307–8.

25 Leopold, *Elihu Root and the Conservative Tradition*, pp. 57–58; Jessup, *Elihu Root*, 2:308.

26 Quoted ibid., p. 75

27 Robert Bacon and James Brown Scott, eds., *Latin America and the United States: Addresses by Elihu Root* (Cambridge, Mass., 1917), p. 270
28 See ibid., pp. 245–67.
29 Quoted in Jessup, *Elihu Root*, 2:375.

Chapter 9: *Commercial Domination*

1 Thomas J. McCormick, *China Market* (Chicago, 1967), pp. 27–28, 34.
2 Charles R. Flint, "Our Export Trade," *Forum*, 23 (May, 1897): 290–97.
3 Albert K. Steigerwalt, *The National Association of Manufacturers, 1895–1914* (Ann Arbor, Mich., 1964), pp. 17–19, 43–51, 56.
4 Stephen M. White, "Our Inadequate Consular Service," *Forum*, 25 (July, 1898):546–47. See also Walter LaFeber, *The New Empire: An Interpretation of American Expansion, 1860–1898* (Ithaca, New York, 1963), pp. 176–85.
5 *Literary Digest*, 17 (Sept. 3, 1898):273, and 17 (Dec. 10, 1898): 685–86; McCormick, *China Market*, pp. 40–51.
6 William Elliot Griffis, "The Pacific Ocean and Our Future There," *Outlook*, 61 (Jan. 14, 1899):111; Whitelaw Reid, *Problems of Expansion* (New York, 1900), pp. 41–42.
7 See remarks of John Foord in "The Commercial Relations of the United States with the Far East," in *The Foreign Policy of the United States, Political and Commercial* (American Academy of Political and Social Science, Philadelphia, 1899), p. 144. (This volume is a compilation of the "Addresses and Discussion" at the Academy's meeting of April 7–8, 1899.)
8 *Cong. Record*, 58 Cong., 1 sess. (1903), 37:263.
9 See Charles S. Campbell, *Special Business Interests and the Open Door Policy* (New Haven, 1951), p. 11.
10 Robert T. Hill in "Commercial Relations with the Far East," *Foreign Policy of the U.S.*, p. 134; John Foord, ibid., p. 151; Reid, *Problems of Expansion*, p. 41.
11 *Literary Digest*, 18 (March 4, 1899):242.
12 Worthington Chauncey Ford in "Commercial Relations with the Far East," *Foreign Policy of the U.S.*, pp. 107–130. Paul A. Varg, "The Myth of the China Market, 1890–1914," *American Historical Review*, 73 (Feb., 1968):742–58, analyzes the falla-

cies of the China myth in terms often remarkably similar to Ford's.

13 Robert T. Hill in "Commercial Relations with the Far East," *Foreign Policy of the U.S.*, p. 134; John Foord, ibid., p. 151; Reid,

14 John Foord, ibid., pp. 144–53; E. R. Johnson, ibid., pp. 158–60.

15 Clarence Cary, "China, and Chinese Railway Concessions," *Forum*, 24 (Jan., 1898):591–605; and Clarence Cary, "China's Complications and American Trade," ibid., 25 (March, 1898): 35–45.

16 Worthington Chauncey Ford in "Commercial Relations with the Far East," *Foreign Policy of the U.S.*, p. 111; Henry Cabot Lodge to Theodore Roosevelt, May 21, 1903, in Lodge, ed., *Selections from the Correspondence of Theodore Roosevelt and Henry Cabot Lodge*, 2 vols. (New York and London, 1925), 2:15; Campbell, *Special Business Interests*, pp. 19–20.

17 August C. Radke, "John Tyler Morgan, An Expansionist Senator, 1877–1907" (Ph.D. dissertation, University of Washington, 1953), pp. 145–46; Shelby M. Cullom, *Fifty Years of Public Service* (Chicago, 1911), pp. 348–51.

18 Radke, "John Tyler Morgan," pp. 148–49, 202–11; David M. Pletcher, *The Awkward Years* (Columbia, Mo., 1962), pp. 125, 177, 185, 326; John T. Morgan, "The Duty of Annexing Hawaii," *Forum*, 25 (March, 1898):11–16.

19 Radke, "John Tyler Morgan," pp. 328–30.

20 John T. Morgan, "What Shall We Do With the Conquered Islands?" *North American Review*, 166 (June, 1898):649; and John T. Morgan, "The Territorial Expansion of the United States," *Independent*, 50 (July 7, 1898):10.

21 Morgan to Bryan, April 25, 1900, quoted in Radke, "John Tyler Morgan," pp. 281–83.

22 See Pletcher, *Awkward Years*, p. 26.

23 Quoted in Claude G. Bowers, *Beveridge and the Progressive Era* (Cambridge, Mass., 1932), p. 69.

24 W. A. Peffer, "A Republic in the Philippines," *North American Review*, 168 (March, 1899):311.

25 Robert Seager II, "Ten Years Before Mahan: the Unofficial Case for the New Navy, 1880-1890," *Mississippi Valley Historical Review*, 40 (Dec., 1953):491–512; Alfred Thayer Mahan, "The United States Looking Outward," *Atlantic Monthly* (Dec., 1890), reprinted in *The Interest of America In Sea Power* (Boston, 1897), pp. 3–30.

26 Truxtun Beale, "Strategical Value of the Philippines," *North American Review*, 166 (June, 1898):759–60; Frank A. Vanderlip, "Facts About the Philippines," *Century*, n.s. 34 (Aug., 1898):555–56.

27 Bowers, *Beveridge*, p. 119; John A. Garraty, *Henry Cabot Lodge* (New York, 1953), p. 204; Foord, "Commercial Relations with the Far East," *Foreign Policy of the U.S.*, p. 148.

28 Adams to John Hay, Nov. 2, 1901, in W. C. Ford, ed., *Letters of Henry Adams*, 2 vols. (Boston and New York, 1938), 2:358.

29 Louis A. Coolidge, *An Old-Fashioned Senator, Orville H. Platt* (New York, 1910), p 286.

30 David J. Rothman, *Politics and Power: the United States Senate, 1869–1901* (Cambridge, Mass., 1966), pp. 48–50, 58; Nathaniel Wright Stephenson, *Nelson W. Aldrich, A Leader in American Politics* (New York, 1930), p. 161.

31 *Cong. Record*, 55 Cong., 3 sess. (1899), 32:1385 (quotation); Dorothy Ganfield Fowler, *John Coit Spooner, Defender of Presidents* (New York, 1961), pp. 233–37.

32 Reid, *Problems of Expansion*, p. 42; Bowers, *Beveridge*, p. 119.

33 *Literary Digest*, 17 (Dec. 10, 1898):686, and 15 (Dec. 11, 1897):964

34 Garraty, *Lodge*, p. 57; Lodge to Theodore Roosevelt, March 30, 1901, in Lodge, *Selections from the Correspondence of Theodore Roosevelt and Henry Cabot Lodge*, 1:487.

35 John R. Proctor, "Hawaii and the Changing Front of the World," *Forum*, 24 (Sept., 1897):34–46; John R. Proctor, "Isolation or Imperialism?" ibid., 26 (Sept., 1898):14–26.

36 Brooks Adams, "Reciprocity or the Alternative," *Atlantic Monthly*, 88 (Aug., 1901):145; Adams, *America's Economic Supremacy* (New York, 1900), pp. 11–12, 19.

37 Ibid., pp. 10–11, 24–25 (quotation on p. 24); Adams, *The New Empire* (New York, 1902), p. 209.

Chapter 10: *Charles Denby*

1 The physical description is based on old photographs. For a character sketch see Dean C. Worcester, *The Philippines Past and Present*, 2 vols. (New York, 1914), 1:311, 326.

2 Charles Denby, *China and Her People*, 2 vols. (Boston, 1906), 1:ix–xvi; Denby to Thomas F. Bayard, July 13, 1886, China Despatches, Vol. 78, Division of State Department Archives,

National Archives; *Dictionary of American Biography*, eds. Allen Johnson and Dumas Malone (New York, 1930), 5:233–34.

3 Charles C. Tansill, *The Foreign Policy of Thomas F. Bayard* (New York, 1940), pp. 422–23; *Dictionary of American Biography*, 5:233–34.

4 Bayard to James H. Wilson, May 16, 1885, quoted in John William Cassey, "The Mission of Charles Denby and International Rivalries in the Far East, 1885–1898" (Ph.D. dissertation, University of Southern California, 1959), p. 202; Wilson to Bayard, Aug. 29, 1885, quoted in Tansill, *Foreign Policy of Thomas F. Bayard*, p. 423. See also Denby to Bayard, July 13, 1886, China Despatches, Vol. 78, National Archives.

5 Charles Denby, "The Doctrine of Intervention," *Forum*, 26 (Dec., 1898):385–87; Denby interview, *Literary Digest*, 16 (Jan. 1, 1898):4.

6 Denby to Bayard, July 13, 1886, China Despatches, Vol. 78, National Archives; Denby to Bayard, Oct. 10, 1885, quoted in Tansill, *Foreign Policy of Thomas F. Bayard*, p. 424.

7 Cassey, "Mission of Charles Denby," p. 205; Tansill, *Foreign Policy of Thomas F. Bayard*, p. 431.

8 Denby to Bayard, July 13, 1886, China Despatches, Vol 78, National Archives. (An account of the Wilson project may be found in Chapter 4.)

9 Ibid.; Denby to Bayard, April 5 and June 3, 1887, ibid.

10 Cassey, "Mission of Charles Denby," pp. 208–13 (quotation from p. 213).

11 Ibid., pp. 215–18; Thomas J. McCormick, *China Market* (Chicago, 1967), pp. 57–58, 67–68.

12 Cassey, "Mission of Charles Denby," pp. 222–27; McCormick, *China Market*, pp. 74–75. (An account of the Wilson-McCook project may be found in Chapter 4.)

13 Denby, *China and Her People*, 2:38.

14 McCormick, *China Market*, pp. 67–68, 73–74.

15 Denby, *China and Her People*, 2:88–89.

16 Ibid., 1:233–34, and 2:87.

17 Ibid., 2:75; Cassey, "Mission of Charles Denby," pp. 150, 156–58; Dean C. Worcester, *The Philippines Past and Present*, 2 vols. (New York, 1914), 1:311.

18 Denby, *China and Her People*, 1:213–16.

19 Ibid., 1:220, and 2:38–39. See also Charles Denby, "The Influence of Mission Work on Commerce," *Independent*, 53 (Dec.

12, 1901):2960–62.

20 Margaret Leech, *In the Days of McKinley* (New York, 1959), pp. 314–22.

21 Ibid., pp. 351–52, 363; Denby, *China and Her People*, 2:153–55.

22 Otis to McKinley, Jan. 16, 1899, William McKinley Papers, Library of Congress; Denby, *China and Her People*, 2:155–58.

23 Ibid., pp. 158–60; Leech, *In the Days of McKinley*, p. 364.

24 Denby, *China and Her People*, 2:158–60; Worcester, *The Philippines Past and Present*, 1:311.

25 Report of the Philippine Commission, Nov. 2, 1899, in Records of the Bureau of Insular Affairs relating to the Philippine Islands, 1898–1935, National Archives,Record Group 350.

26 See Denby interview, *Literary Digest*, 16 (Jan. 1, 1898):4; and Denby, "The Doctrine of Intervention," pp. 385–92.

27 Denby, *China and Her People*, 2:240, 94.

28 Charles Denby, "Why the Treaty Should be Ratified," *Forum*, 26 (Feb., 1899):644; Denby, *China and Her People*, 1:7–8, and 2:96.

29 Charles Denby, "Shall We Keep the Philippines?" *Forum*, 26 (Nov., 1898):281; Denby, "The Doctrine of Intervention," pp. 386–87; Denby, "Why the Treaty Should Be Ratified," p. 647.

30 For examples see Morrison I. Swift, *Imperialism and Liberty* (Los Angeles, 1899), p. 38; James H. Blount, *The American Occupation of the Philippines, 1898–1912* (New York and London, 1912), pp. 273–75; and Richard Hofstadter, "Manifest Destiny and the Philippines," in *America in Crisis*, ed. Daniel Aaron (New York, 1952), p. 195.

31 Denby, *China and Her People*, 2:28.

32 Ibid., pp. 29–30, 43.

Chapter 11: *Charles A. Conant*

1 See obituary, *New York Times*, July 7, 1915; and Charles S. Campbell, *Special Business Interests and the Open Door Policy* (New Haven, Conn., 1951), p. 26.

2 The book was made up of the following articles: "The Economic Basis of 'Imperialism'," *North American Review*, Sept., 1898; "Russia as a World Power," ibid., Feb., 1899; "The Struggle for Commercial Supremacy," *Forum*, June, 1899; "Can New Openings be Found For Capital?"*Atlantic Monthly*, Nov., 1899; "Recent Economic Tendencies," ibid., June, 1900; "The United

States as a World Power—the Economic and Political Problem," *Forum,* July, 1900; and "The United States as a World Power—Their Advantages in the Competition for Commercial Empire," ibid., Aug., 1900.

3 Charles A. Conant, *The United States in the Orient* (Boston and New York, 1900), pp. 3–24.
4 Ibid., pp. 24–29.
5 Ibid., pp. 29–30.
6 Ibid., pp. iii, 61. See also p. 161.
7 Ibid., pp. 63–64.
8 Ibid., p. 175.
9 Ibid., pp. 59–60, 191, 215, 175.
10 Ibid., pp. 120, 158, 114.
11 Ibid., pp. 73, 120.
12 Ibid., pp. 222–23, 1–2.
13 Ibid., p. 194.
14 Ibid., pp. iv–vi, 114.
15 Ibid., pp. 118–20.
16 Ibid., pp. 89, 226.
17 Ibid., pp. 89–90, 197, 225.
18 Ibid., pp. 213, 197.
19 Ibid., 211–16.
20 Ibid., pp. 211–12.
21 Ibid., p. 221.
22 Ibid., pp. vi–viii, 114.
23 William L. Langer, *The Diplomacy of Imperialism, 1890–1902,* 2 vols. (New York, 1935), 1:68.
24 Agnes Murphy, *The Ideology of French Imperialism, 1871–1881* (Washington, D.C., 1948), pp. 118–24.
25 See Samuel Haber, *Efficiency and Uplift* (Chicago and London, 1964), pp. 74, 100–107.
26 Elihu Root to William Howard Taft, July 23, 1901, in Records of the Bureau of Insular Affairs relating to the Philippine Islands, 1898–1935 (Record Group 350), National Archives. See also Conant to Secretary of the Treasury, Oct. 16, 1900, ibid.
27 "Special Report on Coinage and Banking in the Philippine Islands made to the Secretary of War by Charles A. Conant of Boston, November 25, 1901," ibid. (Printed as Appendix G in *Annual Report of the Secretary of War, 1901* [Washington, General Printing Office, 1902].)
28 Taft to Root, Oct. 14, 1901, in Elihu Root Papers, Library of

Congress; Conant to Root, Dec. 11, 1901, and Conant to Lt. Col.
Clarence R. Edwards, Jan. 3 and Jan. 16, 1902, in R.G. 350,
National Archives.
29 Conant to Taft, Aug. 22, 1902, ibid.; Edwin W. Kemmerer,
Modern Currency Reforms (New York, 1916), pp. 309–13,
324–32.
30 See Kemmerer, *Modern Currency Reforms*, pp. 324–32; and
Henry Parker Willis, *Our Philippine Problem* (New York, 1905),
pp. 305–9.
31 See obituary, *New York Times*, July 7, 1915.
32 "The 'Cost of the Philippines'," New York *Journal of Commerce*,
March 1, 1907. Although this is an unsigned editorial, Conant
acknowledged his authorship of it in a note to Col. Edwards
at the Bureau of Insular Affairs.

Chapter 12: *The Anti-Imperialist Movement*

 1 Among them are Theodore Clark Smith, "Expansion After the
Civil War, 1865–71," *Political Science Quarterly*, 16 (1901):412–
36, and Robert L. Beisner, "Thirty Years Before Manila: E. L.
Godkin, Carl Schurz, and Anti-Imperialism in the Gilded Age,"
Historian, 30 (Aug. 1968):561–77.
 2 For a standard biography see Claude Moore Fuess, *Carl Schurz,
Reformer* (Port Washington, N.Y., 1932).
 3 Frederic Bancroft, ed., *Speeches, Correspondence and Political
Papers of Carl Schurz*, 6 vols. (New York and London, 1913),
2:75–78, 93–94, 98.
 4 Ibid., 2:115, 78–96, 99–101.
 5 Ibid., 2:111–12, 97–98, 117–18, 122.
 6 Ibid., 5:191–214.
 7 Ibid., pp. 206–11.
 8 Ibid., 6:27.
 9 Ibid., p. 35.
10 Rollo Ogden, ed., *Life and Letters of Edwin Lawrence Godkin*,
2 vols. (New York, 1907), 2:202–3.
11 For a detailed study of this group, see John G. Sproat, *"The
Best Men": Liberal Reformers in the Gilded Age* (New York,
1968).
12 A standard account of the anti-imperialist movement is Fred
Harvey Harrington, "The Anti-Imperialist Movement in the
United States, 1898–1900," *Mississippi Valley Historical Review*,

22 (Sept., 1935):211–30.

13 Morrison I. Swift, *Imperialism and Liberty* (Los Angeles, 1899), especially pp. 4–8, 92–103, 116–17, 176–85, 346–54. However, not only leftists were militant. The elderly and respectable Edward Atkinson of Boston attempted to send pamphlets violently attacking the Philippine War to soldiers fighting there, only to have them banned from shipment by the Postmaster General. See *Literary Digest,* 18 (May 13, 1899):541–43.

14 Carnegie to Carl Schurz, Dec. 27, 1898, printed in Bancroft, ed., *Speeches, etc. of Carl Schurz,* 5:531.

15 The Gompers position was reflected in numerous editorials in *The American Federationist,* but a particularly succinct summary is contained in "The Future Foreign Policy of the United States," *American Federationist,* 5 (Sept., 1898):136–40, which reprints a speech given by Gompers at Saratoga, New York, on Aug. 20, 1898. Gompers's fear of the anti-labor role of the army is expressed in "Militarism, its purposes partly portrayed," ibid., 5 (Dec., 1898):203–4. The quotation from *The American Agriculturalist* appeared in *Literary Digest,* 17 (Sept. 17, 1898): 332–33.

16 Ibid. (Aug. 6, 1898), pp. 156–58. The general anti-imperialist bias of the German-American press was also noted by Richard Michaelis, editor of the *Chicago Freie Presse*; see Michaelis to W. J. Bryan, Aug. 9, 1899, Bryan Papers, Library of Congress.

17 Sproat, *The Best Men,* p. 271; Robert L. Beisner, *Twelve Against Empire: the Anti-Imperialists, 1898–1900* (New York and London, 1968), pp. 5–17; Delber L. McKee, "Samuel Gompers, the A. F. of L., and Imperialism," *Historian,* 21 (Feb., 1959):187–99; Harrington, "The Anti-Imperialist Movement," pp. 218–19. For a detailed study of mugwump and Republican anti-imperialists, see Beisner, *Twelve Against Empire.*

18 This point is explored in John A. S. Grenville and George B. Young, *Politics, Strategy, and American Diplomacy* (New Haven, Conn., and London, 1966), pp. 102–115.

19 Hoar to Bryan, May 15, 1900; Watterson to Bryan, June 4, 1900; both in Bryan Papers.

20 Jefferson Myers to Bryan, Aug. 25, 1899, ibid.; W. W. Smith to Senator John T. Morgan, Feb. 7, 1899, John T. Morgan Papers, Library of Congress.

21 Hearst to Bryan, dated only "1899," Bryan Papers. Internal evidence indicates that the letter was written in the summer

of 1899.

22 Quoted in *Literary Digest*, 17 (July 2, 1898):2. See Paolo E. Coletta, *William Jennings Bryan* (Lincoln, Nebr., 1964), 1: 220–37, for Bryan's career in this period.

23 William Jennings Bryan, *Speeches of William Jennings Bryan*, 2 vols. (New York and London, 1913), 2:7, 11.

24 Rollo Ogden to Bryan, Aug. 19, 1899, Bryan Papers. See William E. Leuchtenberg, "Progressivism and Imperialism: the Progressive Movement and American Foreign Policy, 1896–1916," *Mississippi Valley Historical Review*, 39 (Dec., 1952):486–88.

25 Harrington, "The Anti-Imperialist Movement," pp. 220–22; Coletta, *Bryan*, 1:233–36; Lodge to Theodore Roosevelt, Feb. 9, 1899, printed in Henry Cabot Lodge, ed., *Selections from the Correspondence of Theodore Roosevelt and Henry Cabot Lodge*, 2 vols. (New York and London, 1925), 1:391–92; *Speeches of William Jennings Bryan*, 2:21. For the adverse reaction of one Democratic Senator to Bryan's treaty position, see Senator James K. Jones to Bryan, Jan. 24 and Jan. 30, 1899, Bryan Papers.

26 *Speeches of William Jennings Bryan*, 2:21–22, 46. See also Bryan to Carnegie, Jan. 13, 1899, and Bryan to Hearst, Feb. 5, 1899, both in Bryan Papers.

27 *Cong. Record*, 55 Cong., 3 sess. (1899), 32:1846; Lala Carr Steelman, "Senator Augustus O. Bacon, Champion of Philippine Independence," in *Essays in Southern Biography*, East Carolina Publications in History, Vol. 2 (Greenville, N.C., 1965), 93–100.

28 *The Autobiography of Andrew Carnegie* (Boston and New York, 1920), p. 364; Hoar to Bryan, May 15, 1900, Bryan Papers; Storey to Hoar, Feb. 28, 1900, printed in M. A. De Wolfe Howe, *Portrait of an Independent: Moorfield Storey, 1845–1929* (Boston and New York, 1932), pp. 227–28.

29 Edward C. Kirkland, *Charles Francis Adams, Jr., 1835–1915: The Patrician at Bay* (Cambridge, Mass., 1965), pp. 179–80; Harrington, "The Anti-Imperialist Movement," pp. 226–28; Schurz to Edwin Burritt Smith, Jan. 17, 1901, printed in Bancroft, ed., *Speeches, etc., of Carl Schurz*, 6:276.

30 Kirkland, *Charles Francis Adams, Jr.*, p. 185. The major frictions inherent in the anti-imperialist movement are explored in Richard E. Welch, Jr., "Senator George Frisbie Hoar and the Defeat of Anti-Imperialism, 1898–1900," *Historian*, 26 (May, 1964):

362–80.
31 Howe, *Portrait of an Independent,* p. 240.

Chapter 13: *Conflict and Consensus*

1 *Cong. Record,* 55 Cong., 3 sess. (1898), 32:20.
2 Ibid., pp. 93–96, 287; (1899), pp. 564–65, 1376–85.
3 Ibid., pp. 1450–51. See also the statement of Senator Thomas Platt of New York, p. 1155.
4 Ibid. (1898), pp. 93, 296–97, 327.
5 Francis Newton Thorpe, "The Civil Service and Colonization," *Harper's New Monthly Magazine,* 98 (May, 1899):861.
6 Amos K. Fiske, "Some Consecrated Fallacies," *North American Review,* 169 (Dec., 1899):821–28.
7 William Graham Sumner, *The Conquest of the United States by Spain and Other Essays,* ed. Murray Polner (Chicago, n.d.), pp. 139, 142, 150–52, 173.
8 Ibid., pp. 70–73, 77–81. These references are from "Earth Hunger, or the Philosophy of Land Grabbing," which Sumner wrote in 1896.
9 William Jennings Bryan, *Speeches of William Jennings Bryan,* 2 vols. (New York and London, 1913) 2:37; Godkin to Moorfield Storey, Jan. 19, 1900, printed in Rollo Ogden, ed., *Life and Letters of Edwin Lawrence Godkin,* 2 vols. (New York, 1907), 2:242–43.
10 Sumner, *Conquest of the United State by Spain,* pp. 145, 229 (quotation); *Cong. Record,* 57 Cong., 1 sess. (1902), 35:4670.
11 Storey to George Marvin, April 16, 1903, printed in M. A. De Wolfe Howe, *Portrait of an Independent: Moorfield Storey, 1895–1929* (Boston and New York, 1932), pp. 230–31; *Literary Digest,* 18 (Jan. 7, 1899):2–3; George F. Hoar, *Autobiography of Seventy Years,* 2 vols. (New York, 1903) 2:317–18.
12 David Starr Jordan, *Imperial Democracy* (New York, 1899), p. 18; Frederic Bancroft, ed., *Speeches, Correspondence and Political Papers of Carl Schurz,* 6 vols. (New York and London, 1913), 5:507; George F. Hoar, "Statesmanship in England and in the United States," *Forum,* 23 (Aug., 1897):720–21. See also Peter Henry King, "The White Man's Burden" (Ph.D. dissertation, University of California at Los Angeles, 1958), pp. 2, 163–65.
13 Christopher Lasch, "The Anti-Imperialists, the Philippines, and

the Inequality of Man," *Journal of Southern History*, 24 (Aug., 1958):319–31; Jordan, *Imperial Democracy*, pp. 56–57.

14 Ibid., pp. 33–34, 56–57, 106.

15 King, "The White Man's Burden," pp. 163–65; Bancroft, ed. *Speeches, etc., of Carl Schurz*, 6:33; Sumner, *Conquest of the United States by Spain*, p. 169.

16 *Literary Digest*, 17 (Nov. 12, 1898):566–67; editorial, "Have We the Capacity?" *Outlook*, 60 (Nov. 26, 1898):753–55; Rev. S. D. McConnell, "Are Our Hands Clean?" ibid., 61 (Jan. 28, 1899):216–19; *Literary Digest*, 17 (Dec. 3, 1898):652.

17 Frances Butler Simkins, *Pitchfork Ben Tillman* (Baton Rouge, La., 1944), pp. 355–57; Hoar, *Autobiography*, 2:305; Lasch, "The Anti-Imperialists, the Philippines, and the Inequality of Man," pp. 324–25.

18 *Cong. Record*, 55 Cong., 2 sess. (1898), 31:3890; ibid., 57 Cong., 1 sess. (1902), 35:4718–21. See also Lala Carr Steelman, "Senator Augustus O. Bacon, Champion of Philippine Independence," in *Essays in Southern Biography*, East Carolina Publications in History, Vol. 2 (Greenville, N.C., 1865), p. 111.

19 Jordan, *Imperial Democracy*, pp. 8–9; Thomas F. Dawson, *Life and Character of Edward Oliver Wolcott*, 2 vols. (New York, 1911), 2:752.

20 Bancroft, ed., *Speeches, etc., of Carl Schurz*, 6:27; Edward Atkinson, "How to Increase Exports," *The Anti-Imperialist*, 1 (June 3, 1899):26–32.

21 *Speeches of William Jennings Bryan*, 2:42.

22 Sumner, *Conquest of the United States by Spain*, p. 173; Hoar is quoted in Mary Augusta Burr, "George Frisbie Hoar: An Imperialist Dissenter" (M.A. thesis, University of Delaware, 1965), pp. 81–82.

23 Quoted in Howe, *Portrait of an Independent*, p. 225.

24 Bancroft, ed., *Speeches, etc., of Carl Schurz*, 5:485, 481; Jordan, *Imperial Democracy*, pp. 12–13, 23–24; Senator George G. Vest, "Objections to Annexing the Philippines," *North American Review*, 168 (Jan., 1899):112; E. E. Morison, ed., *The Letters of Theodore Roosevelt*, 8 vols. (Cambridge, Mass., 1951–54), 2:921.

25 See Fred Harvey Harrington, "The Anti-Imperialist Movement in the United States, 1898–1900," *Mississippi Valley Historical Review*, 22 (Sept. 1935):223–24.

Conclusion

1 Frederic Bancroft, ed., *Speeches, Correspondence and Political Papers of Carl Schurz*, 6 vols. (New York and London, 1913), 6:178.

2 See Dorothy Ganfield Fowler, *John Coit Spooner, Defender of Presidents* (New York, 1961), pp. 240–41; and Julius W. Pratt, *America's Colonial Experiment: How the United States Gained, Governed, and in Part Gave Away a Colonial Empire* (New York, 1951), pp. 154, 164–66.

3 Rounsevelle Wildman to John Hay, Nov. 25, 1898, John Hay Papers, Library of Congress; Russell Hastings to McKinley, May 7, 1899, William McKinley Papers, Library of Congress; Elihu Root to Samuel L. Parrish, Dec. 1, 1899, Elihu Root Papers, Library of Congress.

4 Alleyne Ireland, *Tropical Colonization* (New York and London, 1899); Archibald R. Colquhoun, *Greater America* (New York and London, 1904); James Bryce, "British Experience in the Government of Colonies," *Century Magazine*, 57 (March, 1899): 718–28. Benjamin Kidd, *The Control of the Tropics* (New York and London, 1898), also falls into this category.

5 "The Government of Dependencies," in *The Foreign Policy of the United States: Political and Commercial* (American Academy of Political and Social Science, Philadelphia, 1899), pp. 3–73; Edward G. Bourne, "A Trained Colonial Service," *North American Review*, 169 (Oct., 1899):528–35; "The Government of Dependencies," pp. 16–17, 59. See also Charles Kendall Adams, "Colonies and Other Dependencies," *Forum*, 27 (March, 1899): 33–46.

6 W. B. Devereux to Root, Dec. 16, 1899; James B. Reynolds to Root, Aug. 3, 1899; both in Elihu Root Papers.

7 See Earl S. Pomeroy, "The American Colonial Office," *Mississippi Valley Historical Review*, 30 (1944):521–32.

Bibliography

PRIMARY SOURCES

Manuscripts

Library of Congress
William Jennings Bryan Papers
John Hay Papers
William McKinley Papers
Whitelaw Reid Papers
Elihu Root Papers
James Harrison Wilson Papers
National Archives of the United States
Division of Interior Department Archives, Records of the Bureau of Insular Affairs relating to the Philippine Islands, 1898–1935 (Record Group 350).
Division of State Department Archives, Diplomatic Despatches, Vol. 78.

Public Documents

Richardson, James D. *A Compilation of the Messages and Papers of the Presidents, 1789–1897*. 10 vols. Washington, 1899.
Santovenia, Emeterio S., and Llaverías, Joaquín, eds. *Actas de las Asambleas de Representantes y del Consejo de Gobierno Durante la Guerra de Independencia*. 5 vols. Havana, 1932.
United States *Congressional Record*. 53–58 Congresses.
United States State Department. *Papers Relating to the Foreign Relations of the United States*. 1885–1907.
United States War Department. *Civil Report of Major General John R. Brooke, Military Governor, Island of Cuba*. Washington, 1900.

Periodicals

Century Magazine, 1898–1899
Forum, 1897–1899
Literary Digest, 1897–1900
North American Review, 1897–1899
Outlook, 1897–1899
Public Opinion, 1896–1898

Books, Articles, and Pamphlets

Abbott, Lyman. *Reminiscences*. Boston and New York, 1915.
Adams, Brooks. *America's Economic Supremacy*. New York, 1900.
————. *The Law of Civilization and Decay*. New York and London, 1896.
————. "Reciprocity or the Alternative." *Atlantic Monthly*, 88 (Aug., 1901):145–55.
Adams, Charles Kendall. "Colonies and Other Dependencies." *Forum*, 27 (March, 1899):33–46.
Adams, Henry. *The Degradation of the Democratic Dogma*. New York, 1919.
"After the Treaty, What?" *Outlook*, 61 (Jan. 7, 1899):10–12.
Aldrich, Thomas Bailey. *The Writings of Thomas Bailey Aldrich*. 9 vols. Boston and New York, 1907.
Atkinson, Edward. "How to Increase Exports." *Anti-Imperialist*, 1 (June 3, 1899):26–32.
————. "How to Meet the Increased Cost of Criminal Aggression by a Tax on Thinking." *Anti-Imperialist*, 1 (July 4, 1899):60–62.
Bacon, Robert, and Scott, James Brown, eds. *Addresses on Government and Citizenship by Elihu Root*. Cambridge, Mass., 1916.
————. *Latin America and the United States: Addresses by Elihu Root*. Cambridge, Mass., 1917.
————. *Men and Policies: Addresses, etc., by Elihu Root*. Cambridge, Mass., 1925.
————. *Military and Colonial Policy of the United States, Addresses and Reports by Elihu Root*. Cambridge, Mass., 1916.
————. *Miscellaneous Addresses by Elihu Root*. Cambridge, Mass., 1917.
Bagehot, Walter. *Physics and Politics*. New York, 1904.
Bancroft, Frederic, ed. *Speeches, Correspondence and Political*

Papers of Carl Schurz. 6 vols. New York and London, 1913.

————, and Dunning, William A., eds. *The Reminiscences of Carl Schurz.* 3 vols. New York, 1908.

Bates, George H. "Some Aspects of the Samoan Question." *Century*, 37 (April, 1889):945–49.

Beale, Truxtun. "Strategical Value of the Philippines." *North American Review*, 166 (June, 1898):759–60.

————. "The White Race and the Tropics." *Forum*, 24 (July, 1899):534–36.

Beveridge, Albert J. "The Development of a Colonial Policy for the United States." *Annals of the American Academy of Political and Social Science*, 30 (July, 1907):3–15.

————. *The Meaning of the Times and Other Speeches.* Indianapolis, 1908.

————. *The Russian Advance.* New York and London, 1903.

Blaine, James G. *Political Discussions, Legislative, Diplomatic, and Popular, 1856–1886.* Norwich, Conn., 1887.

Bourne, Edward G. "A Trained Colonial Civil Service." *North American Review*, 169 (Oct., 1899):528–35.

Bradford, Royal B. "Coaling Stations for the Navy." *Forum*, 26 (Feb., 1899):732–47.

Bryan, William Jennings, et al. *Republic or Empire? The Philippine Question.* Chicago, 1899.

————. *Speeches of William Jennings Bryan.* 2 vols. New York and London, 1913.

Bryce, James. *The American Commonwealth.* 2 vols. 3rd ed. New York and London, 1908.

————. "British Experience in the Government of Colonies." *Century Magazine*, n.s. 35 (March, 1899):718–28.

————. "The Policy of Annexation for America." *Forum*, 24 (Dec., 1897):385–95.

Burgess, John W. *Sovereignty and Liberty.* Political Science and Comparative Constitutional Law, vol. 1. Boston and London, 1893.

"Canadian Railroad Question, The, Arguments and Facts submitted to a Committee of the United States Senate by E. W. Meddaugh and A. C. Raymond at a hearing in Detroit, Michigan, May 1, 1891." Pamphlet, Detroit, 1891.

Carnegie, Andrew. "Americanism vs. Imperialism—II." *North American Review*, 168 (March, 1899):362–72.

————. *The Autobiography of Andrew Carnegie.* Boston and

New York, 1920.

———. "Distant Possessions—the Parting of the Ways." *North American Review,* 167 (Aug., 1898):239–48.

Cary, Clarence. "China, and Chinese Railway Concessions." *Forum,* 24 (Jan., 1898):591–605.

———. "China's Complications and American Trade." *Forum,* 25 (March, 1898):35–45.

Chamberlain, Joseph. *Foreign and Colonial Speeches.* London, 1897.

Clark, (Rev.) Francis E. "Do Foreign Missions Pay?" *North American Review,* 166 (March, 1898):268–80.

Colquhoun, Archibald R. *Greater America.* New York and London, 1904.

Conant, Charles A. *The United States in the Orient.* Boston and New York, 1900.

Crampton, Charles A. "The Opportunity of the Sugar Cane Industry." *North American Review,* 168 (March, 1899):276–84.

Crichfield, George Washington. *American Supremacy: The Rise and Progress of the Latin American Republics and Their Relations to the United States Under the Monroe Doctrine.* 2 vols. New York, 1908.

Cullom, Shelby M. *Fifty Years of Public Service.* Chicago, 1911.

Davis, Cushman K. *A Treatise on International Law, Including American Diplomacy.* St. Paul, Minn., 1901.

Denby, Charles. *China and Her People.* 2 vols. Boston, 1906.

———. "The Doctrine of Intervention." *Forum,* 26 (Dec., 1898):385–92.

———. "The Influence of Mission Work on Commerce." *Independent,* 53 (Dec. 12, 1901):2960–62.

———. "Shall We Keep the Philippines?" *Forum,* 26 (Nov., 1898):279–81.

———. "Why the Treaty Should be Ratified." *Forum,* 26 (Feb., 1899):641–49.

Dilke, Charles W. "The Future Relations of Great Britain and the United States." *Forum,* 26 (Jan., 1899):521–28.

———. *Greater Britain.* 2 vols. London, 1869.

"Expansion not Imperialism." *Outlook,* 60 (Oct. 22, 1898):464–66.

"Expansion: One Step at a Time." *Outlook,* 60 (Dec. 24, 1898):996–99.

"Face to Face with Our Destiny." *Christian Herald,* 21 (May 25, 1898):448.

Filipino, A. "Aguinaldo's Case Against the United States." *North American Review,* 169 (Sept., 1899):425–32.

Fiske, Amos K. "Some Consecrated Fallacies." *North American Review,* 169 (Dec., 1899):821–28.

Fiske, John. *American Political Ideas Viewed from the Standpoint of Universal History.* New York, 1885.

Flint, Charles R. "Our Export Trade." *Forum,* 23 (May, 1897): 290–97.

Foraker, Joseph Benson. *Notes of a Busy Life.* 2 vols. Cincinnati, 1916.

Foraker, Julia B. *I Would Live It Again.* New York, 1932.

Ford, Worthington Chauncey, ed. *Letters of Henry Adams, 1892–1918.* 2 vols. Boston and New York, 1938.

Foreign Naval Officer, A. "Can the United States Afford to Fight Spain?" *North American Review,* 164 (Feb., 1897):209–215.

Foreign Policy of the United States, The: Political and Commercial. Addresses and Discussion at the Annual Meeting of the American Academy of Political and Social Science, April 7–8, 1899. Supplement to the Annals of the American Academy, May, 1899. Philadelphia, 1899.

Froude, James Anthony. *The English in the West Indies, or the Bow of Ulysses.* London, 1888.

————. *Oceana, or England and Her Colonies.* New York, 1886.

Giddings, Franklin Henry. *Democracy and Empire.* New York and London, 1900.

Godkin, E. L. "The Conditions of Good Colonial Government." *Forum,* 27 (April, 1899):190–203.

————. *Problems of Modern Democracy.* New York, 1896.

Griffis, William Elliot. "The Anglo-Saxon in the Tropics." *Outlook,* 60 (Dec. 10, 1898):902–7.

————. "The Pacific Ocean and Our Future There." *Outlook,* 61 (Jan. 14, 1899):110–13.

Halstead, Murat. "American Annexation and Armament." *Forum,* 24 (Sept., 1897):56–66.

Hamm, Margherita Arlina. "The Secular Value of Foreign Missions." *Independent,* 52 (April 26, 1900):1000–3.

Harrison, Benjamin. *Views of An Ex-President.* Indianapolis, 1901.

Hart, Albert Bushnell. *The Foundations of American Foreign Policy.* New York and London, 1901.

Harvey, Charles M. *The Republican National Convention, St. Louis, 1896.* St. Louis, 1896.

"Have We the Capacity?" *Outlook,* 60 (Nov. 26, 1898):753–55.

Hawthorne, Julian. "A Side-Issue of Expansion." *Forum,* 27 (June, 1899):441–44.

Hill, David J. "The War and the Extension of Civilization." *Forum,* 26 (Feb., 1899):650–55.

Hoar, George Frisbie. *Autobiography of Seventy Years.* 2 vols. New York, 1903.

――――. "Statesmanship in England and in the United States." *Forum,* 23 (Aug., 1897):709–22.

"Interesting to Shippers, Receivers, etc., etc., A Merchant's Reply and other matter in reference to General James H. Wilson's statement concerning Transportation in Bond over the Railways of the Dominion of Canada." Pamphlet, Chicago, n.d.

Ireland, Alleyne. *Tropical Colonization.* New York and London, 1899.

Ireland, John. "The Religious Conditions in Our New Island Territory." *Outlook,* 62 (Aug. 26, 1899):933–34.

James, William. *Essays on Faith and Morals.* New York, London, and Toronto, 1947.

Jordan, David Starr. *Imperial Democracy.* New York, 1899.

Kidd, Benjamin. *The Control of the Tropics.* New York and London, 1898.

――――. "The United States and the Control of the Tropics." *Atlantic Monthly,* 82 (Dec., 1898):721–27.

Krock, Arthur, ed. *The Editorials of Henry Watterson.* New York, 1923.

Lodge, Henry Cabot. "England, Venezuela, and the Monroe Doctrine." *North American Review,* 160 (June, 1895):651–58.

――――, ed. *Selections from the Correspondence of Theodore Roosevelt and Henry Cabot Lodge, 1884–1918.* 2 vols. New York and London, 1925.

――――, and Roosevelt, Theodore. *Hero Tales From American History.* New York, 1895.

Long, Margaret, ed. *The Journal of John D. Long.* Rindge, N.H., 1956.

Lugard, Frederick D. *The Dual Mandate in British Tropical Africa.* London, 1922.

McConnell, (Rev.) S. D. "Are Our Hands Clean?" *Outlook,* 61 (Jan. 28, 1899):216–19.

McKim, (Rev.) Randolph H. "Religious Reconstruction in Our New Possessions." *Outlook,* 63 (Oct. 28, 1899):504–6.

Mahan, Alfred Thayer. *The Interest of America in Sea Power.* Boston, 1897.

————. *Lessons of the War with Spain, and Other Articles.* Boston, 1899.

————. *The Problem of Asia and its Effects upon international policies.* Boston, 1900.

————. *Retrospect and Prospect.* Boston, 1902.

Mayo, Lawrence Shaw. *America of Yesterday As Reflected in the Diary of John D. Long.* Boston, 1923.

McKinley, William. *Speeches and Addresses of William McKinley from March 1, 1897 to May 30, 1900.* New York, 1900.

Mills, David. "Which Shall Dominate—Saxon or Slav?" *North American Review,* 166 (June, 1898):729–39.

Moffett, Samuel E. "Ultimate World-Politics." *Forum,* 27 (Aug., 1899):665–68.

Morgan, H. Wayne, ed. *Making Peace With Spain: the Diary of Whitelaw Reid (September–December, 1898).* Austin, Texas, 1965.

Morgan, John T. "The Duty of Annexing Hawaii." *Forum,* 25 (March, 1898):11–16.

————. "The Territorial Expansion of the United States." *Independent,* 50 (July 7, 1898):10–12.

————. "What Shall We Do With the Conquered Islands?" *North American Review,* 166 (June, 1898):641–49.

Morison, Elting E., ed. *The Letters of Theodore Roosevelt.* 8 vols. Cambridge, Mass., 1951–54.

Mott, John R. *Strategic Points in the World's Conquest.* New York and Chicago, 1897.

Mulhall, Michael G. "Thirty Years of American Trade." *North American Review,* 165 (Nov., 1897):572–81.

Nevins, Allan, ed. *Letters of Grover Cleveland, 1850–1908.* Boston, 1933.

Olney, Richard. "Growth of Our Foreign Policy." *Atlantic Monthly,* 85 (March, 1900):289–301.

————. "International Isolation of the United States." *Atlantic Monthly,* 81 (May, 1898):577–88.

Pearson, Charles H. *National Life and Character: A Forecast.* London and New York, 1894.

Peffer, W. A. "A Republic in the Philippines." *North American Review,* 168 (March, 1899):310–20.

"Philippine Problem, The." *Outlook,* 59 (May 14, 1898):112–13.

"Possible Colonial Policy, A." *Outlook,* 60 (Nov. 12, 1898):652–55.

"Praise of Wrath, The." *Congregationalist,* 83 (July 21, 1898):70.

Proctor, John R. "Hawaii and the Changing Front of the World." *Forum,* 24 (Sept., 1897):34–46.

_____. "Isolation or Imperialism." *Forum,* 26 (Sept., 1898):14–26.

"Progress of the War, The." *Congregationalist,* 83 (July 21, 1898): 71.

Reed, Thomas B. "Empire Can Wait." *Illustrated American,* 22 (Dec. 4, 1897):713–14.

_____. "The New Navy." *Illustrated American,* 22 (Sept. 25, 1897):392–93.

Reid, Whitelaw. *Problems of Expansion, as Considered in Papers and Addresses.* New York, 1900.

Roosevelt, Theodore. "General Leonard Wood, A Model American Military Administrator." *Outlook,* 61 (Jan. 7, 1899):19–23.

_____. *The Works of Theodore Roosevelt.* 24 vols. Edited by Hermann Hagedorn. New York, 1923–26.

Rowe, L. S. "The Influence of the War on Our Public Life." *Forum,* 27 (March, 1899):52–60.

"Santiago." *Outlook,* 59 (July 9, 1898):610.

"Scenes in Our New Colonial Possessions." *Christian Herald,* 21 (May 18, 1898):431.

Seeley, John R. *The Expansion of England.* Boston, 1920.

Sherman, William T. *Memoirs.* 2 vols. New York, 1875.

Smalley, Eugene V. "What Are Normal Times?" *Forum,* 23 (March, 1897):96–100.

Smalley, George W. *Anglo-American Memories.* Second Series. New York, 1912.

Smith, Goldwin. *Canada and the Canadian Question.* London and New York, 1891.

_____. *Commonwealth or Empire, A Bystander's View of the Question.* New York and London, 1902.

_____. "The Moral of the Cuban War." *Forum,* 26 (Nov., 1898): 282–93.

Smith, (Rev.) Judson. "The Awakening of China." *North American Review,* 168 (Feb., 1899):229–39.

Smith, Theodore Clark. "Expansion After the Civil War, 1865–71." *Political Science Quarterly,* 16 (1901):412–36.

Speer, Robert E. *Missions and Modern History.* 2 vols. New York and London, 1904.

Stanley, Henry M. "Anglo-Saxon Responsibilities." *Outlook*, 63 (Sept. 30, 1899):249–58.

Stead, William T. *The Americanization of the World*. London, 1902.

Storey, Moorfield, and Codman, Julian. "Secretary Root's Record. 'Marked Severities' in Philippine Warfare. An Analysis of the Law and Facts Bearing on the Action and Utterances of President Roosevelt and Secretary Root." Pamphlet, Boston, 1902.

Straus, Oscar. *Under Four Administrations*. Boston and New York, 1922.

Strong, Josiah. *Expansion Under New World Conditions*. New York, 1900.

——. *Our Country*. Edited by Jurgen Herbst. Cambridge, Mass., 1963.

Sumner, William Graham. "The Conquest of the United States by Spain, A Lecture before the Phi Beta Kappa Society of Yale University, January 16, 1899." Pamphlet, Boston, 1899.

——. *The Conquest of the United States by Spain and Other Essays*. Edited by Murray Polner. Chicago, n.d.

Swift, Morrison I. *Imperialism and Liberty*. Los Angeles, 1899.

"Terms of Peace." *Outlook*, 59 (Aug. 6, 1898):813–15.

"Territorial Expansion." *Outlook*, 59 (July 2, 1898):511–12.

Thorpe, Francis Newton. "The Civil Service and Colonization." *Harper's New Monthly Magazine*, 98 (May, 1899):858–62.

Vanderlip, Frank A. "Facts About the Philippines." *Century Magazine*, n.s. 34 (Aug., 1898):555–63.

Vest, George G. "Objections to Annexing the Philippines." *North American Review*, 67 (Jan., 1899):112–20.

Volwiler, Albert T. *The Correspondence Between Benjamin Harrison and James G. Blaine, 1882–1893*. Philadelphia, 1940.

White, Andrew D. *Autobiography of Andrew Dickson White*. 2 vols. New York, 1905.

White, Stephen M. "Our Inadequate Consular Service." *Forum*, 25 (July, 1898):546–54.

White, William Allen. *Autobiography of William Allen White*. New York, 1946.

Willis, Henry Parker. *Our Philippine Problem, A Study of American Colonial Policy*. New York, 1905.

Wilson, James H. "America's Interest in China." *North American Review*, 166 (Feb., 1898):129–41.

——. "An Address on Our Trade Relations with the Tropics

delivered by General James H. Wilson at Boston, Massachusetts, November 9, 1901." Pamphlet, Boston, 1901.

————. *China, Travels and Investigations in the Middle Kingdom.* 3rd. ed. New York, 1901.

————. "Our Relations with Cuba, An Address Delivered by General James H. Wilson at the request of the Commercial Club of Chicago at the Auditorium Hotel on the evening of October 25, 1902." Pamphlet, Wilmington, Del., 1902.

————. "Remarks of General James H. Wilson in Joint Debate with Erastus Wiman, Esq., Before the Board of Trade and the Citizens of Wilmington, Delaware, on Our Relations with the Dominion of Canada, December 13, 1889." Pamphlet, Wilmington, Del., 1890.

————. *Under the Old Flag.* 2 vols. New York, 1912.

Woolsey, Theodore S. *America's Foreign Policy: Essays and Addresses.* New York, 1898.

Worcester, Dean C. "Knotty Problems of the Philippines." *Century Magazine*, n.s. 34 (Oct., 1898):873–79.

SECONDARY SOURCES

Armstrong, William M. *E. L. Godkin and American Foreign Policy, 1865–1900.* New York, 1957.

Auxier, George W. "Middle Western Newspapers and the Spanish-American War, 1895–1898." *Mississippi Valley Historical Review*, 26 (March, 1940):523–34.

Baehr, Harry W. *The New York Tribune Since the Civil War.* New York, 1936.

Bailey, Thomas A. "Was the Presidential Election of 1900 a Mandate on Imperialism?" *Mississippi Valley Historical Review*, 24 (June, 1937):43–52.

Baker, George P. *The Formation of the New England Railroad System.* Cambridge, Mass., 1949.

Beale, Howard K. *Theodore Roosevelt and the Rise of America to World Power.* Baltimore, 1956.

Beisner, Robert L. "Thirty Years Before Manila: E. L. Godkin, Carl Schurz, and Anti-Imperialism in the Gilded Age." *Historian*, 30 (Aug., 1968):561–77.

————. *Twelve Against Empire: The Anti-Imperialists, 1898–1900.* New York, 1968.

Berman, Milton. *John Fiske: the Evolution of a Popularizer.* Cambridge, Mass., 1961.

Blount, James H. *The American Occupation of the Philippines, 1898–1912.* New York, 1912.

Bodelson, Carl A. *Studies in Mid-Victorian Imperialism.* Copenhagen, 1924.

Bowers, Claude G. *Beveridge and the Progressive Era.* Cambridge, Mass., 1932.

Braisted, William R. *The United States Navy in the Pacific, 1897–1909.* Austin, Texas, 1958.

Brown, Robert Craig. *Canada's National Policy, 1883–1900: A Study in Canadian-American Relations.* Princeon, N.J., 1964.

Burns, Edward McNall. *The American Idea of Mission.* New Brunswick, N.J., 1957.

————. *David Starr Jordan: Prophet of Freedom.* Stanford, Cal., 1953.

Burr, Mary Augusta. "George Frisbie Hoar: An Imperialist Dissenter." Master's thesis, University of Delaware, 1965.

Burrow, J. W. *Evolution and Society.* Cambridge, Eng., 1966.

Busbey, L. White. *Uncle Joe Cannon.* New York, 1927.

Callahan, James Morton. *American Foreign Policy in Canadian Relations.* New York, 1937.

Campbell, Charles S. *Anglo-American Understanding, 1898–1903.* Baltimore, 1957.

————. *Special Business Interests and the Open Door Policy.* New Haven, Conn., 1951.

Carrington, C. E. *The British Overseas.* Cambridge, Eng., 1950.

Cassey, John W. "The Mission of Charles Denby and International Rivalries in the Far East, 1885–1898." Ph.D. dissertation, University of Southern California, 1959.

Coletta, Paolo E. "McKinley, the Peace Negotiations, and the Acquisition of the Philippines." *Pacific Historical Review,* 30 (Nov., 1961):341–50.

————. *William Jennings Bryan: Political Evangelist, 1860–1908.* 3 vols. Lincoln, Nebraska, 1964.

Coolidge, Louis A. *An Old-Fashioned Senator, Orville H. Platt.* New York, 1910.

Cortissoz, Royal. *The Life of Whitelaw Reid.* 2 vols. London, 1921.

Cullum, George W. *Biographical Register of the Officers and Graduates of the United States Military Academy.* 4 vols. Boston and New York, 1891.

Curtin, Philip D. *The Image of Africa: British Ideas and Action,*

1780–1850. Madison, Wis., 1964.

Dawson, Thomas F. *Life and Character of Edward Oliver Wolcott.* 2 vols. New York, 1911.

Dennet, Tyler. *Americans in Eastern Asia: A Critical Study of United States Policy in the Far East in the Nineteenth Century.* New York, 1922.

————. *John Hay, From Poetry to Politics.* New York, 1934.

Ellis, Elmer. *Henry Moore Teller, Defender of the West.* Caldwell, Idaho, 1941.

Farrell, John T. "Archbishop Ireland and Manifest Destiny." *American Catholic Historical Review,* 33 (Oct., 1947):269–301.

Faulkner, Harold U. *Politics, Reform and Expansion, 1890–1900.* New York, 1959.

Fowler, Dorothy Ganfield. *John Coit Spooner, Defender of Presidents.* New York, 1961.

Friedlander, Heinrich E. and Oser, Jacob. *Economic History of Modern Europe.* New York, 1953.

Fuess, Claude Moore. *Carl Schurz, Reformer.* Port Washington, N.Y., 1932.

Garraty, John A. *Henry Cabot Lodge, A Biography.* New York, 1953.

Garvin, James L. *The Life of Joseph Chamberlain.* 3 vols. London, 1932–34.

Gelber, Lionel M. *The Rise of Anglo-American Friendship.* New York, 1938.

Gillett, Frederick H. *George Frisbie Hoar.* Boston, 1934.

Gleaves, Albert. *The Life and Letters of Rear Admiral Stephen B. Luce.* New York, 1925.

Goldman, Eric F. *Rendezvous With Destiny.* New York, 1958.

Grenville, John A. S. "American Naval Preparations for War with Spain, 1896–1898." *Journal of American Studies,* 2 (April, 1968): 33–47.

————, and Young, George B. *Politics, Strategy, and American Diplomacy.* New Haven, Conn., and London, 1966.

Griswold, A. Whitney. *The Far Eastern Policy of the United States.* New Haven, Conn., and London, 1962.

Gwynn, Stephen. *The Letters and Friendships of Sir Cecil Spring-Rice.* 2 vols. Boston and New York, 1929.

Habakkuk, H. J. and Postan, M., eds. *The Cambridge Economic History of Europe.* Vol. 6. Cambridge, Eng., 1965.

Haber, Samuel. *Efficiency and Uplift: Scientific Management in*

the Progressive Era, 1890–1920. Chicago and London, 1964.
Hagedorn, Hermann. *Leonard Wood.* 2 vols. New York, 1931.
Hancock, Harold Bell. "The Political Career of John Edward Addicks in Delaware." Typescript. Federal Writers Project, 1939.
Harlow, Alvin F. *Steelways of New England.* New York, 1946.
Harrington, Fred Harvey. "The Anti-Imperialist Movement in the United States, 1898–1900." *Mississippi Valley Historical Review,* 22 (Sept. 1935):211–30.
————. "Literary Aspects of American Anti-Imperialism." *New England Quarterly,* 10 (Dec., 1937):650–67.
Healy, David F. *The United States in Cuba, 1898–1902.* Madison, Wis., 1963.
Higham, John. *Strangers in the Land.* 2nd ed. New York, 1963.
Hobson, John A. *Imperialism: A Study.* London, 1902.
Hofstadter, Richard. "Manifest Destiny and the Philippines." In *America In Crisis,* edited by Daniel Aaron. New York, 1952.
————. *Social Darwinism in American Thought.* Boston, 1955.
Houghton, Walter E. *The Victorian Frame of Mind, 1830–1870.* New Haven, Conn., and London, 1957.
Howe, M. A. De Wolfe. *Portrait of an Independent: Moorfield Storey, 1845–1929.* Boston and New York, 1932.
James, Henry. *Richard Olney and His Public Service.* Boston and New York, 1923.
Jessup, Philip C. *Elihu Root.* 2 vols. New York, 1938.
Karsten, Peter Daggett. "The Naval Aristocracy: U.S. Naval Officers From the 1840's to the 1890's: Mahan's Messmates." Ph.D. dissertation, University of Wisconsin, 1968.
Kemmerer, Edwin W. *Modern Currency Reforms.* New York, 1916.
King, Peter Henry. "The White Man's Burden." Ph.D. dissertation, University of California at Los Angeles, 1958.
Kirkland, Edward C. *Charles Francis Adams, Jr., 1835–1915: the Patrician at Bay.* Cambridge, Mass., 1965.
Koebner, Richard. "The Concept of Economic Imperialism." *Economic History Review,* 2nd s., 2 (1949):1–29.
La Feber, Walter. *The New Empire: An Interpretation of American Expansion, 1860–1898.* Ithaca, N.Y., 1963.
Lambert, John R. *Arthur Pue Gorman.* Baton Rouge, La., 1953.
Lambert, Oscar D. *Stephen Benton Elkins.* Pittsburgh, Pa., 1955.
Langer, William L. *The Diplomacy of Imperialism, 1890–1902.* 2 vols. New York, 1935.
Lasch, Christopher. "The Anti-Imperialists, the Philippines, and

the Inequality of Man." *Journal of Southern History,* 24 (Aug., 1958):319–31.

Laughlin, J. Lawrence, and Willis, H. Parker. *Reciprocity.* New York, 1903.

Leech, Margaret. *In the Days of McKinley.* New York, 1959.

Leopold, Richard W. *Elihu Root and the Conservative Tradition.* Boston, 1954.

Leuchtenburg, William E. "Progressivism and Imperialism: The Progressive Movement and American Foreign Policy, 1898–1916." *Mississippi Valley Historical Review,* 39 (Dec., 1952): 483–504.

Levine, Daniel. *Varieties of Reform Thought.* Madison, Wis., 1964.

Livezy, William E. *Mahan On Sea Power.* Norman, Okla., 1947.

Martin, Edward Sandford. *The Life of Joseph Hodges Choate.* 2 vols. New York, 1921.

May, Ernest R. *American Imperialism, a Speculative Essay.* New York, 1968.

————. *Imperial Democracy: the Emergence of America As A Great Power.* New York, 1961.

McCall, Samuel W. *The Life of Thomas Brackett Reed.* Boston, 1914.

McCormick, Thomas J. *China Market: America's Quest for Informal Empire, 1893–1901.* Chicago, 1967.

McKee, Delber L. "Samuel Gompers, the A. F. of L., and Imperialism, 1895–1900." *Historian,* 21 (1959):187–99.

McLean, Joseph E. *William Rufus Day: Supreme Court Justice from Ohio.* Baltimore, 1946.

Mechan, J. Lloyd. *The United States and Inter-American Security, 1889–1960.* Austin, Texas, 1961.

Miller, Dorothy R. "Josiah Strong and American Nationalism: A Reevaluation." *Journal of American History,* 53 (Dec., 1966): 487–503.

Millis, Walter. *American Military Thought.* New York, 1966.

————. *The Martial Spirit.* Cambridge, Mass., 1931.

Morgan, H. Wayne. *William McKinley and His America.* Syracuse, N.Y., 1963.

Murphy, Agnes. *The Ideology of French Imperialism, 1871–1881.* Washington, D.C., 1948.

Neale, Robert G. *Great Britain and United States Expansion, 1898–1900.* East Lansing, Mich., 1966.

Neilson, James W. *Shelby M. Cullom, Prairie State Republican.*

Urbana, Ill., 1962.

Nevins, Allan. *Henry White: Thirty Years of American Diplomacy.* New York, 1930.

Nichols, Jeannette P. "The United States Congress and Imperialism, 1861–1897." *Journal of Economic History,* 21 (Dec., 1961): 526–38.

Nye, Russel B. *This Almost Chosen People.* East Lansing, Mich., 1966.

Ogden, Rollo, ed. *Life and Letters of Edwin Lawrence Godkin.* 2 vols. New York, 1907.

Olcott, Charles S. *The Life of William McKinley.* 2 vols. Boston and New York, 1916.

Pennanen, Gary. "American Interest in Commercial Union with Canada, 1854–1898." *Mid-America,* 47 (Jan., 1965):24–39.

Perkins, Dexter. *A History of the Monroe Doctrine.* Boston, 1955.

Perry, Bliss. *Life and Letters of Henry Lee Higginson.* Boston, 1921.

Pike, Frederick B. *Chile and the United States, 1880–1962.* Notre Dame, Ind., 1963.

Pletcher, David M. *The Awkward Years.* Columbia, Mo., 1962.

Pomeroy, Earl S. "The American Colonial Office." *Mississippi Valley Historical Review,* 30 (1944):521–32.

Power, Thomas F. *Jules Ferry and the Renaissance of French Imperialism.* New York, 1944.

Pratt, Fletcher. *Eleven Generals: Studies in American Command.* New York, 1949.

Pratt, Julius W. *America's Colonial Experiment: How the United States Gained, Governed, and in part Gave Away a Colonial Empire.* New York, 1951.

————. *Expansionists of 1898: the Acquisition of Hawaii and the Spanish Islands.* Baltimore, 1936.

Quint, Howard H. "American Socialists and the Spanish-American War." *American Quarterly,* 10 (1958):131–41.

Radke, August Carl. "John Tyler Morgan, an expansionist Senator, 1877–1907." Ph.D. dissertation, University of Washington, 1953.

Rauch, Basil. *American Interest in Cuba, 1848–1855.* New York, 1948.

Reuter, Frank T. *Catholic Influence on American Colonial Policies, 1898–1904.* Austin, Texas, and London, 1967.

Richardson, Leon Burr. *William E. Chandler, Republican.* New York, 1940.

Robinson, William A. *Thomas B. Reed, Parliamentarian*. New York, 1930.

Rothman, David J. *Politics and Power: the United States Senate, 1869–1901*. Cambridge, Mass., 1966.

Russ, William A., Jr. *The Hawaiian Revolution, 1893–1894*. Gettysburg, Penn., 1959.

Sage, Leland L. *William Boyd Allison, A Study in Practical Politics*. Iowa City, Iowa, 1956.

Samuels, Ernest. *Henry Adams: The Major Phase*. Cambridge, Mass., 1964.

Schott, Joseph L. *The Ordeal of Samar*. Indianapolis and New York, 1964.

Seager, Robert, II. "Ten Years Before Mahan: The Unofficial Case for the New Navy, 1880–1890." *Mississippi Valley Historical Review*, 40 (Dec., 1953):491–512.

Seed, Geoffrey. "British Reactions to American Imperialism Reflected in Journals of Opinion, 1898–1900." *Political Science Quarterly*, 73 (June, 1958):254–72.

_____. "British Views of American Policy in the Philippines Reflected in Journals of Opinion, 1898–1907." *Journal of American Studies*, 2 (April, 1968):49–64.

Semmel, Bernard. *Imperialism and Social Reform, English Social-Imperial Thought, 1895–1914*. Cambridge, Mass., 1960.

Simkins, Frances Butler. *Pitchfork Ben Tillman*. Baton Rouge, La., 1944.

Snyder, Louis L. *The Imperialism Reader: Documents and Readings on Modern Expansionism*. Princeton, N.J., 1962.

Sproat, John G. *"The Best Men": Liberal Reformers in the Gilded Age*. New York, 1968.

Sprout, Harold and Margaret. *The Rise of American Naval Power, 1776–1918*. Princeton, N.J., 1939.

Steelman, Lala Carr. "Senator Augustus O. Bacon, Champion of Philippine Independence." In *Essays in Southern Biography*, East Carolina Publications in History, vol. II. Greenville, N.C., 1965.

Steigerwalt, Albert K. *The National Association of Manufacturers, 1895–1914*. Ann Arbor, Mich., 1964.

Stephenson, Nathaniel Wright. *Nelson W. Aldrich, a Leader in American Politics*. New York, 1930.

Stevens, Sylvester K. *American Expansion in Hawaii, 1852–1898*. Harrisburg, Pa., 1945.

Strauss, William L. *Joseph Chamberlain and the Theory of Imperialism.* Washington, D.C., 1942.

Stromberg, Roland N. *Collective Security and American Foreign Policy.* New York, 1963.

Swanberg, William A. *Citizen Hearst.* New York, 1961.

Talbot, E. H., and Hobart, H. R. *Biographical Directory of Railway Officials of America.* Chicago and New York, 1885.

Tansill, Charles C. *The Foreign Policy of Thomas F. Bayard, 1885–1897.* New York, 1940.

Teng, Ssu-yu, and Fairbank, John K. *China's Response to the West.* Cambridge, Mass., 1954.

Thayer, William Roscoe. *Life and Letters of John Hay.* 2 vols. Boston, 1915.

Thistlethwaite, Frank. *America and the Atlantic Community: Anglo-American Aspects, 1790–1850.* New York, 1959.

Tuchman, Barbara. *The Proud Tower: A Portrait of the World Before the War, 1890–1914.* New York, 1966.

Tyler, Alice Felt. *The Foreign Policy of James G. Blaine.* Minneapolis, Minn., 1927.

Urban, C. Stanley. "The Ideology of Southern Imperialism: New Orleans and the Caribbean, 1845–1860." *Louisiana Historical Quarterly,* 39 (Jan., 1956):48–73.

Van Deusen, Glyndon. *William Henry Seward.* New York, 1967.

Varg, Paul A. *Missionaries, Chinese, and Diplomats: the American Protestant Missionary Movement in China, 1890–1952.* Princeton, N.J., 1958.

————. "The Myth of the China Market, 1890-1914." *American Historical Review,* 73 (Feb., 1968): 742–58.

Vevier, Charles. "American Continentalism: An Idea of Expansion, 1845–1910." *American Historical Review,* 65 (Jan., 1960): 323–35.

Walters, Everett. *Joseph Benson Foraker: An Uncompromising Republican.* Columbus, Ohio, 1948.

Warner, Donald F. *The Idea of Continental Union: Agitation for the Annexation of Canada to the United States, 1849–1893.* Lexington, Ky., 1960.

Weinberg, Albert K. *Manifest Destiny.* Baltimore, 1935.

Welch, Richard E., Jr. "Senator George Frisbie Hoar and the Defeat of Anti-Imperialism, 1898–1900." *Historian,* 26 (May, 1964): 362–80.

Wilgus, William J. *The Railroad Interrelations of the United States and Canada.* New Haven, Conn., 1937.

Wilkerson, Marcus M. *Public Opinion and the Spanish-American War.* Baton Rouge, La., 1932.

Wisan, Joseph E. *The Cuban Crisis as Reflected in the New York Press.* New York, 1934.

Worcester, Dean C. *The Philippines Past and Present.* 2 vols. New York, 1914.

Younger, Edward L. *John A. Kasson: Politics and Diplomacy from Lincoln to McKinley.* Iowa City, Iowa, 1955.

Index